The Practitioner Inquiry Series

Marilyn Cochran-Smith and Susan L. Lytle, SERIES EDITORS

Ethical Issues in Practitioner Research
JANE ZENI, Editor

Because of the Kids: Facing Racial and
Cultural Differences in Schools
JENNIFER E. OBIDAH &
KAREN MANHEIM TEEL

Action, Talk, and Text: Learning and
Teaching Through Inquiry
GORDON WELLS, Editor

Teaching Mathematics to the New
Standards: Relearning the Dance
RUTH M. HEATON

Teacher Narrative as Critical Inquiry:
Rewriting the Script
JOY S. RITCHIE & DAVID E. WILSON

From Another Angle: Children's Strengths
and School Standards
MARGARET HIMLEY with
PATRICIA F. CARINI, Editors

Unplayed Tapes: A Personal History of
Collaborative Teacher Research
STEPHEN M. FISHMAN &
LUCILLE McCARTHY

Inside City Schools: Investigating Literacy
in the Multicultural Classroom
SARAH WARSHAUER FREEDMAN,
ELIZABETH RADIN SIMONS,
JULIE SHALHOPE KALNIN,
ALEX CASARENO, and the
M-CLASS TEAMS

Class Actions: Teaching for Social Justice in
Elementary and Middle School
JoBETH ALLEN, Editor

Teacher/Mentor: A Dialogue for
Collaborative Learning
PEG GRAHAM, SALLY HUDSON-
ROSS, CHANDRA ADKINS,
PATTI McWHORTER, &
JENNIFER McDUFFIE STEWART,
Editors

Teaching Other People's Children: Literacy
and Learning in a Bilingual Classroom
CYNTHIA BALLENGER

Teaching, Multimedia, and Mathematics:
Investigations of Real Practice
MAGDALENE LAMPERT &
DEBORAH LOEWENBERG BALL

Tensions of Teaching: Beyond Tips to
Critical Reflection
JUDITH M. NEWMAN

John Dewey and the Challenge of
Classroom Practice
STEPHEN M. FISHMAN &
LUCILLE McCARTHY

"Sometimes I Can Be Anything": Power,
Gender, and Identity in a Primary
Classroom
KAREN GALLAS

Learning in Small Moments: Life in an
Urban Classroom
DANIEL R. MEIER

Interpreting Teacher Practice: Two
Continuing Stories
RENATE SCHULZ

Creating Democratic Classrooms: The
Struggle to Integrate Theory and Practice
LANDON E. BEYER, Editor

ETHICAL ISSUES
IN
PRACTITIONER RESEARCH

EDITED BY JANE ZENI

Foreword by Susan Lytle

Teachers College, Columbia University
New York and London

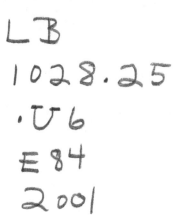
Published by Teachers College Press, 1234 Amsterdam Avenue, New York, NY 10027

Library of Congress Cataloging-in-Publication Data

Ethical issues in practitioner research / edited by Jane Zeni.
     p. cm. — (Practitioner inquiry series)
   Includes bibliographical references and index.
   ISBN 0-8077-4001-2 (cloth : alk. paper) — ISBN 0-8077-4000-4 (pbk. : alk. paper)
    1. Education—Research—Moral and ethical aspects—United States.   I. Zeni, Jane, 1945–
II. Series.
   LB1028.25.U6 E84 2001
   370′.7′2073—dc21   00-057742

ISBN 0-8077-4000-4 (paper)
ISBN 0-8077-4001-2 (cloth)

Printed on acid-free paper
Manufactured in the United States of America

08   07   06   05   04   03   02   01   8   7   6   5   4   3   2   1

Dedicated to Lou Smith—
his pioneering work in collaborative action research
and his gentle mentoring
have guided many of us through our careers.

CONTENTS

Foreword   ix
    SUSAN LYTLE
Introduction   xi
    JANE ZENI

PART I SCHOOL-BASED RESEARCHERS

1. Drafting Ethical Guidelines for Teacher Research in Schools   3
   MARIAN M. MOHR

2. "Tuesday Night" Revisited: Learning to Survive   13
   LESLIE TURNER MINARIK

3. Coming to Know My Place   24
   WANDA C. CLAY

4. Teacher Research: A Wolf in Sheep's Clothing   35
   LINDA HAJJ

5. Who Owns the Story? Ethical Issues in the Conduct of
   Practitioner Research   45
   The Clayton (Missouri) Research Review Team: CATHY BECK,
   LAURA DUPONT, LORI GEISMAR-RYAN, LINDA HENKE,
   KATHRYN MITCHELL PIERCE, AND CATHERINE VON HATTEN

Reflections on School-Based Research   55

PART II UNIVERSITY-BASED RESEARCHERS

6. "A Root Out of a Dry Ground": Resolving the
   Researcher/Researched Dilemma   61
   SHARON SHOCKLEY LEE

7. Action Research on Action Research: Emancipatory Research
   or Abuse of Power?   72
   SALLY BARR EBEST

8. The Ethics of Accountability in Action Research   83
    OWEN VAN DEN BERG

9. When Evaluation Turns Sour: Quandaries of the Individual Case   92
    LOUIS M. SMITH

Reflections on University-Based Research   105

**PART III   COLLABORATIVE
SCHOOL-UNIVERSITY RESEARCH**

10. The Ethics of Cultural Invisibility   113
    JANE ZENI AND MYRTHO PROPHETE, WITH NANCY CASON
    AND MINNIE PHILLIPS

11. Insiders and Outsiders: Perspectives on Urban Action Research   123
    JACQUELYN C. HARRIS, MICHAEL LOWENSTEIN, AND ROSALYNDE SCOTT

12. Negotiating Two Worlds: Conducting Action Research
    Within a School-University Partnership   136
    MARILYN M. COHN AND SUZANNE KIRKPATRICK

Reflections on Collaborative Research   149

Epilogue A Guide to Ethical Decision Making for Insider Research   153
    JANE ZENI

References   167
About the Editor and Contributors   175
Index   181

FOREWORD

The last decade or so has seen a remarkable resurgence of interest in insider investigations of teaching, learning and schooling—variously known as practitioner research/inquiry, teacher research, and action research. Within the movement, many have seen the power of these "indigenous" inquiries to question and transform business as usual in schools and universities. This book explores some of the critical ethical issues and dilemmas that come with the territory but are rarely documented or shared beyond the local setting.

In the increasingly politicized arena of educational change projects, it is no surprise that relationships among the many and various participants are more and more complicated. Classroom teachers, administrators, parents, community members, school staff, district leaders, and university faculty—in various combinations—are now working together to construct and reconstruct relationships that intentionally make traditional boundaries between teachers and learners, schools and communities, and districts and universities much more porous and negotiable. It is also increasingly evident that there is much at stake for schools, districts, and universities in these new collaborative relationships, and in taking on the challenge of envisioning new relationships between research and practice.

In pulling together these particular stories, Jane Zeni draws from her own long and deep experiences as a member of several inquiry communities. It is no accident that this, the first full-length volume devoted to ethical issues, emerges from the work of school- and university-based practitioners who have made commitments to creating and sustaining inquiry collectives as sites for surfacing and struggling with these issues over time. It provides a revealing window on the ongoing work in these and several other communities. Practitioner research is intentionally defined in a broad manner and then spun out in distinctive ways by differently positioned educators, including classroom teachers, university professors, building and district-level administrators, professional development leaders, and coordinators of field experiences.

Zeni's introduction provides a valuable historical and conceptual framing that cuts across the three major sections of the book: chapters by both school-based and university-based researchers, and chapters about collaborative school–university research. Each story illuminates a particular issue related to the researcher's location and positioning in an institution, research relationships, interpretation and representation of others' experiences, as well as to the many concerns arising from publication for wider audiences and institutional expectations within and across settings.

The various chapters thus provide quintessentially local and vivid accounts, but also "telling" cases for those engaging in action research in other locales. Indeed, raising readers' consciousness of ethical dilemmas as a way to stimulate conversation within and across communities seems to be one of the primary purposes of the collection as a whole. These stories provoke; they seek not to forward a set of "best ethical practices" but rather to render the bumpy terrain as experienced by interesting and thoughtful people deeply involved in the daily work.

Jane Zeni's final chapter offers a clear invitation for the many people involved in this work to take closer, more systematic looks at their own practices and contexts. Her "Guide to Ethical Decision Making for Insider Research" emerged from discussions in the Teacher Educator Seminar of the Action Research Collaborative in St. Louis about the requirements of human subjects reviews and policies of ethical research generated by professional organizations. Framed as a set of questions that emanate from the concerns of institutional review boards, it provides a rich rendering of what may be at stake in insider research in and on practice. Furthermore, as a grounded conceptual framework, the guide also provides a compelling agenda for everyone who values this kind of work to try to document, analyze, and communicate from multiple perspectives about the ethical issues and dilemmas that arise.

This is a book that resonates strongly with my belief that, as people committed to activist research and educational change, we need to take the lead in questioning and studying our own research practices and in arguing in our own institutions for structures and procedures that support rather than undermine new configurations of research and practice. Figuring out how to represent ethical issues within one's own workworld is hard enough. Re-representing these issues for an audience beyond one's own community adds layers of complexity both for the local community and for readers hoping to learn something for their own contexts. As one of the editors of the Practitioner Inquiry Series and as someone who also lives and worries about these significant dilemmas, I am truly grateful to Jane Zeni and her collaborators for being willing to take on these challenges.

Susan Lytle

INTRODUCTION

Jane Zeni

For the past 14 years, I have grappled with ethical dilemmas in research into my own practice as a college teacher and in collaboration with K–12 teacher-researchers. We have learned together as we tried to cope with the unexpected, sometimes troubling, consequences of our inquiries.

The growing popularity of practitioner research in educational reform means that more people are launching inquiries in schools with less formal grounding in either research methods or ethical safeguards. The advice dispensed in the available literature has not been particularly helpful. Publications on research ethics tend to be dense and scholarly, addressed to researchers in the universities rather than in the schools. More important, such guides usually ignore the situation of the insider. As a result, they miss the ethical dilemmas most often encountered by teachers studying their own classrooms.

Ethics in the special case of practitioner research first came to my attention when an ethics review committee rejected a dissertation proposal I had advised; the teacher planned to write fieldnotes and document the learning of his own students. The committee cited concerns about the protection of "human subjects"—a label that struck me as inappropriate, if not offensive.[1] I protested that the researcher had proposed an analysis of normal classroom practice, and that the responsibilities of teachers to students were deeper and more personal than whatever was implied by the term "subjects." The dean of research then made the obvious suggestion: "Why don't you draft some guidelines better suited to the review of qualitative research, especially research by educators in their own contexts?" I brought the challenge to the St. Louis Action Research Collaborative, where members who taught at all levels from the primary grades to university discussed the issues in seminars and conference sessions.

In time, it became apparent that the ethical dilemmas facing practitioner-researchers tended to be ambiguous, context-sensitive, and therefore resistant to generic regulations. I did, however, produce a guide with heuristic questions that have proved useful in teacher research groups and graduate courses (Zeni, 1998; also the Epilogue in this volume). This book project developed as I started looking for answers in the concrete stories of educators who have negotiated the ethical complexities of research into their own practice.

WHOSE DILEMMAS?

Ethical dilemmas seem to be complicated by the very nature of the practitioner-researcher role. The insider has responsibilities and relationships that are fundamentally different from those of an outsider doing research in schools.

Teacher-researchers, for example, struggle with issues of loyalty, confidentiality, and trust. They ask, "How do I handle this new role without alienating my colleagues or my administrators?" They wonder, "Will my students benefit from my research or will I be using them for my own gain?" They know that after this inquiry is complete and this report is written, their own professional life will continue in the same setting.

Consultants to collaborative research projects face other dilemmas, whether they work in school-based professional development or on university faculties. Many feel caught in a squeeze between the ethical concerns of the schools and the research regulations of the academy. They ask, "How can I support and empower teacher-researchers while I direct them in a degree program?" If they promote action research as professional development, they wonder, "Can we really institutionalize reflection?" If they publish collaboratively with K–12 teacher-researchers, they question the ethics of their own knowledge, power, and language.

Then there are the hidden dilemmas, the ones researchers in any role may fail to see because these dilemmas are built into their major research tool—themselves. As school demographics change, a teaching force that is largely middle-class, female, and European American faces a student population that is increasingly composed of "other people's children" (Delpit, 1995). Practitioners need to begin their inquiries by asking, "How can I recognize my own cultural baggage so that I can really see my students?"

My own practice has given me access to many inquiring teachers. As founding director (1978–1997) of St. Louis's Gateway Writing Project and member of the Action Research Collaborative, I have worked closely with several multiyear investigations.

The first, in the mid-1980s, was an inquiry I initiated with the help of teachers who were integrating computers into writing classes. We came to see not only the potential of new technology to support the writing process but also the risk of further dividing schools into "haves" and "have-nots." My research led me to design new Writing Project courses and to publish *WritingLands: Composing with Old and New Writing Tools* (1990).

From 1987 through 1993, I assisted team leaders Joan Krater and Nancy Cason in action research that profoundly affected their suburban district. Troubled by the underachievement of many African American students, these secondary school teachers set out to build culturally inclusive classrooms—and learned much about themselves. We coauthored *Mirror Images: Teaching Writing in Black and White* (Krater, Zeni, & Cason, 1994).

I played a smaller consulting role in the Urban Sites Network under St. Louis team leaders Rosalynde Scott and Michael Lowenstein. In eight U.S. cities during the early 1990s, National Writing Project teacher-researchers documented their students' learning, shared successes and frustrations, and discovered their own power to improve the system (Urban Sites Network, 1996).

My perspective has been broadened by participation since 1987 in a faculty exchange between the University of Missouri and the University of the Western Cape in South Africa. There, Owen van den Berg had established an action research master's program for teachers working to transform their classrooms into democratic communities and to prepare for the fall of apartheid.

Through projects such as these, I have come to recognize some of the ethical risks that may lurk behind the progressive goals of action research. In fact, the rapid growth of teacher research projects, groups, and grants may pose the greatest ethical risk to this movement. As a case in point, picture the following scene.

A regional conference on practitioner research has drawn 200 teachers from K–12 and university settings as well as a number of administrators. The conference coordinator and I are gratified that a state-level professional development leader has been attending the sessions and seems impressed. He agrees to say a few closing words to the group. "I want to congratulate all of you on an exciting conference. Your involvement in action research is at the cutting edge of what we are trying to do for education in this state." We are pleased and encouraged by his remarks. He continues, "In fact, I hope to see the day when action research is recognized as *the* mode of professional development and when every school district in this state requires teachers to complete one action research project per year." Speechless and embarrassed, we close the conference wondering what went wrong.

I believe that those of us who do practitioner research must engage in serious dialogue on ethical issues. As we attend to university human subjects reviews, school district curriculum and privacy mandates, and state professional development standards, we must ensure that practitioners maintain ownership of their research agendas. If we do not, this powerful movement will be reduced to a pile of bureaucratic rubble.

PRACTITIONER RESEARCH: SOME DEFINITIONS

This book attempts to create such a dialogue about ethics among educators studying their own practice in school and university roles. As editor, I use the term *practitioner research* broadly to include teacher research, action research, and other modes of self-study in education.

Teacher research has been defined by Cochran-Smith and Lytle as "systematic and intentional inquiry by teachers about their own school and classroom work" (1993, p. 23) that challenges the "exclusively university-generated knowledge base for teaching" as well as the image of "teacher as technician, consumer, receiver, transmitter, and implementor of other people's knowledge" (1999, p. 16). Teacher-researchers work together collaboratively, refining their practice and developing their knowledge (MacLean & Mohr, 1999). Hubbard and Power see teacher-researchers as "a wonderful new breed of artists-in-residence" (1993, p. xiii). The term is used in a wide range of U.S. publications, including the quarterly *Teacher Research: The Journal of Classroom Inquiry*, and at the International Conference on Teacher Research, which is sponsored annually by the Teacher Research special interest group of the American Educational Research Association (AERA).

Action research, the term preferred in the British tradition, has been defined as "the study of a social situation with a view to improving the quality of action within it. . . . In action research, 'theories' are not validated independently and then applied to practice. They are validated through practice" (Elliott, 1991, p. 69). Action research involves a "cycle" or "spiral" rather than a one-shot study: "a systematic way of planning an action, 'doing' the action [teaching], observing the action, reflecting on the action, and then planning a revised action" (Davidoff & van den Berg, 1990, p. 32). Since the 1970s, teachers' work has been shared at the Collaborative Action Research Network conference at the University of East Anglia and (more recently) in the U.K. journal *Educational Action Research*.

Practitioner research, whatever its tradition, relies on qualitative or descriptive methods (e.g., participant observation, interviewing, journaling) rather than quantitative, statistical, or experimental methods. It typically results in a classroom ethnography or case study. When Cochran-Smith and Lytle call teacher research "systematic and intentional," they are referring to such methods; their definition excludes the everyday process of being thoughtful or reflective but not "systematic" (1999, p. 22). This heritage is evident in the annual Ethnography in Education Research Forum at the University of Pennsylvania.

Pulling these descriptions together, I would define *practitioner research* as "qualitative research conducted by insiders in educational settings to improve their own practice":

Who?   Insiders, stakeholders
Where? In their own workplace
What?   Issues in their own practice
How?   Qualitative methods of inquiry

Why?   To understand themselves and their students
         To solve professional problems
         To change society

Notice the range of answers to the question "why." Noffke (1997) points out that practitioner research, though sharing a common methodology, can serve three quite different goals—personal, professional, and political. Why do research? Practitioners who emphasize "personal" goals would talk about reflection, self-knowledge, and growth; those with "professional" goals would talk about team building, career development, and leadership; those with "political" goals would talk about democratic classrooms, justice, and social change. I think the relative emphasis on these three goals is the basis of much apparent difference in definition.

Whether it is called teacher research, action research, or reflective practice, this movement challenges some dichotomies taken for granted in education. Practitioner research rejects the theory/practice split, because theories emerge and are refined through cycles of practice. It opens the boundary between practice and research, because doing research becomes central to how one teaches. It also challenges the insider/outsider distinction, because teachers or administrators inside a school setting may collaborate with outside consultants, such as university faculty, to explore questions framed by the insiders. Then again, the professors may themselves be insiders who conduct research into their own practice.

RESEARCH ETHICS

Any research involving people and social institutions must involve ethical decision making. For that matter, research is a kind of practice, and any practice (teaching, research) must have ethical implications.

Ethics is the branch of philosophy dealing with decisions about right and wrong actions. Ethics may be used as a synonym for *morality*, although the term *ethics* is currently applied most often to codes of conduct (Kimmel, 1988; Newman & Brown, 1996) published by professional organizations. For example, AERA's Qualitative Research special interest group (SIG) provides *A Casebook for Teaching about Ethical Issues in Qualitative Research* (Mathison, Ross, & Cornett, 1993). The authors say that research handbooks have "overwhelmingly focused on issues of method," but the "deeper issues about how to do good and act right . . . are not satisfied by the application of better techniques" (p. 1). A set of cases for discussion help the reader explore such ethical issues as informed consent, reciprocity, deception, right to privacy, advocacy, research independence, and ownership of data (pp. 3–6).

The principles behind these issues are widely discussed in the social science literature (Beauchamp, Faden, Wallace, & Walters, 1982; Burgess, 1989; Kimmel, 1988; Mason, 1996). Newman and Brown (1996) classify ethical theories by the criteria researchers use to make decisions. These include *consequences*, the greatest good for the greatest number; *rights*, the unconditional value of each individual; and *caring*, a feminist ethic of relationships and context (pp. 24–35). These principles are clearly relevant to practitioner research; however, social science ethics is not widely read in schools or even in educational research courses at universities.

Yet educational institutions are now keenly aware of ethical risks in research. They were shocked into controls, first by the Nuremberg Trials and their revelations of Nazi medical experiments on Jewish prisoners. Closer to home was the Tuskegee syphilis experiment, whose federally funded researchers spent 40 years documenting the course of untreated syphilis among indigent African American men who might have been cured with penicillin (Anderson, 1996, 1998). Today, before launching a project, most would-be researchers must analyze the potential risks as well as benefits to participants. All universities and a growing number of school districts require that a proposal be presented to an institutional review board (IRB), which decides whether human subjects will be protected and whether the researcher has an adequate plan conforming to ethical guidelines.

ETHICS IN PRACTITIONER RESEARCH

The institutional review process, originally designed for experimental research in medicine, has an uneasy fit with qualitative research in education, especially research by insiders in the schools. Because issues often arise in process, it is impossible to make all ethical decisions before getting into the study. Instead, Jennifer Mason (1996) advocates "an active and self-questioning" stance in which "qualitative researchers will not and cannot be satisfied with standardized or codified answers to ethical and political dilemmas" (p. 167).

Such contextually sensitive approaches are described in *The Paradigm Dialog* (Guba, 1990) and in *Qualitative Inquiry in Education* (Eisner & Peshkin, 1990). Lou Smith's chapters in these volumes approach ethics in research, not through general principles but through the discussion of problematic stories. A growing consensus suggests that while providing the "codified answers" required by the IRB, practitioner-researchers must also engage in a dialogue about their personal values and about the impact of the study in this concrete situation. As Mohr (1996) argues, teachers cannot base ethical decisions on objectivity (as in statistics) or anonymity (as in sociology); instead, they must use principles of responsibility and accountability. Soltis (1990) explains, the unique relationship of teacher to student created a specific moral situation, one in which the student placed trust in the teacher and had a legitimate expectation of being taught . . . , of not being . . . harmed in any way, and, in general, of having his or her own well-being, not the teacher's, function as the guiding value. (p. 247)

As awareness of the implications of this role grows, ethics has become an explosive issue in scholarly communities that emphasize practitioner research. I offer here two recent examples, one from composition and one from women's studies.

In *College Composition and Communication* (Feb. 1998), Paul Anderson reveals some dilemmas that have smoldered in teacher research newsletters and listserves. A consultant to the U.S. Office for Protection from Research Risks (OPRR), Anderson discusses a 1995 OPRR directive stating that research formerly exempt from institutional review—studies of "commonly accepted educational settings, involving normal education practices"—must now be examined (pp. 69–70). Journals that have relied on the exemption of most classroom research are changing their editorial policies. Yet "important ethical issues are not covered by the federal policy," such as the "intellectual property rights" of students and of colleagues in a research group (p. 83). Anderson alerts writing teachers to the new regulations and also urges them to look deeper—to the more serious dilemmas of insider research.

Gesa Kirsch, in *Ethical Dilemmas in Feminist Research* (1999, p. x), suggests three checkpoints on a continuum of ethical issues: "location," "interpretation," and "publication." Although she writes primarily of outsider research, her use of qualitative methods and feminist theories of personal knowing also speak to insiders studying their own practice. I would add two more checkpoints for insiders: relationships and institutionalization.

I have based the following definitions on the work of Kirsch and adapted them for practitioner research:

Location: What a researcher brings to the inquiry—gender, race, class, roles, status in the institution. How do these aspects of culture connect or divide a researcher from colleagues, students, other participants?
Relationships: The human dynamics, friendships, and professional responsibilities that may be threatened or enhanced by the research. To whom is the researcher accountable?
Interpretation/definition: How the researcher represents the subjective experience of others to consider multiple perspectives. How do various participants define the issues?
Publication: Texts, forms, and voices that bring the research to a wider public. How does the researcher tell a complex story truthfully and respectfully to varied audiences?

Institutionalization: Legal and procedural expectations in the university, school, or other setting. What guidelines apply when research involves more than one institutional culture? I will be referring to this list in my commentaries on the chapters to follow.

In a 1996 article, I described ethical risks as windmills and wild beasts that may beset the Don Quixotes of educational reform. These monsters can rarely be slain with a single stroke, like a signature on a consent form. Action research calls for a process of ethical review, with different ethical checks at different points in the research. For example, a teacher may send a brief letter in September to inform parents and students that she plans to write fieldnotes and videotape some group work in an effort to improve learning. But if the teacher wants to present these data at a conference in April or to analyze them for a publication in July, more explicit written consent is needed.

OVERVIEW

In this volume, a diverse set of practitioners will address the ethical issues they have encountered in doing research. The contributors—classroom teachers, university professors, building- and district-level administrators, professional development leaders, coordinators of field experiences, and others—share a commitment to dialogue. Avoiding the jargon of the academy, they write for a diverse audience of educators.

The Voices

I believe that *voice* is fundamentally an ethical issue in writing about education. A university researcher, for example, may collaborate with school people but report the findings in a mode of discourse that excludes the uninitiated. When that happens, any critique of the research by the stakeholders is effectively silenced. I would argue that those of us who work in the intellectual spaces between schools and universities have an ethical obligation to write in a style that communicates to both audiences.

Even the simple decision to use the pronoun *I* has ethical implications. In the natural sciences, it is conventional to write something like "the rats' growth was monitored," not "I monitored the rats' growth." That researcher is not accountable to the rats, nor will they read and evaluate the report. We as action researchers cannot hide behind statements like "the decision was made" or "a test was given" or "the fourth grader was disrespectful." When writing about the complexities of our own social context, we need to say whether the principal, parent, or teacher made that decision; whether the school psychologist or the teacher-researcher gave that test, and which human in authority—and under what conditions—interpreted that child as disrespectful.

All the contributors to this volume thought carefully about the impact of publication on an audience that might include teachers, parents, children, school boards, and others in the settings where they work. Four (two school-based and two university-based) chose to disguise the school, district, or both and to use pseudonyms for key individuals in the story. The other eight authors, after considering the ethical implications and referring drafts for review, chose to name schools, districts, and all adults. (Given our topic, there are few close-up views or quotations of children. However, these authors tend to use pseudonyms for K–12 and college students and real names for graduate students and other adult professionals.) In a few cases, "naming names" led to minor changes in wording or tone. A story of snarled communication might be published, for example, but some comments about colleagues might remain in the field journal.

The Chapters

As editor, I have invited chapters from people whose research I know and admire. Most are inquiring practitioners from the St. Louis area with whom I have shared the excitement and also the pain that often accompany the personal, professional, and political commitment to research. I wanted their stories in this book.

Other authors I know through conferences and publications. I contacted Sandra Hollinsworth, Susan Lytle, and Marian Mohr and asked them to suggest teacher-researchers in their geographical areas who have confronted ethical dilemmas and whose stories need to be heard more widely. Thanks to their help, this collection shows the range of voices, roles, and perspectives that make action research both powerful and problematic.

In 1999, I shared my questions about ethics with an encouragingly large audience at the International Conference on Teacher Research. Later I sent out the same questions on XTAR, the action research listserve. (These two groups draw researchers from beyond the mainstream of AERA, philosophically as well as culturally.) Written responses from members of both groups confirmed my impression that people who teach in schools and people who work in universities tend to see ethical dilemmas differently. The chapters in this book are grouped on the basis of context to highlight these different perspectives.

Part I, "School-Based Researchers," has contributors from Missouri, Virginia, and California—elementary school teacher-researchers as well as people studying their own practice in professional development roles. Framing the section are chapters that describe the process of developing ethical guidelines at the district level. Although these authors have connections with university researchers, they are writing about ethical decisions by practitioners in schools and the impact of these decisions on school policies. Many of the school-based authors have been involved with the National Writing Project (NWP). As Cochran-Smith and Lytle observe (1993, p. 11), classroom research took root early among writing teachers because it resonated with their own practice of process, collaboration, and journaling.

Part II, "University-Based Researchers," contains work of two kinds. In some chapters, academics explore ethical issues in studying their own practice in university settings. Other chapters examine such roles as consultant, practicum student, or program evaluator—roles which bring the university's ethical codes into the school setting. Most authors from the St. Louis area have been involved, to some degree, in the Action Research Collaborative. In particular, all the university-based authors have taken part in the ARC Teacher Educator Seminar. I doubt that this book would have been written at all if it were not for this seminar, whose members have worked together since 1992. We meet each month, faculty from as many as nine area colleges and universities, to share our writing and to discuss problems in our practice of doing and teaching action research. Issues of ethics—and our emerging chapter drafts—have been the focus of many seminars.

Part III, "Collaborative School-University Research," presents chapters by researchers in different locations who explore together their ethical decisions. These coauthored pieces may resemble a dialogue more than a formal essay. McCarthy and Fishman (1996) praise such multivoiced texts as "forms that honor diversity, empower the voices of researchers and informants, and enhance participants' chances for understanding and change" (p. 173). Contributors experiment with styles and genres to represent the multiple perspectives valued in action research.

In reflections ending each part, I try to tease out the common themes and contrasting choices made by the authors. The epilogue my "Guide to Ethical Decision Making for Insider Research" and a comprehensive reference list. The guide first appeared in *Educational Action Research* (1998); extensively revised, it now reflects what I have learned through this project.

The Purpose

My hope is that this volume will be more than an academic discussion document; it is designed as a resource for problem solving by practitioners doing research. School districts are becoming more and more concerned that action research may pose certain risks to student privacy and teacher integrity. The mix of stories, analysis of issues, and guidelines for action will support school district professional development libraries, teacher inquiry teams, and individual action researchers.

I also hope this book will find its way into graduate schools of education. A growing number of teachers whose notion of research is grounded in school-based inquiry are objecting to university textbooks that present only traditional, outsider research designs. The essays are appropriate for qualitative methods courses or for guidance in action research dissertations.

Throughout this project, I have been guided by the concrete dilemmas in my own experience and the experiences of colleagues in the schools and universities. As in the practice of law, business, and medicine, principles for the ethical conduct of practitioner research in education must emerge, story by story, from an analysis of cases. Let us turn, then, to the stories.

NOTE

1. Most of us who do practitioner research work in educational institutions that require some sort of ethics review, and the label "human subjects" has become standard. Some contributors to this book use the term when referring to institutional reviews. It is not, however, what they would choose to call their students and colleagues.

Part I

SCHOOL-BASED RESEARCHERS

Chapter 1

DRAFTING ETHICAL GUIDELINES FOR TEACHER RESEARCH IN SCHOOLS

Marian M. Mohr

In this chapter I will present a statement of ethics developed for a school system in Frederick County, Virginia. I drafted the statement with the help of an assistant superintendent, a building administrator, and a group of high school teacher-researchers. My emphasis, however, will be less on the draft itself and more on the process of writing and learning that produced it.[1]

EXPLORATORY WRITING

For the moment, my class of 10th graders was quietly writing. They were not an easy group to work with, but I looked forward to seeing them each day. Teaching them was like reading an interesting book and wondering what would happen next, wondering how it would happen and how the writer would show it happening. It was also like writing a book. I was the managing editor of the text we wrote together, and chapters developed day by day, not always as I expected.

I sometimes revised my plans in midlesson as I observed my students' responses. When something seemed noteworthy, especially a particularly wise comment by a student, I grabbed my research log from my desk and wrote it down. They had grown used to my interest in how they progressed through their learning. Occasionally one would even say to me, "You need to write this down." In oral and written evaluations of our work, we continued our dialogue about teaching and learning.

I taught, and I rethought. I acted, and I observed at the same time. I was not a stage actor performing before my students; I was myself as a thinker and learner. My students were not my human subjects; they were more like coworkers—all were necessary to the research. The kind of personal interaction we relied on demanded and depended on my teaching them responsibly and acting toward them ethically. They were teenagers required by law to be in school. I was employed by the community to teach them and to evaluate and grade what they learned.

My values and theirs, my power and theirs, my personality and theirs, my background and theirs—all were present in our classroom. The improvement of my teaching and their learning was the goal of my research; teaching and learning did not exist to further my research. As I learned how to teach them and they learned how to learn from me, we were drafting the ethical guidelines of my research. The process begins in dialogue in the classroom.

DEVELOPING IDEAS WITH COLLEAGUES

When I am in a discussion with other teacher-researchers, they describe experiences similar to mine with the 10th graders, and we learn from each other ways to integrate our teaching and researching. We talk about writing observations of our classes and examining our students' behavior as data. We compare letters we have written to parents about our research or notes we have composed asking permission to quote a student's work. One teacher might share the names her students have suggested for themselves to be used in her forthcoming article. We ask each other for sources of ideas that we know did not originate with us, and are lost in our memories, files, and bookshelves of professional reading.

To many teachers, what I have described will sound familiar—normal practice—and it will sound like teacher research, but not like an exploration of ethical issues. I think that is because, historically, teaching has not been viewed as research any more than research has been viewed as something a teacher would do. When teachers are viewed merely as conduits, research ethics are irrelevant to their practice. Even when teachers begin to conduct research, it is sometimes difficult to see ethics as an issue. To discuss it seems to be participating in criticism of teachers, as if they are not ethical people in their relationships with students, along with everything else they are thought to do wrong.

Ethical issues may also be overlooked when teacher-researchers are thought by their school district to be doing something right. At present, many school districts with complex requirements for outside researchers desiring to conduct research in their classrooms do not require the same procedures for teacher-researchers. It is only when teacher research comes to be valued as research that ethical questions emerge. Thinking about the ethics of teacher research, therefore, requires rethinking the meaning of both teaching and researching. On a recent journey to extend my understanding of ethics, I came to understand this need for redefinition.

REDEFINING AND REVISING

Having just shifted from over 20 years of high school teaching to working as a researcher in a grant-funded teacher research program in my school system, I became a new member of the American Educational Research Association (AERA). It is not a coincidence that I came to AERA only after I stopped teaching high school. Teachers in grades K–12, or in community colleges, may not see what happens at AERA as pressing. I had long been active in conferences concerning my own discipline, English teaching, but AERA was new territory.

At my first AERA conference, I heard Yvonna Lincoln (1995) speak about ethics and standards of quality for qualitative research. She could have been talking about teacher research when she carefully described "critical subjectivity" to heighten self-understanding. She could have been talking about teacher-researchers when she spoke about the importance of "voice," hearing from the "unheard from" rather than speaking for them. I appreciated her emphasis on the idea that research takes place within a community and must serve that community. I could picture many teacher-researcher classrooms, mine included, when she described the "intense sharing" that may go on between the researcher and the researched.

I had heard the characteristics Lincoln attributed to quality research discussed in slightly different terms many times in my years of working with fellow teacher-researchers. We had discussed role tensions—the tugs between the various "communities" our research involves. We also had discussed dilemmas—the unsolvable problems that must be weighed and balanced by inquirers into their own practices. We are doubly bound to ethical behavior, I thought, as teachers and researchers. How we treat our students and colleagues is a measure of the quality of both our teaching and our researching.

Lincoln, however, did not seem to be including teachers in her definition of researcher. Nevertheless, her talk helped me redefine research in a way that permitted me to connect standards of quality and ethical behavior. I went to Lincoln's presentation in the first place because my colleagues and I had learned the methods of qualitative research from her, among others, in order to conduct our classroom studies. We had needed to go beyond our original ideas about research—statistical studies and bell-shaped curves of data far removed from our daily lives as teachers. I planned to attend other sessions by authors of the books I had read to extend my definition of research.

One panel presentation about ethics had an emphasis on quantitative research. I picked up a large stack of documents describing standards from various institutions including AERA and the Department of Education. Because they had not addressed the subject in their remarks, during the question period I asked if any of the speakers had ideas about ethical standards for teacher research. The chair of the panel said that for an answer to my question I need only read the current issue of the *Educational Researcher*, an AERA monthly journal.

I was stunned because, as an eager new member, I had already read the article and knew that the author, E. David Wong (1995), asserted that researching and teaching are not compatible. He believes that each requires a different kind of knowledge—one theoretical and one practical—and generates a different kind of inquiry—one contributing to a theoretical knowledge base and the other limited to an understanding of one's own practice. He refers to his own stance as that of a "researcher/teacher" and describes his sometimes difficult experience in the classroom as a university researcher who spends time in schools.

A few months later another article appeared in response to Wong's, as exciting as a new installment of a serial novel. Suzanne M. Wilson (1995), also a university researcher, asserted that research and teaching are not two different roles, but a relationship. As a teacher-researcher, she uses the skills and knowledge of both teaching and researching, looking intentionally and in different ways at what she does as a teacher.

Although her remarks came much closer to describing my own experience, I also have felt the tensions described by Wong. I see connections between teaching and researching, but the connections raise questions about the nature of each. The questions are challenging; they are political, ethical, and epistemological, as well as practical. They hover around a central question: How do teachers learn?

Most teachers begin their formal learning about teaching in colleges and universities. After they learn to do research in graduate programs, are teachers incapable of conducting it in their classrooms? Are they only to consume the knowledge produced by knowledge producers? What if that knowledge turns out to be false to what they observe in their classrooms? If that happens, is it because the teachers either misunderstood the research or are incompetently appropriating the findings?

If teachers learn by this appropriating process, is teacher research only a staff development effort? Do teachers' research findings matter beyond their own classrooms? What if teachers began conducting their own staff development based on their research? What will happen to university research and researchers if teachers begin conducting research that matters?

My thinking was full of such questions and connections. Is practical knowledge of lesser value than theoretical knowledge? Are the knowledge producers all university researchers? Does the status of the producers demand such separation between research and practice? Or is it Aristotle? Are separate knowledges harmful to our understanding of how teaching and learning take place? Do teachers, having only practical knowledge, teach students only practical knowledge?

My thoughts suddenly turned to my students. What is the quality of the relationship between teacher-researcher and student? Will their new relationship add to the definition of teaching or to the understanding of student learning? Are teacher-researchers pulled in too many directions to be effective? Or are they given direction by their research stance? Does their power over students make their data suspect? Or are they able to forge a research partnership with their students that teaches them how a learner behaves?

The more I thought about what I had learned at the AERA conference, the more I knew that in seeking to understand the ethics of teacher research, I was changing my ideas of both research and teaching. One evening a few weeks later at a teacher-researcher group meeting, we were each trying to represent our current research thinking in a diagram and sketch. Mine looked like the parting of the Red Sea, itself labeled "Research Ethics." One side was the past, with old definitions of teaching and research; the other was the present and future, with revised definitions. I wrote a term on the "Past" side and tried to redefine it on the "Present and Future" side. (See Figure 1.1.) When I showed my primitive sketch to the rest of the group, they could see the connections. When I asked how, aside from help from Moses, we could arrive at ethics that include these changes, one teacher said, "By having lots more discussions like this."

WRITING THE FIRST DRAFT

At this point I knew that rethinking and revising would always be needed to establish ethical principles for teacher research and that teacher-researchers, their students, and their colleagues who are school administrators and university researchers must share the decision making. Also, in all efforts of this kind, someone would have to write the first draft.

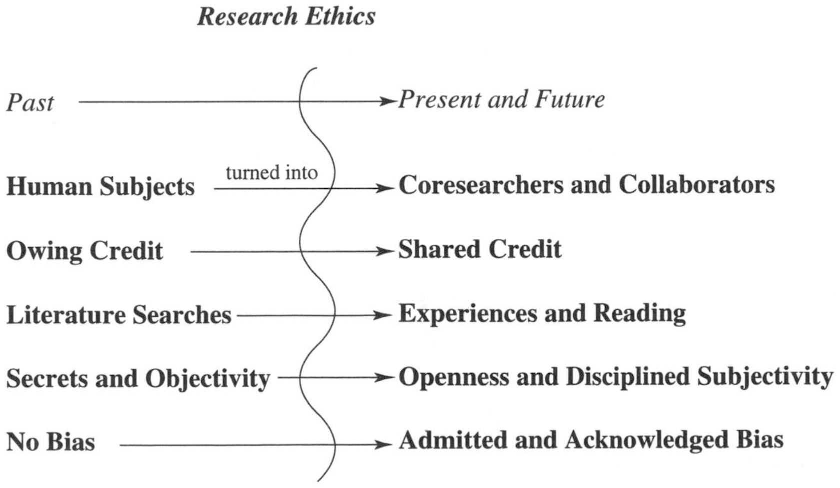

Research Ethics

Past ———————————→ *Present and Future*

Human Subjects —— turned into ——→ **Coresearchers and Collaborators**

Owing Credit ———————→ **Shared Credit**

Literature Searches ————→ **Experiences and Reading**

Secrets and Objectivity ——→ **Openness and Disciplined Subjectivity**

No Bias ————————→ **Admitted and Acknowledged Bias**

FIGURE 1.1. Research Ethics

The draft presented in this chapter originated because a group of teachers in Frederick County, Virginia, and I were conducting classroom research with the support of the district and the Assistant Superintendent for Instruction, Patricia Taylor. After discussion with Taylor and the research group from James Wood High School—Lisa Byers, Jane Campbell, Fran Jeffries (a building administrator), Theresa Manchey, Vicki Pitcock, Victoria Santucci, and B. J. Westervelt—I wrote a first draft. We all discussed it, and revisions were incorporated. Eventually, a statement was decided upon and adopted for use in the Frederick County schools. The research group agreed that I could circulate this version to other teacher-researchers seeking to write guidelines of their own.

After the original drafting process, members of the Fairfax County Public Schools Teacher-Researcher Network made suggestions to be incorporated. Teacher-researchers of the Prince William County Institute (of the Institute of Educational Transformation of George Mason University) also contributed suggestions. As an AERA member, I joined the Teacher Research special interest group and circulated the draft in their newsletter with permission to copy and revise as necessary. Responses received from this group were duly added. The whole process took place over two to three years and gradually led to some consensus among the contributors.

One point on which all agreed was the need for a background statement that explained teacher research, particularly how it both resembles and differs from more conventional research in schools. Everyone also agreed that an explanation of how a teacher both teaches and conducts research would be helpful. The explanations included in the draft below attempt to describe the value of teacher research to schools and its function as an extension of teaching. Our goal was to support and encourage ethical teacher research of high quality.

This draft may not be new to those who belong to any of the teacher research networks mentioned above. Occasionally, I see part of the statement in another document or publication, and my colleagues and I are pleased that it has provided other teacher-researchers with a basis for developing their own ideas. The draft that follows is the version of the statement that I prefer at the time of this writing.

———

TEACHER-RESEARCHER STATEMENT OF ETHICS

Background

Classroom research is conducted by many teachers as part of their day-to-day work and is seen by them as an integral part of their teaching and as a way to increase and improve their students' learning. They are formalizing, as researchers, what they already do, as teachers, by systematically documenting and analyzing their work and that of their students. Their students are collaborators in their research and may help to plan data collection, conduct data analysis, and draft findings based on the analysis.

Teacher-researchers' data grows dynamically as the research progresses. They identify their own assumptions and biases as they work, seeking a disciplined subjectivity and a clear statement of the research context. Their research is part of their professional development, and they work with respect for their students, their educational colleagues, and the community.

Teacher-researchers may conduct studies as assignments in university classes, through grants funded from outside the school system (by a professional organization, for example), as school-sponsored efforts to benefit their district, or as self-sponsored projects to answer their own questions about teaching and learning. Each of these situations involves slightly different ethical responsibilities.

Whatever the context, teacher-researchers' primary responsibility is to their students, and they and their students are the primary beneficiaries of their work. When teacher-researchers have a commitment to the professional world beyond their classroom—to their school districts and to education in general—they take on additional responsibilities common to any researcher.

In summary, teachers' research contributes to improved teaching and learning in classrooms and provides much-needed information to educational research in general. Teacher-researchers take part in the discourse of their profession. Because of the public nature of teachers' responsibilities and the nature of teacher research itself, ethical standards for the research require cooperative discussion. The five statements that follow have been developed by teacher-researchers and school administrators in an effort to encourage teacher research while maintaining the highest ethical standards.

Statement of Ethics

1. The Teacher-Researcher Role. Teacher-researchers are teachers first. They respect those with whom they work, openly sharing information about their research. While they seek understanding and knowledge, they also nurture the well-being of others, both students and professional colleagues.

2. Research Plans. Teacher-researchers consult with teaching colleagues and appropriate supervisors to review the plans for their studies. They explain their research questions and methods of data collection and update their plans as the research progresses.

3. Data Collection. Teacher-researchers use data from observations, discussions, interviews, and writing that are collected during the normal process of teaching and learning. They secure the principal's permission for broader surveys or letters to solicit data. They also secure permission if they need to use data already gathered by the school to which they would ordinarily have access as part of their teaching responsibilities such as standardized test scores.

4. Research Results. Teacher-researchers may present the results of their research to colleagues in their school districts and at other professional meetings. When they plan to share their conclusions and findings in presentations outside the school or district, they consult with their local supervisors. They are both honest in their conclusions and sensitive to the effects of their research findings on others.

5. Publication. Teacher-researchers may publish their reports. Before publishing, teacher-researchers obtain written releases from the individuals involved in the research, both teachers and students, and parental permission for students 18 years old or younger. The confidentiality of the people involved in the research is protected.

The draft status of this statement is to accommodate as many ideas from teacher-researchers in various teaching situations as possible. Draft circulation also acknowledges that such statements are not owned, but exist as documents for all to revise and make use of to support and encourage the best teacher research. Particular school systems or organizations supporting teacher-researchers in their work may wish to add more specific guidelines to meet their needs.

———

GOING PUBLIC

There are many questions to be answered about teacher research, so the drafting process continues; but there are also school districts where teacher research has been conducted, used as staff development, published in professional journals, and consequently where ethical and quality decisions have been and are being made. I purposely couple the words *ethical* and *quality* because I think that in teacher research the quality of the study is highly dependent on the ethics with which the study was conducted. In every part of the research process—from revising the question to analyzing and writing about the data—the ethical stance of the researcher has an impact on the results.

For example, a research question such as "Why won't my students do their homework?" differs ethically from a question such as "What happens when I assign my students homework?" The latter question could lead to a study of homework, to useful staff development for the school and community about issues relating to homework, and possibly even to some ideas about using it more successfully as a help in learning.

Even when teacher research is accepted as normal practice, as it makes its way into the life of the school, new issues arise. What kind of relationship exists between teachers in a school who are conducting research and those who are not? What is the best way for a principal and faculty to make good use of the teacher research conducted in their school? How will the parent community react to the teachers' research? Collected teacher research in a school can become the basis for decision making, planning, and program evaluation.

In the high school where I taught for many years, each year's first faculty meeting opened with a new attendance policy. In some cases, more paper work was required; in others, the point was to have less. Some years, teachers were required to call the homes of absentees; other years, we were not to call home. Sometimes absenteeism was to be reflected in students' grades, other times not. I never heard anyone speak of research that had been conducted to try to understand why the absenteeism existed or what might be an effective way to reduce it. We were simply switching systems because some statistics indicated that we had an absentee rate that some other statistics determined was too high.

Although I tried not to be cynical about the various systems, I had a hard time remembering which one was currently in use, and besides, I had a system for my own classes that I thought worked pretty well. No one had asked me or any other teacher in the school what system we thought might work, and no teachers had done any research on the question. I want to teach in a school where decisions are made on the basis of carefully analyzed data—teacher- and student-collected data that tells why and how things happen. In this school, decisions about policies would be made with the help and knowledge of teachers, students, and their parents.

But if that is the kind of school I desire, I must also advocate ethical standards for teacher research that are developed through the participation of the people involved. The quality that unites all educators is not cynicism, but a belief in the possibility of change. When we learn something new, we are changed. Teacher-researchers are working to achieve this kind of learning for themselves and their students, and their participation in the decisions that affect their ability to teach and learn is an ethical requirement.

My own participation in the explorations and revisions that have been discussed has left me with another set of guidelines about the process itself. They don't qualify as a final draft, I know, but in any endeavor when the collaborators are this different and distant, the first draft writers don't own the final drafts that emerge. I have learned that the talking, writing, and reviewing in different contexts—classrooms, schools, meetings of colleagues, and professional meetings—and the draft guidelines put out for the professional community to use and revise are all parts of an essential process. When I participate in discussions of teacher research ethics I can offer that process and these basic assumptions about how it works:

1. Teacher research ethical guidelines are the same basic ethical guidelines followed by any researcher in any situation, but they exist in a different context—the classrooms and schools in which teachers teach and conduct research—and that context cannot be ignored by the guidelines.

2. Ethical guidelines need to define both *teaching* and *researching* in relation to teacher research. A good way to begin is by describing how teacher research concepts of teaching and researching differ from those the readers might be familiar with from their education or the media.

3. Effective guidelines are written for a wide audience, including the school board and parent community as well as professional colleagues. Guidelines are more easily understood by those unfamiliar with teacher research if they are written with a limited amount of educational jargon and without condescension.

4. Research colleagues outside of the K–12 public school systems need to educate themselves about teacher research so that they can use their experience in colleges, universities, and educational institutes to assist in the development of ethical guidelines. Teachers in graduate programs are often interested in teacher research and are also in a good position to help draft ethical guidelines.

5. A framework that follows and describes the process of teacher research is a useful way to write the guidelines because those who read them can then understand what happens when teachers conduct research in their classrooms and how research should be conducted in an ethically responsible manner.

6. Ethical guidelines need to recognize the public nature of teacher research and anticipate both its local uses and the possibilities of professional publications and presentations.

My assumptions about ethics are themselves based on the idea that the most important quality of teacher research is its emphasis on understanding teaching and learning in classrooms. Schools that encourage their teacher-researchers send, to both students and teachers, a valuable message of respect for and interest in their learning. In the face of editorial pronouncements, political threats, reform demands, and harsh judgments of schools by those who know little of life within them, such a message is itself an ethical statement.

NOTE

1. All references to people and places in this chapter use their real names to recognize their contributions to my thinking.

Chapter 2

"TUESDAY NIGHT" REVISITED: LEARNING TO SURVIVE

Leslie Turner Minarik

The following piece was written some years ago, during a time when the stress of being a new teacher in an urban elementary school caused me many sleepless nights. A member of my teacher research group, Dr. Sam Hollingsworth, suggested that I write down my thoughts.[1] And so one Tuesday night, though I hated writing and hated getting out of bed even more, I found myself at the computer trying to exorcise my frustrations. I wrote until tears ran down my face and eventually made it to bed to fall asleep.

Over the years, each time I have come across this piece, I have shed tears for my young students. Today I realize that the issues I unknowingly outlined would push me to action, then discourage me until I retreated to my classroom again. They were issues I, of necessity, learned to cope with to survive as a teacher. And they were issues that would eventually convince me to do my own research.

"Tuesday Night" was the discovery of my voice. It was encouraged by the teacher research group of which I am still a member. But in 1990 I was just beginning as a researcher; later, our group published several papers (including Hollingsworth, Teel, & Minarik, 1992) and a book, *Teacher Research and Urban Literacy Education* (Hollingsworth, 1994).

That night's writing started me on a journey to research school reform. But the mindlessness of those in power continued, and I eventually stopped trying, happy and embarrassed to rediscover the joy in my classroom. "Tuesday Night" helped me clarify my purpose as a teacher and determine where my allegiance lay. In this essay, I will read the story again, reflecting on where I have been and where I am going.

TUESDAY NIGHT

[*Written to myself in my third year of teaching*]
May 16, 1990

I'm tired. I wasn't so tired earlier. It is not a physical weariness. It is a case of wanting to forget—an emotional weariness. But I can't sleep.

I came home with my bag, full as usual. Tonight I planned to review the rest of the year and get an idea of what the children should work on before we leave for summer vacation. I want to make sure we don't miss anything. I want the end of the year to be important for them. They deserve a good send-off to third grade. I'll miss them. All of this goes through my mind. Instead of my work I'll probably read my mystery book which I keep on my nightstand just for these occasions when I need to forget, for awhile, what is happening in the "environment" I spend my days in. If the environment were just my room and the children, I wouldn't feel this way. The reality is that the "educational environment" is my room and the children AND the administration AND the community. And I keep hearing the words of a gentleman from a "department of education" who, when addressing teachers' stories, said that "we must teach them to be better teachers faster." As if we teachers do not also wish the same thing. As if we are not painfully aware of our shortcomings.

I am trying to forget the phone call I got from a parent. I have worked so hard with her son to get him to read. I have called the parents at home a number of times to get their support and to work with them. She is upset. I was trying to get my own daughter dinner when I got the call. I stopped to listen to her. She's never initiated a phone call before. My daughter's dinner was cold by the time I finished listening to her. The mother is still mad because the district announced last week that our school [building] will be closed at the end of the year. During the October earthquake our auditorium/lunchroom was damaged. The earthquake happened as my daughter and I were en route to school for the first- and second-grade potluck. Several primary teachers thought it would be a good idea to have the children perform in October and have a potluck so that we could see the parents. They don't usually come to school. We made it to school that night and we ate and performed with the parents and teachers who came and remained despite the disaster. Little did we know how great the damage was. Seven months later (seven months of children eating in the classroom, of teaching with milk on the floors and sticky food on the tables, of having children eating breakfast in the office hall), we got word of the closure.

This parent pulled her child out of school because she was afraid the building was unsafe. I was sorry to see him go. She called tonight because she wanted to transfer her child to another school or to teach him at home which requires a lot of paperwork. However, she was also considering taking him out of school for three weeks on vacation and letting him come back for the last week. She wanted to know if she could do this. I told her I didn't know. She's mad and thinks that I'm giving her the runaround. I don't know the district's rules. I'm a teacher. I think about what the kids should know. I haven't studied the district's policies in this area. I've studied her son and his reading skills. We go around and around. I still can't give her a definite answer. She would like me to prepare three weeks of work for her son in the event that she can keep him enrolled in my class, but not have him in my class. But earthquakes are rare. "This is an unusual encounter with a parent," I tell myself.

When they announced that we would have to move, it didn't bother me. So much goes on in this environment that you learn to take things in stride or to try to forget them. Several teachers met informally after school to talk through some of the issues. As we did, we began to think about how much work it would be to pack everything up and to move it. When are we supposed to do this? While we teach? After school when we plan and prepare? During summer? I had to clean and scrub out the pit of a room when I was hired, and I have moved rooms every year since then. This summer I even snuck into my room and scrubbed and painted it. Teachers aren't allowed to paint their rooms, but then the district won't paint them either. I thought, "Certainly I will be in this room for several years. I can come back to school next year and start off totally focused on teaching." I pounded posters on the walls. It looked so nice. So—I'll pack everything. They say we'll have to move into portables. The other school site needs a lot of work. They say to pack what we really need on top for the beginning of the year. Perhaps we will have to move again in the middle of the year. I begin to feel tired at the thought of it.

As I was leaving school today, I heard that if we don't get another vote on the school board for the bond issue that the school district will go into receivership. The superintendent will most likely quit at that point. There is serious question as to whether the important vote can be gotten. I wonder how disastrous this will be. Maybe they won't have the money for the portables that we need to teach in. In one of my classes the children and I were reading about how children in Africa have school outside, sometimes under a tree, except in the rainy season of course.

I begin thinking of another student. He transferred into my room late in the year. He was so depressed and out of touch with school. He got into bad trouble and yet he had turned around. Last week when I ran into him in the hall he had a smile on his face. His mother brought him to school to say she was pulling him out. Perhaps she was going to have him

move in with her. She must have lived nearer another school. He wanted
to tell me. The reasons behind this action are common. We talk about
them at school. But we don't print them. Maybe we can't. He and his
younger sister were living with his mother's friend while she [his mother]
was in a drug rehab center. The friend put the younger sister's hand on a
hot burner to teach her a lesson about lying. The child had also been ex-
torting money from other first graders at school. But she was a survivor.
You had to give her credit for that. Her older brother wasn't. He was like
a black hole turning in on himself. This day they were back with their
mother. He seemed happy.

I heard today that he and his little sister are in foster care now after
only one week with the mom. I remember that when he was in my class
someone very special came to work with him each Friday. His reading
was so much better. He came to school each day. He smiled. Now he is
gone. I can't help him now. I feel he is lost and in spite of the tears I am
shedding now, I will try to forget all about this because if I hurt too much
for him I can't do a good job. I have to stay to teach the others.

There were more stories to tell about parents this week. I won't re-
peat them. My husband will listen, but you can't burden people too much
with this stuff. The other teachers are so supportive, but I think even we
know we must be careful about unloading too much on each other. A person can only ask for so much support. You ultimately must learn to deal
with this environment.

A colleague and I had thought about working together next year. We
want to do some peer coaching and thought of writing an integrated sci-
ence/language arts curriculum for our second-grade classes. Teaching has
taught me a lot in a short time. It has taught me to be flexible. I am
VERY flexible now. However, I seem to be more impatient some days
than I used to be. But the reality is that here, in this environment, being
impatient for things to get better doesn't pay. It pays to be flexible. So my
colleague and I will plan and then see how much we can accomplish
given all the other "situations" that always occur within this educational
environment which don't have anything directly to do with helping children to learn.

They are making budget cuts. We don't know what this will mean. It
is hard to get supplies now. But the good news last week was that they
said that our principal would stay with us next year. I had drafted a letter
to request that they leave our principal. After all, how could they move
him? How could someone else be thrown into this? He was doing so
much. The staff signed it and we got a quick response. It came the same
morning that we were told we would move. Well, at least he would be

there to help. Our teachers learn to be thankful for whatever good news comes their way. Our teachers are flexible and not very picky.

But this week they told us he would not stay. A school in an upper-middle-class neighborhood doesn't like their principal. They will be sent ours. Their parents are vociferous. Ours are silent. They didn't say this was the reason they were transferring him, of course, but it is the truth. Our meeting with the superintendent was futile. Our questions about this decision only riled him. He finally shook his finger at us and said, "Teachers don't make decisions." So we learned something new this week. It is best not to put too much faith in what the district says. Nor is it wise to be too hopeful about effecting change. We are just teachers, after all.

The children are wonderful. That is the only unchanging truth. That is why I do what I do. And I keep hearing the voice of the nice gentleman who wanted us to learn to be better teachers and do it more quickly. Does anyone from the "outside" ever spend any time in a classroom? Maybe they all want to forget what is happening in our schools more than I do tonight.

I feel better now. I don't know why. Maybe I can sleep now.

"TUESDAY NIGHT" REVISITED

March, 1998

When I was asked for this piece, it took me a while to find it. Reading it always brought back so many memories I'd cry all over again. I didn't cry this time. I wonder what that means.

There have been no more major earthquakes, but I still get asked to pack up and move. I am more flexible and more patient. I listen to little the district says, because I trust less. I don't write protest letters anymore—well, not often. I still give my daughter cold dinners. Except tonight she is making dinner for me so I can finish some work for school. I am much better at shutting off the insanity of what happens or doesn't happen outside my classroom. I sleep better. Perhaps I have learned how to be a better teacher in the most efficient way. Younger, idealistic, caring teachers look so tired and struggle so much.

The children are still wonderful. And despite everything, they are there most every day, and I am there with them every day.

February, 1999

So what are the ethical issues raised by my experiences as a teacher-researcher? I think I was fortunate that my research came later in my teaching, after I had formulated a very clear and strong understanding of who I was and what my mission was.

Student Advocacy

I knew I was primarily an educator, a teacher, an advocate for my students. I had heard many people call themselves educators, thus implying that they were interested in students, but in fact giving priority to other demands. Once I had defined myself as an advocate for children, I gladly tackled ethical dilemmas related to teaching. While other teachers debated whether to follow district curriculum mandates or whether to follow what experience had taught them their students needed, I did not.

During this time of defining myself and finding my voice, I became more aware of how school districts operate. Administrators listen to the "state" or to "downtown" or to powerful members of the community whose voices are scarier than teachers. Who were they listening to when they took the principal away from a faculty and student body who had been in chaos for close to a year? Who do they listen to when they bemoan our low test scores yet refuse to buy practice tests to prepare the students? What are they thinking when they send out a memo entitled "Testing Tips"—"Provide your students with a nutritious beverage and snack"? (Should teachers buy them out of their own pockets? Perhaps the author of this tip didn't bother to think that far.)

District-sponsored in-service, though well intentioned, tends to deal with new curriculum by supporting it uncritically in the face of clear problems. Such workshops may be presented by those who have taught and done research but now work as consultants for textbook companies. I remember the day when some of us teachers asked about limited-English students who couldn't read the text. We were assured that "if the child sat with the book for a year and listened to the other students, they would learn to read." A colleague and I looked at each other, secretly shook our heads, and decided to get books that our students could read. Naively we asked the district, expecting support because they had just sent out memos on our dismal reading results. Their response: "Students should all be reading on grade level." Who were they listening to? the state? the textbook consultant? Rather than honest, critical, professional discussions about how and what we must do to help children, there is often abdication.

By then I was no one's employee. I had loyalty only to the students. So I just "borrowed" the books that my students needed from book storage rooms, and I taught what I needed to teach with a new clearness of purpose. I did not wrestle with such minor ethical decisions.

Doing the Right Thing

My teacher-researcher group was of like mind. Although we taught different grade levels, from elementary school through university, we all were bound by our commitment to our students. Our monthly conversations revolved around a myriad of topics, but our goals were to find better ways of working with students, regardless of constraints that might be placed on us, and to explore honestly our own biases.

Although my research has not focused on issues of class or race, the ethical necessity of studying our own practice is especially serious for teachers in large, urban, culturally diverse schools where most students qualify for free lunch and teachers of color are underrepresented. This is even more true now as some people argue that those of us who are White cannot research children of color.

Caring teachers have no ethical option but to do the right thing. A friend, Hugh Sockett, describes our profession as a "moral" one. If teachers embrace that philosophy, decisions become easier, though the answers may be painful. Around the time that I wrote "Tuesday Night," I attended a workshop for an alternative math program. Some teachers in the audience spent many minutes explaining that they couldn't use what appeared to be a developmentally sound program because it wasn't part of the district's math curriculum. The presenter said, "Sometimes you have to lock your door and do the right thing." She soundly advised those of us who caught her words to put a few "approved" math texts near the door in case "someone" should walk in. It was such a novel comment that I have remembered it all these years and passed it on to student teachers and new teachers: "If you believe that you have a moral obligation to teach your students to the best of your abilities, then your ethical decisions must be guided by your knowledge of your students and by best practice—whether approved or not."

Of course, this puts the burden on the teacher to find the best practice, to engage in dialogues that are enlightening and self-critical. I have little tolerance for teachers who will make no changes even when methods are obviously not working. I recently heard a teacher say she was "following guidelines," making her seven-year-old students "sit by themselves silently, with a book in their hands, for 20 minutes during Sustained Silent Reading period—though I know they would benefit from reading out loud and discussing what they read." We teachers cannot wait for an enlightened person to come and release us to do the right thing. Are we not empowered by virtue of our experience and expertise to make these decisions or at least to begin a dialogue?

Monthly meetings with my teacher-researcher group provided a link to the world of education beyond my site and my district. And they pushed me to look critically at my practice as well as at myself. These wonderful, now-close friends, the presenter who refreshingly spoke the truth, the framing of our role as a "moral" one, all gave me support to find my own answers. There are many valid reasons for doing action research. It is unfortunate to be prompted because one cannot trust those "in power." But perhaps that is the best reason to begin.

Systemic Reform?

For a few years I believed in school reform, starting at the bottom. I had no concerns about speaking up and writing critiques. For years I followed a well-documented research project from Mills College that dealt with attempts by area high school teachers to make reforms (Abbey, Connor, & Squires, 1995). For various reasons, including changes in administration, their attempts at lasting school reform failed. *Schools for the Twenty-First Century*, by Phillip C. Schlechty (1990), helped me understand why. He stresses vision: "Restructuring requires that one's loyalty be bound to principles and visions, not to individual leaders" (p. 10). The book concludes:

> Leaders with a clear understanding of their organization's purpose, a realistic under-
> standing of their organization's capacity to achieve this purpose, and a compelling
> vision of how their organization could be made to pursue this purpose effectively
> are in short supply. The difficulty is that—in schools more than in most organiza-
> tions—creative leadership is discouraged at the top as well as the bottom. (p. 154)

When I read this, it clarified my belief that there was more to be done than working with students if teachers were to fulfill their moral and ethical commitment. Unfortunately, I made little impact; so in time I stopped, discouraged.

But look at Schlechty's words and substitute *teachers* for *leaders*. What I read is encouragement to think clearly about our purpose and what we teachers realistically can do so that students learn well, in a supportive environment. Such a vision can allow us to succeed even in an environment that does not feel comfortable nor encourage creativity. Thus from a defeating experience I found encouragement to move forward in my classroom. Renewing one's commitment is critical to surviving.

Classroom-Level Reform Through Action Research

When I let go of school reform, I wanted to look thoughtfully at what was happening in my own classroom. Action research gave me a systematic way to deal with my concerns over certain teaching practices. My efforts were supported by my research group and by others who believed in teacher knowledge and creativity, in teachers' ability to research their own practice rather than depending on traditional research handed down from an institution.

When it was mandatory to teach whole class reading, I began to research homogeneous groupings for a segment of the day. And while I still put the district-approved texts by the door, I used whatever materials benefited the students I had in a given year. Teachers know if they wait long enough, what they are doing that they're not supposed to be doing, may well be approved. So now, lo and behold, phonics and reading groups are "in" again.

In the ever changing world of curriculum, I believe that, as ethical teachers, we must constantly reconnect with our vision and look into the eyes of those to whom we are loyal—the children. We should learn about new research but look at it critically and pursue our own research. In following this path I have not been very frustrated. It is relatively easy to do what we must when we know why. I have thought about my purpose for years now and believe I can defend myself. Yet I've felt an ethical conflict when talking with new teachers. I hesitate to ask them to stick their necks out, although we teachers must at some point—if we are to do what is best for our students.

Doing action research has helped me to change my own practice, as I have described in my published study entitled "Gender Equity in an Elementary Classroom: The Power of Praxis in Action Research" (Minarik & Lock, 1997). When I discovered the depth and source of inequity in my classroom, I was compelled to intervene, continuing the research to monitor my attempts to correct the problem.

The University Connection

Although my research has sometimes challenged school district policy, it would probably be considered safe by human subjects review boards at universities. Such committees might ask, "Will you gather data on your normal educational practice and on changes in curriculum, instruction, and assessment that you could make . . . according to your own professional judgement?" (See Epilogue.) I can answer "yes," so my research would fall into the category that needs minimal review.

I have had access to a university and a research group for help in monitoring such ethical issues. The university offered the advice to change or code student names and disguise school locations because anonymity offers protection from many ethical risks. Members of my group have been able to work out issues of acknowledgement among ourselves. I consider myself fortunate in having a university connection.

Yet I don't believe my situation is typical. In the Epilogue, "A Guide to Ethical Decision Making for Insider Research," Jane Zeni begins, "Practitioner research has become a major mode of inquiry in American education." I disagree. I work in a very large school district, and it has no formal acknowledgement nor support for teacher research. This also seems to be true of neighboring districts. For those teachers who connect with a university program, huge doors are opened. Ethical issues are discussed with more experienced members. There is access to publishing and help in framing the work in language suited to publication. And in a teacher-friendly environment, teachers wrestle less in getting credit for their work.

For those who work on their own, ethical guidelines may well not be common knowledge. Paul Anderson (1998) warns that new action researchers may not be aware of ethical issues they may face in doing person-based research. If action research is in fact exploding, then it is necessary to consider how to disseminate information on ethics to those who are not university connected.

On the other hand, when I attended my first AERA meeting in the early 1990s, I recognized another concern. Too many people involved in educational research at universities remain too far from the subjects they write about. I saw that teachers were often ignored even when their students were observed by outside researchers. How ethical is research when teachers' experiences and interpretations are excluded from the analysis? I have seen some changes since I began attending AERA. Clearly K–12 teachers must be involved in collaboration with those at universities if action research is to grow until it truly becomes a major force in shaping teacher practice.

Teacher-researchers and university researchers need one another. Without a university connection, it is unlikely that teachers' work will be published. If their voices are not heard, teachers will continue to be relegated to the lower rungs of the educational ladder. Fortunately the style of university research is now being debated, and research partnerships are increasing.

Change

I support the discussion of ethical issues, but I hope such debates do not discourage teachers from doing research. In my experience, teacher research has been one of the most powerful tools I have possessed to improve my practice. Few in-service programs have so profoundly changed my teaching for a sustained period of time. (It is said that less than 5% of what one hears in a workshop results in long-term implementation.)

Teacher research adds the critical factor of motivation—the teacher chooses the topic. Research also demands close observation. I think I am a good observer of the many conversations and events that go on each day in my room, but I am always surprised at how much more I see when I am doing a study. Teacher research supports the reflection that good teachers already rely on, helping them to modify a myriad of details in the classroom. It encourages a teacher to reach out for information and help. The research I have done, the connections that have resulted, and the conversations in my teacher-researcher group have nurtured my growth as a teacher.

REFLECTION

The writing of "Tuesday Night" seemed at the time a simple exercise in releasing frustration. I see now that it was a survival tactic. It was a way of laying out issues that I would need to wrestle with if I was to continue to teach in what often seemed like chaos and insanity. Defining and building on my loyalty to students above all has helped me to filter the many issues, including those of ethics, and to prioritize the many demands that are made by administrators and the state. Time and a clear vision have taught me patience, flexibility, and problem-solving skills. Writing "Tuesday Night" was a way of finding my voice, and that was the beginning of my empowerment as a teacher.

With support from my group—Sam, Anthony, Jennifer, Mary, and Karen— and also from Robyn, Diane, Anne, Jim, and others, doing research was a logical next step. It has opened new avenues that will prevent burnout and encourage growth. It has also taught me to choose my battles, to continue asking questions, and to rekindle my vision.

NOTE

1. On this chapter, references to members of my teacher research group use their real names to recognize their contributions to my thinking. Other people, places, and institutions are unnamed to protect their privacy.

Chapter 3

COMING TO KNOW MY PLACE

Wanda C. Clay

It was the fall of 1998 and I thought I had reached an understanding of my place as an instructional supervisor and practitioner-researcher in an urban middle school. I discovered, however, that my place was not as clear as I had believed. A routine event showed me once again just how unclear my place was.

I had been working with the language arts department on the writing program for what seemed like forever. They had finally developed a checklist that reflected types of writing as well as specific products by grade level. I was given this checklist at the end of the 1997–1998 school year and considered it a good beginning. When school began in September, I returned to the checklist and asked the department head, "Okay, how many of these products will be retained in the writing folders, and how many will display examples of process?" (Our feeder high schools had requested that students' folders should contain products that displayed attention to process.) The department head met with the teachers and presented my questions. One response revealed that my place as a practitioner-researcher was not clear to the teachers and possibly not even to me. One sixth-grade language arts teacher said, "What does Wanda want? I think she should just come and tell us exactly what she wants!" I still had not reached the place where the questions I posed were viewed as part of an inquiry process and not the demands of an instructional supervisor.

THE ETHICS OF A PRACTITIONER-RESEARCHER

Smith (1990a) say *ethics* as "refer to a complex of ideals showing how individuals should relate to one another in particular situations, to principles of conduct guiding those relationships, and to the kind of reasoning one engages in when thinking about such ideals and principles" (p. 141). Initially, I had some difficulty writing this chapter. I tried to focus on ethics as if it were a thing separate from the acts that define it. I am a middle school instructional supervisor responsible for supporting and assisting teachers as *they* improve instruction. I am also a researcher studying my actions as a supervisor. Since the primary functions of my role center on instructional improvement—change—I am a change agent engaged in action research.

Noffke and Stevenson (1995) define *action research* in part as "the ongoing process of identifying contradictions, which, in turn help to locate spaces for ethically defensible, politically strategic action" (p. 5). Because they are insiders, action researchers tend to encounter certain ethical complexities.

Most outside researchers aim for detachment from the community under research, avoiding relationships with subjects or informants that could muddy the waters of data collection and analysis. Yet the action researcher must develop and then analyze the relationships that facilitate effective change.

As an action researcher, my perspective is different from that of an outside researcher. Yet it is also different from the traditional school-based action researcher—the teacher. I am neither a teacher nor an outside expert conducting research on teaching. Because of my role, my actions involve proposing change that would benefit the total school community.

My premise is that the ethics of action research is really the merger of the ethically defensible actions of the practitioner and the ethically defensible actions of the researcher. And at the center of that ethically defensible action is the relationship between the practitioner-researcher and the other practitioners in the research setting.

LEADERSHIP AS ETHICALLY DEFENSIBLE ACTION

In September 1994, I began conducting systematic research of my practice as an instructional supervisor in order to identify ways to improve my practice. My original research question was this: "Using group development as my primary method of assistance, can I, in the role of Instructional Coordinator at Urban Prep, support and assist teachers as they improve instruction?"[1] I began my study by reorganizing the entire staff into small groups and teams. This reorganization changed my relationships with the staff.

At the start of my research, I believed I was analyzing *my* situation—how I as a practitioner assisted teachers in groups as they planned and implemented well-designed, well-thought-out instruction. But in fact, my actions and the changes I proposed involved ways that *we* could make it better. Thus my initial questions and plans did not include a critical examination of the myriad consequences my own actions would produce. Although I believed my question and my research focused on positive change for the total school community, my actions often contradicted this espoused belief. As a result, the changes I proposed, although warranted, were not necessarily welcome.

Over the course of my 3-year study, I encountered a variety of resistance and opposition to my actions as a change agent. Of course there were many reasons: opposition to change of any kind, lack of consensus on what needed changing, unwillingness to work for change, mountains of failure with previous change attempts, and an incomplete understanding of the factors that effect change. Regardless of the reason, as a practitioner I was responsible for facilitating change as best I could. Ultimately, my central ethical concern became the problems that surfaced in my relationships with others at the school. Most of those ethical concerns—the opposition and resistance—were derived from the beliefs of other practitioners about what constituted the legitimate responsibilities and actions of a change agent.

As a researcher I was responsible for studying and analyzing the "best efforts" of the practitioner. Over the years, I have attempted to identify the ethical principles that should inform my action research relationships. Time and time again, two questions have emerged as central. The first involves the extent of my authority and power to set a change agenda: "How does a practitioner-researcher establish a climate and process for defining improvement and reaching agreement or consensus without coercion—real or perceived?" The second question emerges from the first and examines the types of associations I develop with other practitioners: "What does the practitioner-researcher have to do to maintain positive working relationships with teachers who feel they are being forced to consider change?" Certainly there have been other questions. These two, however, reflect how I continuously strive to understand my ethically defensible place in action research relationships. "Coming to know my place" is not a declaration of my arrival. It is a statement of my ongoing journey as an action researcher.

ETHICALLY DEFENSIBLE ACTION: NEGOTIATING AUTHORITY

In my role as an instructional supervisor, I was given authority by the policymakers in the River City district to propose a change agenda. On many occasions, the agenda was set by the policymakers and was in fact nonnegotiable. Yet my position as the "messenger" for the policymakers was only one aspect of my ethical dilemma with power and authority.

There were hordes of issues that were negotiable in my proposals. And it was these negotiable issues that resulted in the most disturbing conflicts regarding perceptions of my "power." One recurring dilemma involved the "autonomy" of the teacher.

Curriculum development is one of the five major tasks I perform as an instructional supervisor. Each department in the school works through a process of brainstorming a skeleton curriculum plan, selecting materials, and drafting a formal curriculum. The curriculum implementation year in the science department was 1994–1995. In the weekly department meetings, we engaged in a continuous dialogue regarding appropriate strategies and materials. My process in those meetings was primarily to facilitate the discussions and consolidate any written products into a draft of the curriculum guide. I also shared journal articles on issues I thought relevant to the discussion.

In every curriculum project, I tried to facilitate the development of a scope and sequence. The principal and I had discussed the need for consistency and continuity of experience at each grade level. For the science department, identifying the content of laboratory experiences proved a major concern.

In April 1995, I implemented a norming activity, giving each science teacher a form to list their lab experiences from September through March. In a note to the teachers, I explained that the goal was "to identify what *is*—those experiences that are common at each grade level—and to begin the dialogue about what *ought to be*—those experiences for the future." I then wrote a research memo reflecting on this norming activity. An excerpt from that memo illustrates this type of ethical challenge:

When we met as a department Tuesday afternoon I sensed there was a problem. I had been given the lists of lab experiences the day before and had reviewed them. The seventh- and eighth-grade teachers had collaborated the entire year and so the lists were almost identical. The sixth-grade lists, however, were markedly different. I began the discussion by asking them to pair off and examine their lists. I explained that several students had indicated that some of their lab experiments were repeated from one grade level to the next.

Bill York, an eighth-grade teacher, said, "Well, that shouldn't be. We are dealing with different content at each grade level." I told him I thought that the problem had occurred because of our concern for standardized testing, and that some teachers may have reviewed content. I then said to the group, "One way to avoid this happening in the future is to reach consensus about the lab experiences that should occur at each grade level. Just like we agreed on which units from the three texts should be covered, we should agree on common lab experiences." Tom Flowers, the sixth-grade teacher, was outraged. He started his display by saying he didn't believe that any students had experienced the same lab experiments. I asked him if he thought the students were making it up. He continued by saying, "I just don't believe any students said that." I continued by asking him just exactly what was he implying, was he saying I was lying? He verbalized his discontent by saying, "I resent this, you are interfering with my creativity and spontaneity." I asked him how identifying common experiences with his colleagues was interfering with his creativity. I also asked him how much spontaneity was appropriate in the design of educational experiences for our young people.

I understood his resentment, yet it was obvious that the two sixth-grade teachers were at odds. The fact that the sheets turned in by everybody else were similar indicated that they had either talked or were on the same wave-length. I had not intended this activity to be seen as "telling" the science teachers what the labs should be. I thought doing this activity so late in the year, after the majority of the experiments had been conducted, would indicate this. I was mistaken. I told Mrs. Battle [the principal] that I didn't believe the two sixth-grade teachers were quite ready for this kind of norming. (Clay, 1998, pp. 134–136)[2]

I believed I was posing questions that were worthy of examination. I did not intend to infringe on anyone's rights. But time and time again, I was faced with questions about the rights of individuals versus the rights of the collective. Should teachers have complete autonomy in selection of content? Would this autonomy infringe on the rights of students and parents who expected equity in content and instruction? Whose interest should the school be serving? Was I in fact simply imposing my beliefs rather than negotiating mutually accepted solutions? I encountered resistance not only when I asked which content had been selected, but also when I asked why specific content was selected.

This type of ethical challenge was not limited to individuals. Some events involved pairs or small groups of teachers. Their resistance represented a kind of collective collusion and left me feeling quite powerless. This excerpt from my dissertation describes yet another example:

I felt more confidence with language arts curriculum development than with any other subject matter because I was trained as a secondary English teacher, and I had experience teaching at the high school and college level. My specific knowledge and experience, however, proved to be the source of conflict in the language arts department [in 1996]. . . .

The process involved six classroom teachers, plus a student teacher, the librarian, the language resource specialist, and me. I assumed a participant's role in the initial stages. Since we had five strands or themes of content, we divided into five dyads, or "buddies" as Vivica Nelson [department head] called them. Each dyad was to collaborate on a strand and generate goals and objectives.

Each week a dyad was scheduled to present its strand. The remaining members of the department would critique the strand, offering suggestions, asking questions, or providing clarification. After the five strands were presented and critiqued, we began selecting primary textual materials. This process created the greatest degree of conflict in the department. . . .

The literature texts were either genre-based anthologies or thematically organized anthologies. Which should we choose—a genre anthology or a thematic anthology?

In one meeting, each dyad took a set of textual materials and reviewed them. In the next meeting, we took turns discussing our reasons for selecting or rejecting that particular text. I selected a text with a thematic approach [to review]. I stated my personal beliefs regarding the genre approach versus the thematic approach clearly. I believe the teacher has the right to consider both approaches and I stated this. I also stated my problem with thematically organized texts: "The textbook company makes the decision for you. They choose the themes. Whereas with a genre anthology, you are free to choose your own theme."

My explanation and my "role" in the textbook selection process seemed to disturb the two new staff members, Mrs. Vernon and Mr. Vincent. I suppose my concerns regarding the thematic anthology were presented with more passion than those regarding a genre anthology. I discussed the matter with Mr. Lukee [the language resource specialist] because I certainly did not want to be accused of "choosing" the books for the department. I had been accused of that once before. After my dialogue with Mr. Lukee, I developed a textbook review form that followed the framework of our curriculum. I distributed it to the staff and asked them to use it in their final textbook selections. I thought this would help the two new teachers in particular to understand that my concerns were not personal, but related to the goals of our curriculum. It really didn't seem to matter because after the voting occurred, Mrs. Vernon commented to another language arts teacher, "Why didn't you tell me this was a done deal?" She still felt I was responsible for choosing the primary text.

It was not until after we selected texts in social studies that I realized how different my role was for the two departments. I never looked at the textbooks in social studies, and Chad [Newman, seventh-grade social studies teacher] developed the selection form for the teachers. I have to rethink my position with the language arts department. Although I feel my specific content knowledge should be an asset and not a liability, I may be engaging in actions that are seen as just that.

Vivica Nelson had a different view. When I interviewed her in the summer of 1997, she described the problem as, "Simple, we didn't choose the books they wanted." I did order one set of materials and the teacher's edition for the textbook the two new teachers selected, a compromise which seemed to resolve the conflict for them. I am, nevertheless, still concerned. . . .

The two new language arts teachers were vocal regarding their "displeasure" with my role in the curriculum development process. Although I never intended to be coercive, in hindsight, my knowledge of the subject matter could easily have been considered an exercise of inappropriate power, particularly by the new teachers. (Clay, 1998, pp. 392–394)

The issue of who should determine content was a symptom of a greater problem: Who should have authority for change. As I reflected on the data, I constantly asked myself what I was doing or saying that led the other practitioners to believe I had power over them or that I was trying to limit their personal power. As the researcher, I was analyzing my actions, trying to identify the best practices, and trying to engage in collaborative processes. But to the other practitioners, my questions were seen as unwelcomed challenges to the established practices and my collaborative processes were seen as just something "new." During my analysis, I discovered something very alarming. I discovered I did have power; the power to make people "uncomfortable." This was not my goal. In fact it contradicted my goals as a researcher and a practitioner.

As the practitioner I had to address this contradiction frequently. The real power I possessed was in my ability to ask the "best" questions and to render the familiar strange. But as the researcher, I faced a dilemma: Why was a tool that was supposed to "empower" the practitioner threatening their "autonomy" and leaving them feeling powerless? I believed my resolution was in helping other practitioners see the power in this process. But what was my responsibility when they weren't ready to formulate the questions? I continue to face episodes like the scene in the language arts department, and each time I search for solutions that are fair and just and actions that are ethically defensible.

ETHICALLY DEFENSIBLE ACTION: NEGOTIATING FELLOWSHIP

My ethical dilemmas with power also involved dilemmas with my circle of influence and my associations with other practitioners. Practitioner-researchers are members of the research context. This membership over the years results in varying degrees of friendship and philosophical compatibility with others.

During the first and second year of the study, my focus was on group development. My interactions with individuals emerged primarily from the group activities. Therefore, any dilemmas I faced with individual practitioners I perceived as an outcome of the new group processes.

The changes I proposed in fact created at least two different groups—those who accepted membership in the groups and those who didn't. Many teachers chose to leave the school. I was devastated as a practitioner and a researcher. Since this was not an expected outcome, nor an acceptable one, I focused my attention on ways to prevent the exodus. But as I continued my research, I became quite concerned with the teachers who remained and professed compatibility with the changes.

As I began to increase my interaction with the individuals, I discovered that the issue of power or coercion was once again at the center of my ethical dilemmas. The following excerpt from my dissertation describes this dilemma.

On Monday, December 2, 1996, during a conversation with Mrs. Dutton and Mrs. Eddy in the cafeteria, Mrs. Dutton introduced the possibility of two distinct groups [of teachers] within our Urban Prep culture.

She labeled them "the traditional group and the nontraditional group," and went on to indicate differing behaviors associated with those two groups: "The members of the nontraditional group are subject to response from the traditional group that is not always positive. In fact, if the traditional group perceives that the nontraditional group is voicing an opinion or presenting a problem different from the traditional group, then they [the nontraditional group] are considered pawns of the administration, or the IC or something." (Clay, 1998, p. 406)

I was at first amazed by the description of "traditional" and "nontraditional." It was obvious that those who shared a philosophical compatibility with the changes being made were perceived as going against the status quo. I wondered if there was some truth to the beliefs. Were the nontraditional group members pawns? Were they receiving less-than-positive responses from the traditional members because of a perception of elevated status? How could I as the researcher address these concerns? These questions led me to a heightened concern for all individuals—the traditional and nontraditional.

As my lens shifted to individual teachers, I began to experience more and more conflict in my relationships. I considered most of my relationships a type of professional fellowship, yet there were certainly several staff members I did consider friends. Often these differences in bonds—real or perceived—were at the center of those conflicts.

One of my friendlier professional relationships posed an ethical dilemma that seemed almost like a nightmare. It involved the interactions between two staff members who were both viewed as "having my ear" or "seeing as I saw." One, however, was viewed as "my friend." It was an expectation of that friendship that posed the dilemma for all three of us:

My dilemma with Vivica Nelson [7A language arts] and Chad Newman [7A social studies] was one I thought I had encountered from time to time over the past several years. This time, however, it was a great deal more severe. In the past, the conflict appeared to stem from differences in personality. It was frustrating because our groups were contrived, so forming groups based on "affection" or "personality" was difficult. This time it was a question of perceived inequality.

I had my first indication that something other than personality was at the base of the feud between Chad and Vivica during the 11th week of school. After the initial World-in-Motion workshop with the Society of Automotive Engineers, the conflict began to heat up. I approached Vivica and asked her, "What exactly is the problem?" She began to tell me that I didn't really know Chad, and he wasn't the person I thought he was: "He lies." I responded, "Who is he lying to?" She said, "To you and Mrs. Battle." She then went on to describe an incident that I knew nothing about. I told her that the situation was getting silly and they needed to resolve it.

Still, the problems between them continued. Every day for the 2-week period between November 18 and November 25, 1996, Vivica found a way to tell me something "negative" about Chad, so I finally approached Chad and asked him what was the problem. His response was, "I don't know." When Vivica approached me with another "Chad tale," I had had enough. I told her, "I don't care. I am sick of your obsession with Chad. You keep saying Chad is the problem and I just don't understand. What I do understand is that Chad isn't talking about you. Chad isn't coming to me every day with some tale about Vivica. I don't want to hear any more." I was angry and Vivica knew it. She wrote a fable describing her conflict with Chad. (Clay, 1998, pp. 406–407)

After reading the fable, I went to Mrs. Mooney [the administrative assistant]. She too had been receiving an "earful" from Vivica on the "deceitful Chad." Vivica was not only my colleague, she was also my friend. I knew from the fable that she considered my attention to Chad a kind of betrayal. I had been unsuccessful in my attempts to address Vivica's needs [so I asked Mrs. Mooney] if she would mediate and she agreed. . . .

Team 7A began having a second team meeting on Thursday mornings. Although the original purpose was conflict mediation, after several weeks, Mrs. Mooney indicated that "Vivica is her usual self, sullen and quiet. We can't seem to get at the real problems." The conflict continued and the World-in-Motion project only fueled the flames of a very volatile situation. (p. 410)

I wrote a research memo in late March, 1997:

I had a discussion with Abner [Conway, 7A science teacher] about "teaming" and the "dysfunctional nature" of 7A. We both agreed that Chad might lack some social skills, but we could not find a reasonable answer for Vivica's obsession with him. Abner indicated that he thought the group was improving until "they" heard Chad comment to a group of engineers that he had done all the work for the World-in-Motion project. I asked Abner if in fact he had heard that, or if someone else had relayed it to him. Abner conceded, "Maybe that was taken out of context, we didn't hear what was said before that, maybe he was talking about a specific part of the project." Abner agreed to continue working on the "team's cohesiveness." I think I was brutally honest regarding my feelings. "Vivica has only liked two people in my eight years of working with her. Or rather two people she was required to work with. Those two are you and Torrie Perry." All the others had "something wrong with them" in Vivica's eyes, and they all met with her wrath. My question for Vivica is, "Based on your comments and your behavior as perceived by other people, do you think we are justified in believing you have difficulty working with others?" I didn't share this with Abner, but I think I will share this with Vivica. It is time.

Mrs. Battle has had just about enough of Vivica's behavior. She said to me, "I think I'm going to tell her, if she can't work as a part of a team then she needs to find another school." I really don't want this, but I cannot continue protecting her. If she were anybody else I would have turned Mrs. Battle loose a long time ago. I tried explaining when she wrote me that note saying, "I'd rather have a friend than a team." This isn't about friendship, it's about professional responsibilities. (pp. 410–412)

Again I found myself asking questions about my responsibility in the change process: "How can I create an atmosphere where bonding with me or supporting the changes proposed are not perceived as tools of manipulation?" After my first and second years at Urban Prep, certain teachers voluntarily transferred to other schools. Each time I asked if the potential benefits for the total community were worth sacrificing individuals. And each time I searched for ethically defensible action.

Facing these dilemmas in my role as practitioner-researcher, I sometimes felt torn in two. I wrote the following research memo as a dialogue between the Researcher ("R") and the Practitioner ("P"):

R: Okay, so the second year is over. How do you feel?

P: I don't know, kinda funny. I know that the changes we made had a profound impact on the people who left, yet I don't feel responsible in the same way I did last year.

R: How so?

P: Well, last year I wanted small miracles. I mean I thought everyone would buy into the changes, and our context would be transformed. But this year I knew we were engaged in a struggle. I mean people were fighting change left and right, and I accepted that I was seen as the maker of change.

R: And you are okay with that?

P: I'm getting there. I keep remembering what Kyle Foster said in the Kiva [a group process I designed in an effort to build more open communication]:
"It's like when I look at this school, I look at us like the Chicago Bulls. Not only did we do it last year, we are going to do it this year. But we always have to keep coming up to that level again, that championship level to put these kids out here. We are doing something right. I was on a corporate team. We were at each other's throats—but our CEO took us on a retreat, made us all live with one another for a weekend, solve the individual little one-on-ones. But remember—[In this district] *we* are the Chicago Bulls."

R: Okay, and so?

P: I have to accept that it isn't easy and there will be casualties of reform. My so-called power doesn't afford me the opportunity to work miracles. (Clay, 1998, pp. 290–291)

COMING TO KNOW MY PLACE

For the practitioner conducting research, it is precisely the relationships—insider to insider—that pose the most significant ethical dilemmas. And for the action researcher, one who seeks to "change the situation" (Carr and Kemmis, 1986), the lines between coercion and collaboration, imposition and negotiation, are often blurred by the pursuit of just and fair practices.

Again and again I found myself examining my conduct, always reflecting on my aims and purposes. I asked a colleague to read one of my research memos and comment. The memo addressed my concern with power, asking "Am I pushing my agenda? Or am I providing content for reflection?" Her response was simple and direct:

> Yes, you do impose your ideas on the population of Urban Prep. (Don't panic.) It's because the majority of the staff have a "method" that is obsolete in practice outside their classroom/world. As part of your job description, self-inflicted or otherwise, you are to help us "go toward the light," expand on ideas rather than teach on "automatic pilot." Many have gotten so comfortable on "A.P." that we have forgotten how we taught when we first started, and that the world (inside of school and outside) has changed; that we need to adjust and function within this change effectively. Your implementation is sneaky. You make "strong" unsuggestive suggestions as a means of getting us to try (reach, stretch . . . think?) . . . (personal letter, 1997)

That is the place I am striving to know, the place where there is "light" for all staff. I am seeking a place where we are all free to explore and expand those ideas that are good for the total school community; where the bonds between researcher and practitioner do not serve as obstacles to the goals of improvement; and where professional fellowship strengthens the negotiations for change. Coming to know my place as an action researcher—a negotiator of change—has become a quest for ethically defensible action and my lifelong professional journey.

NOTES

1. Names of people, places, and institutions [Urban Prep and River City] in this chapter were changed to protect the privacy of the staff.

2. Excerpts from my original dissertation have been shortened somewhat but are otherwise verbatim.

Chapter 4

TEACHER RESEARCH: A WOLF IN SHEEP'S CLOTHING

Linda Hajj

I wasn't prepared for the transformation in my own teaching and learning or for the changes that would occur in my classroom as a result of my teacher research. Nor did I know the impact it would have on my school culture. "It doesn't matter where or when it takes place, or whether it is more or less complex. Education has always been a political act" (Freire, 1993, p. 127). If I had read this quote before teacher research, I would never have understood it. I had no context or background knowledge about politics and education other than voting in local school board elections. Now, it speaks to me loudly and clearly.

Teacher research and its ethical and political companions? I never envisioned them showing up on the doorstep of my classroom. I've taught for 23 years in grades K, 1, 4, 5, and 6 in diverse settings both overseas and in the United States. In 1994, I was a fifth-grade classroom teacher in Virginia's Fairfax County schools.[1] I was experienced: I thought I had heard, seen, and felt just about everything in education. But teacher research changed my professional life. It all began that year when I decided to enroll in a master's program to gain certification as a reading specialist. A cohort group of 30 teachers, organized by Fairfax County, moved through the program in a 3-year cycle. We were taught predominantly by professors from Virginia Polytechnic University.

The first professor in our master's program gently explained how research was a requirement of her class. Moans filled the room as we wondered how we would find the hours to sit in the university or public library and balance our teaching and family lives. As she explained teacher research in more depth, I discovered it could be about my own fifth-grade classroom, that it wasn't just reading and taking notes about others' ideas. On that cool, crisp September night

I skipped happily along the path to my car ready to embark on this teacher research journey.

As I pursued my classroom research over the next 3 years, however, the dilemmas that arose caused it to morph from that innocent beginning into a wolf-like appearance. My research became aggressive. It didn't want to stop. It was hungry as its range widened. One year's research began spilling into the next. It was relentless as my perspective on my learners and my teaching changed. It hunted for ways to become reality.

Before I became a teacher-researcher, I had quite happily buried myself in the everyday occurrences of my classroom and left the politics outside my door—at least that's where I thought it was. Education as a political act had eluded me while I avoided unpopular decisions and refused to question authority. I felt empowered within my own walls but unaware of how I could influence my own teaching, my students' lives, and the culture of my school.

After joining the master's program, I became increasingly literate about education theory. An important influence on my research and teaching was La Vergne Rosow's *In Forsaken Hands: How Theory Empowers Literacy Learners* (1995). She says, "Power is knowing you have both the right and the responsibility to question the unquestionable" (p. 7). My reading during those 3 years in books and educational journals gave me the opportunity to hear other voices with similar concerns who, like me, questioned their practice.

I had started to roam. I was thinking outside the day-to-day occurrences in my classroom and was hungry for more reading and interaction with my colleagues in the master's program. I was no longer within the same teaching culture. Reading and hearing rich descriptions of classrooms by teacher-researchers and other educators (such as Patrick Shannon, Lucy Calkins, Linda Rief, Nancie Atwell, Marilyn Cochran-Smith and Susan Lytle, Regie Routman, Shelley Harwayne, Victoria Purcell Gates, Kathryn Au, and Dixie Lee Spiegel) awakened my political consciousness. Literacy is power—for teachers as learners and students as learners.

I saw my struggle to be a part of a new learning community as parallel to that of my classroom of student learners. As I joined in discussions with my newfound colleagues, I felt more connected to them. We shared commonalities in our classrooms and in our own struggles to fit into our school-based cultures. I felt my own students struggling to be a part of their new classroom as I watched them engage in group projects and negotiate their learning and positions within the classroom community.

FIRST-YEAR EXPLORATIONS

I began my research by looking at how community formed in the classroom and its implication for educators. Although I didn't know it at the time, I had begun to reflect on my everyday practice, and I had begun to make decisions based on my observations, reflections, and student conversations. My teaching changed as I came to know myself more as a teacher and to know more about my students.

My first year's research centered on creating a community of learners. I posed two questions:

- What is it that happens in the classroom to create a community of learners?
- What is the teacher's role in creating and sustaining this community?

There were some consequences of my research that had nothing to do with my questions. I immediately felt myself becoming distanced from my teaching colleagues in my school setting. The more I moved inward and tried to break down walls inside my classroom, the more barriers went up outside that room. My master's program classroom of teachers were becoming my colleagues. My research became my mentor and collaborator. Today I would ask a new question:

- Does teacher research, when not a school team effort, actually interfere with collaboration and teamwork?

Although immersed in my classroom and supported by colleagues in the master's program, I felt isolated within my school setting. Issues that arose in my research seemed to be divisive rather than supportive of teamwork and collaboration. As I pursued the community questions, my interest and motivation thrived solely on my learners. My classroom became a "closed society"—a private scene in a way because of the stories we shared and the way we came to know each other's needs. I developed my lesson plans based on day-to-day interactions with my students.

Collaboration among school teams, so widely espoused, actually seemed to interfere with my classroom. Whenever colleagues and I tried to plan together, I could only participate superficially in helping to create a general framework. I could not think about switching classes or grouping students for instruction. How do teachers share students without being somehow connected to their whole classroom experience? How does one explain how a student works as a writer? How does one tell about the rich comment made during discussion of a novel? I had heard that teaming would save me planning time and help me develop subject expertise. I could not justify using another teacher's plans, though, because I couldn't guarantee we'd all be on the same page.

The Wolf Appears—Taking a Stand

One of the first dilemmas that arose in my search for community involved a group of labeled students who were pulled out of my classroom each day. The program had always worked that way, and so it began as usual that year. I had observed the work of these students and had wondered why they couldn't stay within the community of learners they had come to know. We were learning how to support each other and I had begun to read stories and build experiences and projects to put us on common ground. An entry from my first year's research stated how I felt about these students:

> At this point I discovered how unhappy I was with the LD [learning disabilities] pull-out program. We could not become a community of learners if members were constantly absent. They were missing important connections to what we did. (Since I integrated reading and writing across the curriculum, I couldn't really say this is where one subject begins and the other ends. I did not fit the traditional classroom model of teaching in little increments of time except in math.) They would become the labeled "others" and never quite fit if I didn't work hard at including them. These students were also beginning to complain about leaving the classroom. I felt their learning could be supported at a higher level and I began to make excuses each day why they couldn't leave at a certain time.

It was hard work. I now concerned myself greatly with all the students' learning. I invited the learning disabilities teacher to join in my classroom whenever possible. I respected the needs of the students and tried to adapt tests and projects to fit them. Perhaps their other teacher wasn't setting high expectations? I saw the students completing similar assignments required of their classmates when in my regular classroom. Gradually, I saw an attitude change: there was a willingness to try. I saw pencils moving that were previously still, and I saw new friendships and a support network forming. It wasn't easy, but I felt inclusion of these students was working. School administrators visited my classroom. Other teachers, however, were beginning to feel the repercussions of my inclusion model. It had worked well for me. I wanted it and I worked hard to sustain it. Could this model now be mandated for other staff?

Administrators want success for all the learners under their care. Teachers want the same success. What works for one doesn't always work for all, though. My research about learning communities was important for me and significant for my learners. But other teachers became anxious when they heard the word *inclusion* both inside and outside the school walls.

I didn't know my research would bare its teeth that first year as it did. My teaching changed and ultimately the lives of my students. In the introduction to my research report that first year, I stated: "Together and individually we had made a difference and we had effected change beyond and within ourselves."

I had taken a stand based on my classroom research, knowing, and observations. A quote from William Ayers supports my feelings. "Teaching is a deeply personal experience, but at its heart a social activity, even a political act" (in Schubert & Ayers, 1999, p. 155).

Politics had indeed crossed the door of my classroom. Unknowingly, I had invited it in through my research. Ethics had also come on board as my research spilled into the school culture. Research was a highly satisfying personal experience. I saw my teaching and my students in a new way. At the same time it was disturbing. I seemed to stand out as "different" among my colleagues and in my school culture.

Empowered but Cowering

I was empowered by that first year's research about forming community in my classroom, especially after sharing it with a wider audience of colleagues and educators at a roundtable conference especially arranged for our master's program. I had invited two colleagues from my school. One was the assistant principal and the other was the school librarian.

Soon, the wheels were in motion for a teacher-researcher group at my school. I discovered through our assistant principal that Fairfax County already had an active Teacher-Researcher Network in place. Working among colleagues in a school setting sounded like the support I had envisioned. Maybe those walls that I had felt go up outside my own classroom would disappear in this school-based group. The assistant principal at our school greatly facilitated the forming of the group, and we learned we would be supported by county funds. The involvement of the assistant principal in our research group gave us validation. She would be conducting her own research about supporting beginning teachers.

I struggled, along with other members of our newly formed teacher-researcher group, to identify the question I wanted to pursue in my own classroom. I was empowered, but still I cowered at the memories of that first year's experience. I felt reluctant to share openly about the changes my research had already brought about in my own classroom and in my own teaching. I think that first year of research was so intense and personal for me that I didn't think I could relate it to the group. I also didn't want to intimidate anyone. I didn't want anyone to feel they had to model their research after mine. As in my previous classroom experience, I was negotiating my place in this new community of learners. I needed to have some common experiences and establish trust among my colleagues.

THE SECOND-YEAR JOURNEY

In my second year of teacher research I had a difficult group of students to focus on, as I had been told by staff and administration. (I first needed to dispel the myth of "the class from hell" and make sure they didn't live up to their reputation!) It didn't take me long to assess that I had some students who were really struggling with their reading. Baseline classroom data I had gathered and standardized testing verified my assessment. I knew how to teach fifth grade and the map was in my head. What I was discovering, though, was that I needed a new route to get the struggling learners invested in print. If I headed down the same road I had taken before, I knew that half of my students were not going to be on the bus. How would I improve their reading and motivate them to play the game of school? What did I need to know? How would I create winners?

I came to know these least-invested students through daily observations and journal writing. From observing simple routines to monitoring assignment notebooks, I recorded what worked. I also felt I needed to update my knowledge base about strategies for beginning readers. I enrolled in a course that was intended for first-grade teachers and found it extremely beneficial. When I reported this in my research group, someone commented that other staff could benefit from the current information. With the assistant principal's leadership, we were able to establish a school-based course in which she and the reading teacher were instructors. This was something I never imagined could result from teachers researching. We were influencing our own staff development and impacting our students as we learned.

As community formed in my new fifth-grade classroom, I progressed in my knowledge of what worked with these struggling readers. I began to feel that this group, with another year of the same guidance by someone who knew them, might make even greater strides in their learning. I wanted them to make maximum literacy gains before middle school. I remember thinking how bold this idea was. Already I was staking out my territory and eying the future. In my journal I expressed my sadness as I watched the year unfold for my previous class; I wished I could have made more of a difference in their learning. This journal entry had a great influence on me.

The Wolf Returns—Going Public

I began an active campaign to put a 2-year model in place. This became my second official political act (the first was including my learning disabilities students in my regular classroom). From my daily reflections and year-long research came the realization that I needed to stay with these struggling students even if it meant moving with them to the next grade level. I had established routines, rules, and consistencies that I found supported them. I was persistent, always searching for methods and materials that worked for them across the curriculum. I saw growth, some loving of the game, and winners; I knew where to go next! After my second year's teacher research I wrote:

I know that a one-size-fits-all curriculum does not advance the learning of these least-invested students. It takes a tremendous amount of patience, understanding, and know-how to try to guide them down the learning road. I know that it will take the next year's teacher another 6 weeks to establish routines and become familiar with their learning needs. They can't afford much delay. I feel these learners need stability in their school life. It doesn't necessarily benefit them each year to start over anew. They need the continuity of learning with someone who knows them. I will actively seek to move up with them to the next grade.

A related ethical issue caused me some sleepless nights. (Imagine, the wolf followed me home!) One member of our school-based group was a sixth-grade teacher. Not only would my research affect his grade-level team, but later it would directly impact his teaching assignment. I felt excited about where my research was leading but reluctant to share it in the group. I trusted this teacher not to discuss it with his colleagues. Yet I was feeling, "Here you go again—stirring up the pot!" Should one's research be kept private for the good of the whole?

My discovery of needing more time to advance the students' learning caused me to write to our principal. The campaign had begun. I informed her of the decision I felt needed to be taken. (It was one I had already made in my mind and in my journal. I had been preparing myself.) I explained how I needed her support. I continued through the year with follow-up notes and included published research that supported the practice of teachers spending more than one year with their class. I suggested meetings with the grade levels affected to explain the model. I knew this was going to be difficult but didn't realize how scary it would feel.

Support and Separation

At the first meeting with the fifth- and sixth-grade teachers the principal announced my plan and let me present the model I wished to implement. The atmosphere was strained; my research was going to cause change in two grade levels. I stayed focused on the student implications. The principal then asked the grade-level teams to meet and come up with a response, deciding who would change grade levels if the model were implemented.

Again, by being a teacher-researcher and acting on my research, I had isolated myself. Again, I felt that the good of the whole was being sacrificed in some way. Why couldn't things stay the same? My research was beginning to widen its range and encroach upon the existing school culture. Did this 2-year model belong in other grade levels? How can a school work for the success of all students and respect the individual teaching styles of staff? Where does a teacher's allegiance belong? These were questions I asked in my mind but could not pursue, as I focused on the needs of my class.

I met again with the fifth- and sixth-grade teams, and my colleagues shared their reasons against the model.

1. The current sixth-grade team of teachers worked well together.
2. The students needed to change teachers because they would face change in middle school anyway.
3. The teachers would have to teach new material and that meant additional time spent in planning.

The principal did not support them. She granted me permission to move up with the class. The teacher-researcher from the sixth-grade team was asked to move down a grade as I carried my class up. There wasn't a conflict between us, but somehow I felt guilty for impacting his teaching. The sixth-grade team then proposed that I team with them in teaching subject blocks, but I had to disagree because that would defeat what I had been trying to accomplish. It was clear that my colleagues did not want the self-contained model and that I would not be a player on their team.

At the end of this same teacher research year, another dilemma surfaced. The county had supported our research by granting several half-day subs so we could write and meet together. We wrote up our individual research and wanted to share it with the faculty. We decided to invite staff to attend one roundtable discussion during a faculty meeting at the end of the year and submitted our plans to the principal. Unfortunately, she felt the program should be orchestrated a bit differently: She decided attendance would be mandatory at two back-to-back sessions. Our research group was no longer in control of the meeting, and the guests didn't feel "invited." This is not the way we envisioned our sharing. Forcing the attendance seemed to widen the rift that was already there among the staff. Before, we had been an oddity that some didn't understand; now we were even less understood as we were forced upon everyone.

THIRD-YEAR BUMPS

Another issue reared its head during the third year of teacher research. Again, we formed a school-based group. As mentioned previously, the assistant principal's involvement had made us feel validated. She was an active teacher-researcher. She also felt that change in schools was possible if teacher research could be connected to the school plan. She was hoping to pursue this since her job was to keep the school plan rolling and some of us served on the school plan committee.

At our second meeting, the assistant principal announced she could not join the teacher-researcher group because higher powers felt it interfered with her duties during the school day. Although we met one half-day each month to discuss our research progress, most of our writing and work was done on our own time. I almost resigned from the group because of what I felt was unfair use of power. In fact, I wrote a letter advocating the reinstatement of the assistant principal but, on her advice, decided not to send it and not to pursue the issue any farther.

I was asked to take on the leadership role. After that, I felt different in the group. I knew some of the politics behind the scenes but couldn't share it with the other staff. I had relied on the assistant principal because she was an experienced researcher and mentor. We had been able to recruit some young, less-experienced teachers because of her close work with them. Now they were feeling unsupported by the administration.

Throughout the year, I worked hard to maintain the structure and leadership to facilitate the group. In trying to keep everyone else on board, however, I felt I spent less time thinking about my own research. I began seeking a new role, possibly in a different school, for the following year. I was feeling that I had accomplished a tremendous amount personally but was not confident that I could influence the school culture more. I did complete my report, which told about my journey with my students and other political acts I had committed during my 3 years of research. My conclusion in the report was that I didn't want to follow the status quo. Patrick Shannon (1992) says it well:

> Teachers' political naivete concerning literacy, teaching, and schooling actually contributes to their students' and their own predicament. . . . Their acts contribute to or challenge the status quo in literacy education, in schools, and in society. All teachers are political, whether they are conscious of it or not. (p. 2)

This brings me back to my first-year research about learning in community. I had written in the introduction:

> I've learned that without a sense of community among teachers, little seems to be accomplished. In isolation one doesn't grow. One needs the input of others, the support, the criticism, the acceptance—then the learner can move on to new experiences and learning truly begins.

REFLECTIONS AND IMPLICATIONS

If I knew then what I know now, I wouldn't change much in my story. What I would do is to bring more understanding and less docility to the field. I would be more prepared for some of the untamable aspects of teacher research and better able to support those around me. I now know that teacher research is empowering and powerful.

Teachers must have the freedom to continue reflecting upon and examining their classroom practices. Rosow (1995) explains, "Empowerment is not bred in a vacuum. It lives and breathes in an unrestrictive environment that recognizes and respects that the human brain must think to grow" (p. 272).

All learners need to think in order to grow. All teachers need to think about their practices on a daily basis. But this learning for students and staff cannot be mandated from above. The ability to think creatively and to use problem solving is what sets humankind apart from other animals and machines. As is evidenced in the current top-down standards and high-stakes testing, many classrooms across America are exterminating thinking among both teachers and students. What I call "drill and fill" classrooms are becoming the norm. We dialogue about how much time we have to drill and fill as much information as possible into children.

If it had not been for teacher research, I would not have continued to grow in my thinking and to challenge my own teaching. Despite the ethical and political issues created, teacher research is necessary to sustain a learning community. It continues to be a great awakening.

I would urge other teachers to read, seek, and find their own learning. I would also urge them to join with a community of colleagues to talk about their classrooms and practices. Teachers *can* coexist with wolves and even learn from them!

Patrick Shannon (1995) aptly sums up the situation of a teacher-researcher: "Although I feel I must walk softly concerning teaching and public issues, I will carry a stick. That stick will be my pencil" (p. 466).

NOTE

1. References to my district and to my district-sponsored teacher-researcher group in this chapter use real names to recognize their contributions to my thinking; specific people and institutions are unnamed to protect their privacy.

Chapter 5

WHO OWNS THE STORY?
ETHICAL ISSUES IN THE CONDUCT
OF PRACTITIONER RESEARCH

The Clayton (Missouri) Research Review Team:
Cathy Beck, Laura DuPont, Lori Geismar-Ryan,
Linda Henke, Kathryn Mitchell Pierce,
and Catherine Von Hatten

Among the Haida people of the Pacific Northwest, history and culture are recorded in oral stories. These stories are told by one generation to the next. They belong to the Haida people, to individual clans and to particular families within the clans. Individuals are ethically required to seek permission from their family members before sharing a family story, or from their clan elders before sharing a clan story. The Haida people have a well-developed code of ethics to help them answer the questions, "Whose story is this?" and "Who has the right to share this story?" Today, those engaged in collaborative, school-based inquiry are struggling with similar issues. In our district, we have been infusing our work with an inquiry perspective and an ethical consciousness so that all members will ask themselves, "Whose story is this?" and "Who has the right to share this story?"

This chapter chronicles the School District of Clayton's efforts to create a culture of inquiry, one that embeds practitioner research in the ongoing work of the district.[1] The authors of this chapter are members of the district's Research Review Team. Cathy is a middle school teacher; Laura is an elementary principal; Lori is the coordinator of the early childhood program and our action research collaborative; Linda is assistant superintendent; Kathryn is a multiage elementary teacher; and Catherine is the professional development director. As members of the Research Review Team, we highlight the ethical dilemmas that led to the creation of structures designed to ensure consideration of ethical issues throughout our work.

Almost a decade ago, our district began to build a culture of inquiry. In 1991 following a year of study and conversation with administrators and teacher leaders, assistant superintendent Linda Henke presented a vision document to the Board of Education. This vision called for a focus on creating "a learning community—a place where every adult and child is actively engaged in learning, a place where children are apprenticed to skilled learners who are studying with them." The document described "a constructivist culture" emphasizing the importance of reflective practice and suggesting teachers become active researchers of their own classrooms. The acceptance of this document by the Board of Education was important primarily because it formalized a district focus on inquiry resulting in major changes in the learning culture.

Interestingly, we did not immediately turn to research as a tool to support teachers in questioning their practice. Instead, reflective practice in the district accelerated through the Clayton Writing Project, a summer institute designed to study pedagogy, but perhaps more importantly to support teachers in finding their own voices to tell personal and professional stories. Over time, as we uncovered the power of writing to build professional meaning, we began to weave it into the way we do our work. New teachers are introduced to reflective practice and journaling during orientation, and teachers keep reflective journals during a year-long experience that follows the granting of tenure. This focus on writing about the work of the classroom is reinforced by a district publication, *Curriculum Quarterly*, which for several years has served as an important vehicle for teachers to share their perspectives on learning and teaching.

As more and more teachers found their voices for writing about their classrooms, the possibilities for classroom-based research began to emerge. Action research seemed a natural next step from teachers talking about their work with their peers. The movement from narration to questioning was a subtle but important shift.

In 1993, the Clayton Action Research Collaborative (Clayton ARC) began as an informal group of teachers and administrators who came together on a regular basis to explore mutual interests. Since its inception, the Clayton ARC has nurtured diverse teacher research projects. A sampling of topics reveals a wide range of interests: struggling readers, integrated learning at the high school level, the ecological impact of people on a local arboretum, and the role of gender in shaping learning. The impact of these individual research projects rippled out from classrooms; districtwide programs such as our support program for beginning readers were based in part on data collected by Clayton ARC participants.

Curriculum that grew from a constructivist orientation of necessity required teachers to act as researchers. Increasingly, we began to incorporate research into our institutional processes—especially in the areas of curriculum and professional development. Members of curriculum committees began to gather artifacts, record classroom discussions, and observe one another. These and other practitioner research strategies have become routine tools in the work of curriculum committees.

We realized that in a learning community professional development begins with teachers' questions. These questions more often than not tie directly back to classroom practice and involve teachers in both formal and informal research methodologies. As a result, district professional development moved away from large groups listening to a speaker to small groups of teachers who gathered to study their questions.

As we have grown comfortable with all that a research lens can provide us, we have discovered it also perches us squarely on the horns of a dilemma. Research informs our practice in critical ways, helping us to see what otherwise might not be seen; however, at the same time we find ourselves struggling with ethical issues that arise from the same methodology that illuminates with such rich detail our classrooms and broader learning community. The following research story captures a turning point in our consideration of the ethical issues involved in school-based practitioner research and the dissemination of its results.

RESEARCH STORY

In 1992, we brought Kathryn Mitchell Pierce to our district to pilot a multiage classroom. As with any pilot in the district, the proposal included an evaluation component. Board of Education members were particularly interested in a cost analysis and an assessment of test score data. Teachers, administrators, and parents had additional questions. Our multiage study group developed a longitudinal evaluation plan using interviews, surveys, and achievement test data.

In addition, the district contracted with Jane Zeni, an experienced educational ethnographer from a local university, to provide a qualitative study of the pilot program. The questions that guided Jane's research were derived from those being explored by the multiage study group and included issues often raised by board members, prospective parents, and teaching colleagues.

A research team was formed that included Kathryn; Phyllis Stoecklein, the building principal; Linda; and Jane. The team developed a general structure and framework for the study. Although Jane created the final document, the work reflected a collaborative endeavor.

The team decided to use case studies as a major component of the research design. For each of the major questions, Kathryn and Jane selected 2–3 children as potential case studies. The final report, therefore, included detailed discussion of individual children in the classroom.

The report was presented to a group of administrators and teacher leaders who review curriculum documents prior to their presentation to the Board of Education. And then the ethical dilemmas surfaced. Kathryn became increasingly aware of the implications of sharing this document with a wider audience. How would parents feel if they heard other parents or school board members talking about "a struggling older student" and recognized the student as their own child? An international child was the focus of a case study on how students can be integrated into an existing classroom group and how the needs of a limited English speaker might be met in a multiage classroom. There would be no question as to the identity of the student being described.

The research team considered changing the demographic information about the case study children in order to protect their privacy. First drafts of these revisions were equally problematic because the research team recognized that once the demographics had been significantly changed, the case study would lose integrity. Race, gender, age, and academic performance were central to the study. Altering these descriptors would significantly compromise the research.

The research team's solution was to request that Jane create a public document that summarized the key elements of the fuller study. This appealed to all involved for several reasons:

• The privacy of the children could be reasonably protected.
• The significant outcomes of the study could be shared with a wider audience.
• The length of the summary document was more manageable for use with a wider audience.
• Those most closely involved with the study itself had access to the detailed information from the case studies that would allow them to make adjustments in the classroom.

After the team presented the report to the Board of Education, conversations began about the feasibility of publishing information from the study beyond the school district. This created a tension between the desire to share what had been learned with a wider audience and the responsibility to protect the identity of the children. With the classroom teacher's name and school affiliation used in conjunction with the article, the data could be traced to the individual children. And whose story was this?

Jane Zeni had invested considerable time and energy to the project; she was the primary author of the final documents. Kathryn Mitchell Pierce, however, contributed significantly to the design, analysis, and reporting of the study. The district had paid for the project. Who controlled the right to tell the story? What if Jane wanted to use parts of this experience, in combination with other ethnographies of language teaching and learning, in a professional article in which the district would not be named directly? Was she obligated to obtain permission from the district, the parents, and Kathryn? What if Kathryn or Jane wanted to write about the experience of engaging in collaborative research, using this study as an example? Did Jane have the right to use the data gathered in the district to pursue her own research interests, and then publish the findings—whether or not the district was recognizable or named directly?

The multiage story illustrates issues emerging as the district nurtured a culture of inquiry, expanded teachers' professional responsibilities and opportunities for collaboration, and increased the complexity of the questions we asked ourselves. At the time, our policy held that all research completed in the Clayton schools required Linda Henke's approval. She found herself increasingly frustrated with questions such as those raised by the multiage research, and she was concerned that such complex issues required more than her single perspective. Linda's lens was that of a central office administrator, providing a broad look at the questions and research. She worried, however, that she was missing important information. Linda wanted to ensure multiple perspectives by including the voices of classroom teachers, building administrators, and university partners in the process. Across the district, those of us involved with action research in our classrooms and buildings also struggled. Conversations at our ARC meetings focused more and more on ethical dilemmas in research and publication. We realized that we could no longer proceed on a case-by-case basis; we needed some framework to support our work. We felt a responsibility to be more explicit about our beliefs and intentional in our actions as they related to teaching and research. And so the Research Review Team was born.

OUR EMERGING VISION

The Research Review Team includes both teachers and administrators with an interest in advancing research in the district. The team supports our culture of inquiry by ensuring that all research conducted in the district

- honors our primary responsibility of educating all children
- advances our understanding of teaching and learning and the health and well-being of all members of our learning community
- follows agreed-upon standards for high-quality educational research
- respects the rights of all members of our learning community and those of the school district

The team's intent from the beginning was to support researchers in their endeavors rather than serve merely to point out design errors or problems. We feared creating a cumbersome, bureaucratic process that might shut down creativity and inquiry rather than promote it. Consequently, the Research Review Team focused on the following items:

- developing and maintaining research guidelines that encourage research and provide effective oversight
- reviewing and approving research proposals
- reviewing final research reports and plans for going public
- reviewing and approving practicum arrangements with universities and colleges
- supporting district conversations about critical issues in educational research
- increasing awareness of research opportunities and funding

The emerging review process supports teachers in examining potential risks that their research poses for students or for the teaching and learning environment. The research review model is based on a continuum from least restrictive to the most restrictive guidelines. The level of restriction is related to the type of research and to the relationship of the researcher and audience to the district. For example, teachers engaged in reflective practice in their own classrooms would follow the least restrictive guidelines for review. Nondistrict researchers conducting research to be shared with a wide audience would follow detailed guidelines to ensure the least disruption to the learning and working environment and the most benefit to our students. Research falling between these two ends of the continuum would require varying levels of review.

The inquiry process frequently yields more questions than answers. In our case, as we explore the ethics of research in our district, we are challenged by several intriguing issues. Implicit in each of these burning questions are tensions—tensions that reflect our desire to support a culture of inquiry while protecting the rights of all members of our learning community.

How Do We Help Teachers Recognize and Accommodate the Transition From Good Teaching to Research? As part of good teaching, we think professionally about our work in classrooms and reflect on our practices in many ways. At times, our practice raises questions that take us beyond good teaching and reflective practice. The shift from good teaching to research calls for a greater intentionality of purpose, more systematic documentation and data-gathering strategies, heightened focus on the inquiry process, and a broadened collaboration or wider audience.

Teachers who engage in reflective practice need to know when the shift from good teaching to research has occurred. It should not be a guessing game, one where teachers wonder when they have crossed the line. We have developed the following set of questions to help teachers recognize the shift:

- Is this information beyond the information I "normally" gather as an ongoing part of good teaching?
- Have I considered how my students' parents might feel about the information I am gathering and sharing about their child?
- Do I intend to change my practice based on the findings?
- Is it possible that others will want to know about or use my ideas?
- Do I plan to share examples of students' work outside the district?
- Do I plan to publish anything about my current inquiry, or is it possible that I may do so in the future?

As increasing numbers of teachers engage in research, our district has committed time, staff, and financial resources to support their work. Staff members have access to research grants, the support of experienced teacher-researchers, and funds to attend conferences to share their work with audiences outside the district.

How Do We Embrace a District Curriculum Vision While Supporting New Questions? In a culture of inquiry we stay focused on doing what is best for students. Children's learning and well-being may potentially be affected by conducting research in our schools. Teachers' research questions may require significant changes in practice that either continue to meet district core content and student outcomes or may, in fact, depart from established curriculum. Each research question requires careful consideration of potential risks that may include disruption to instructional time, deviation from the district curriculum, and the impact of departing from established district and parental expectations.

Members in a dynamic and well-functioning organization share a vision. This is expressed through a mission, guiding principles, expectations, and practices that support a clearly established curriculum. Research and other forms of collaborative inquiry are integral to our efforts to realize our vision. As we read proposals, the Research Review Team considers certain questions:

- Is the research aligned with the district's guiding principles?
- What are the potential benefits and risks to those involved?
- Is the researcher willing to share findings and participate in the broader conversation about curriculum in the district?

Within these conversations, members of our learning community build trust and take on responsibility for challenging our own and others' ideas. In this environment we can ask questions that may reveal our own vulnerability and address issues that have potential to significantly change practice. The tension lies in pursuing a shared curriculum vision while simultaneously encouraging a critical stance toward that vision. A recent example: we approved an elementary teacher's research project that included a radical departure from our literacy curriculum to explore whether isolated, explicit instruction in grammar for African American students improved their writing. In order to minimize the risks, the teacher was asked to revise the format, conducting the research in a before-school optional program with district financial support. The teacher shared her results with the district literacy committee and later through a district workshop to invite further conversation.

How Do We Embed Research in the Broader Work of the District?

Creating a culture of inquiry extends far beyond our Action Research Collaborative. We have worked hard to embed a speculative stance into three major processes that support our work: curriculum development, professional development, and career development and teacher evaluation.

Curriculum committees in each of the disciplines meet monthly as part of our continuous improvement model. One of their most important responsibilities is to investigate specific ways to improve the teaching and learning in their area. Frequently this includes questions that become research proposals. Currently, for example, the math committee is studying the development of number sense in primary students and the literacy committee is examining why we see more girls than boys participating in advanced English classes at the high school. Increasingly, we are finding committees also engaged in studying student work samples and teacher lesson designs as part of the curriculum conversation focusing on student learning.

As inquiry became more and more integral to "the way we do things around here," we discovered the need to redesign professional development. For the past 2 years we have asked all district employees to organize themselves into year-long learning teams that focus on answering specific questions related to their practice. Over 40 teams are currently at work in our district. We post these teams' topics on the district web site so all of us can be informed of the broad spectrum of ongoing study.

The value of continuous learning also is evident in our career development and teacher evaluation process where, from the first day of orientation to the district, teachers are encouraged to become reflective practitioners. The career development process includes opportunities for action research, dialogue journals, observations of other teachers, and an innovative post-tenure career grant program. This program encourages teachers to apply for grants to support their learning by providing released time, summer work, consultation with other professionals, and tuition. All of this helps create a generative culture where adult learning is valued. In the end, we believe this is the most critical feature of a culture that focuses on improving student learning.

How Do We Protect the Rights of Students and Families While Encouraging Teacher Research? Educational researchers frequently move beyond the classroom walls when they collect data and share findings. Teacher-researchers may discuss their work with colleagues within our own district and share findings with a wider audience in presentations and publications. Gaining informed consent from students and parents is critically important. Measures to ensure the confidentiality of the students involved in a research study often require a delicate handling of the data while they are being analyzed and discussed with collaborators and broader audiences.

For example, Kathryn Mitchell Pierce has a system in her classroom that permits parents to be informed and involved in decisions regarding their students' work. At the beginning of the school year, Kathryn uses the classroom newsletter and curriculum night to inform parents that research is an integral part of her teaching. Examples of previous publications are made available throughout the year for parents' review. Parents are asked to sign a blanket release giving Kathryn permission to collect samples of student work created in the context of regular classroom activities. These samples, she explains, may become part of a professional presentation or publication intended to support professional conversations of colleagues beyond the district. At the same time, parents are invited to select a pseudonym for their child, if preferred.

Before including student work in a publication, Kathryn returns to parents for permission to use a specific sample of their child's work for a specific publication. A copy of the article to be submitted for publication, along with a copy of the student work to be included in the article, are provided to parents so that they can see clearly how their child's work is being presented to others. Once the publication has been released, parents receive copies of the final document. In addition, the publication is announced in the classroom newsletter and other parents are invited to request copies for their own reading.

This graduated process of consent, coupled with ongoing information about how Kathryn's research and teaching are connected, allows parents to see how teacher research supports her ongoing professional development and how her publications contribute to larger professional conversations.

How Do We Ensure Effective Research Partnerships Beyond the District? Several district initiatives have benefited from collaboration with colleagues from the field. Currently our district has plans to broaden our learning community to include enhanced relationships with educators from area universities and colleges as well as partner districts. We believe that partnerships with university faculty and students and with teachers from other districts will broaden our lenses and offer new perspectives on teaching and learning. These partnerships will benefit our students, support the district in solving knotty problems, and contribute to the profession well beyond our district's boundaries.

Effective partnerships, however, will require a shared set of understandings between the district and university partners. To engage in the complexities of practitioner research requires agreements about methodology, parental consent, dissemination, and ownership. In addition to making general agreements about research partnerships, the university and district partners will also need to negotiate specific agreements appropriate for each project.

The issues addressed above as part of "insider" research are far more complex as we widen the circle of colleagues to "outsiders." Questions arise around the level of control our district has in the design and implementation of research as well as the dissemination of findings. As we continue to embed research into the way we do our work, the question "Whose Story Is It?" evolves and takes on new meaning.

NOTE

1. All references to people, places, and institutions in this chapter use real names to recognize their contributions to our work.

REFLECTIONS ON
SCHOOL-BASED RESEARCH

Because I believe that action researchers based in schools see ethical issues quite differently from those in universities, Parts I, II, and III of this volume are organized by context. The categories I adapted from Gesa Kirsch (1999)—location, relationships, interpretation, publication, institutionalization—will serve as a framework for the commentary following each of these three sets of chapters.

LOCATION

To conduct a systematic inquiry in a social setting, a researcher must be conscious of what she brings to that inquiry, such as gender, race, class, role, and power in the institution. How does the researcher's position differ from that of students, colleagues, parents, administrators, and others he may describe?

Practitioners need to locate themselves in their research. For example, Leslie Minarik is a European American teacher working in an urban school with children of color; Wanda Clay is an African American leader of a magnet school with a racially mixed faculty. Mohr and Hajj (Fairfax County, Virginia) and the Clayton (Missouri) Research Review Team work in more affluent suburban schools with majority White students. Location inevitably shapes the perspectives of researchers.

Although all the contributors to Part I are school-based, their roles are varied: classroom teachers, building-level and district-level professional development leaders, and a collaborative group including teachers and administrators.

Note too that each of these school-based authors has university links. Minarik and Hajj meet regularly with a teacher research seminar and a university consultant; Mohr's seminars in Fairfax County, Virginia, carry credit; Clay's school reform project was her dissertation research. The Clayton team relies mainly on district credit, but also hires university consultants. In Part I, however, the practitioner sets the research agenda, writes the report, and draws on outside resources as needed.

RELATIONSHIPS

The key ethical issue for school-based practitioner-researchers seems to be relationships. Principles drafted by the teams in Fairfax County and in Clayton place great emphasis on the researcher's responsibility to students and parents. Both districts see practitioner research as a natural feature of a curriculum focused on writing process, constructivism, and inquiry. Although each researcher chooses a topic, teams work in harmony toward common goals; relationships are strengthened.

A different note is struck by researchers working individually. Although they meet with seminars or consultants, Hajj, Minarik, and Clay have no teammates in their buildings. All report ethical tensions in their new roles as researchers. Colleagues and administrators may see them as disrupting the work of the school in their pursuit of data (Clay was urged to chant, "No more innovations!"). At the same time, doing research brings these individuals a new awareness of the politics in education and their own power to act (what Hajj calls the "wolf in sheep's clothing"). Minarik chooses to "do the right thing"—what her research has convinced her is best for her students—quietly ignoring the curriculum mandates of the month.

Despite differences in the support they themselves feel, these school-based researchers agree that their primary ethical commitment is to educate their students. Whether speaking for a district-level team (Mohr: "Teacher-researchers are teachers first") or as individuals (Minarik: "My only loyalty was to my students"), they base their ethical decisions on this standard.

INTERPRETATION/DEFINITION

It is dangerous to assume that one's insider location automatically brings insight. As Fred Erickson says (in Cochran-Smith & Lytle, 1993), "Neither the insider nor the outsider is gifted with immaculate perception" (p. ix). How does a researcher represent the subjective experiences of others?

Among the authors in Part I, Clay faces this dilemma as she struggles to analyze the responses of teachers to her efforts at professional development. She decides to ask colleagues to write minutes, memos, and informal comments, which she then incorporates in her own text. But her position of leadership and apparent power in the school make it difficult for her to solicit honest feedback and avoid the appearance of coercion; most of her voluminous data must be gathered from her own perspective.

School-based researchers can gather multiple perspectives mainly through collaboration. Mohr and the Clayton team describe a meticulous process of talking and drafting and dialoguing among insiders with different roles, views, and status in the district. What emerges in these chapters is a consensus; perhaps the main story is the process of building that consensus.

Another interpretive issue deals with taken-for-granted definitions. Hajj starts to explore the concept of *community* in her fifth-grade classroom, only to recognize that the community she has shared with colleagues is being eroded by her more intense bonding with her new teacher research community. Other chapters explore multiple meanings of *administrative support, confidentiality,* and *power.*

PUBLICATION

School-based researchers have long been advised to "protect" their students and classrooms by using pseudonyms and composite descriptions when they publish. Often this advice comes from academic consultants. Three of the five contributors to this section, after reflecting on their own situations, chose to use real names. I suspect that school-based researchers are less willing than those at universities to trust in anonymity for protection. Their skepticism is appropriate since the author's name and school affiliation on the report make pseudonyms a rather thin disguise. In fact, elementary teacher Donna Nelson and her colleagues shocked an audience at the International Conference on Teacher Research (1999) by reporting that their personal journals and fieldnotes had been subpoenaed as evidence in child custody cases. It might be wiser for school-based researchers to start with the assumption that any student, colleague, or administrator they describe may be recognized and that anything they write may become public. (See also van den Berg's chapter in Part II.)

Which voices and genres best fit an unknown audience that includes both insiders and outsiders? Most teacher-researchers choose a conversational voice modeled on the workshop leader or presenter. Chapters in this section rely heavily on narrative. But authors have textured their stories with embedded memos, documents, dialogues, and commentaries; the chapters by Mohr and Minarik are actually reflections framing an earlier text.

INSTITUTIONALIZATION

What happens when practitioner research becomes part of an institutional culture of inquiry? The projects in Fairfax County, Virginia (Chapter 1), and in

Clayton, Missouri (Chapter 5), show the value of long-term, district support and ethical guidelines developed through collaboration. In such a context, action research does not alienate a teacher; it is a norm in the school culture.

But remember the professional development leader who hoped to require every teacher to do one action research project per year. Can we institutionalize reflection? Wanda Clay documents her attempt to build a culture of inquiry in her building. After her plan for seminars and teams is stalled in a power struggle, the new instructional leader realizes that her seasoned teaching staff is not convinced that their practice needs to be improved—at least, not by her. Today, 3 years later, most of the tension is gone (as are several teachers who requested transfers); staff who choose to work at this school are committed to the program.

The Clayton team relies on widely shared views of curriculum, pedagogy, and professional development leading to an unusual climate of trust. One of the tenure-year options for teachers in this district is a dialogue journal reflecting on their practice. Assistant superintendent Linda Henke personally responds to this reflective writing. Henke is respected as a practitioner and supporter of research, and her teachers express enthusiasm for the journaling. But it is easy to imagine ethical abuses if an administrator with other values took on the role of respondent.

Is institutionalizing inquiry an asset or a threat to practitioner ownership? It depends, I believe, on the professional context and the cast of characters working there.

CONCLUSION

School-based researchers do not tend to use the language of "ethical dilemmas." Instead, they talk about their struggles with unfamiliar roles, conflicting loyalties, and strained relationships. Outside consultants need to listen and to recognize the underlying ethical issues.

Part II

UNIVERSITY-BASED RESEARCHERS

Chapter 6

"A ROOT OUT OF A DRY GROUND": RESOLVING THE RESEARCHER/ RESEARCHED DILEMMA

Sharon Shockley Lee

"In the Old Testament in Isaiah 53:2, it talks about 'a root out of a dry ground.'" Thus Principal Alvin Haines concluded the final interview for my dissertation, an ethnography of the "white knight" principal.[1] He explained:

> When you pull a root outta dry ground, it comes out clean. There's no dirt on it. But when you pull a root outta wet ground, it's dirty. Research is like that. Some research is nice 'n clean, but not what you've been doin'. Ya get your guts in it as well as your head. Ya build relationships. Ya start carin'. Ya muck around in people's lives, and ya get dirty. Ya get hurt. Ethnography's like that, Sharon. It's not a root that ya can pull "out of a dry ground." (Lee, 1992, pp. 226–227)[2]

For 31 years, this aging principal of European descent and rural, southern, religious upbringing had served the Riverside School District located just outside a major midwestern city. For 12 years, Alvin Haines had been principal of Roosevelt School, located south of a small river known by insiders as the "Mason-Dixon Line." Below this line, schools served primarily poor and working-class children of African descent. There he established a strong reputation as a "white knight," a rescuer of troubled schools.

I studied Haines during his final 2-year assignment as principal of Washington School, also south of the "Mason-Dixon Line." During the study, ethical dilemmas emerged that no one had anticipated. I uncovered and reported troubling data regarding the principal's unethical and illegal practices. Alvin

Haines's threatened lawsuit and the involvement of university attorneys jeopardized the research project and completion of my degree.

In this chapter, I reflect on ethical dilemmas emerging from my dissertation, *Hegemony in an Elementary School: The Principal as Organic Intellectual* (1992), and forthcoming book, *Unmasking the White Knight: Emerging Perspectives and Images of the Principalship.* According to Louis Smith (1990a), *ethics* refers to a "complex of ideals showing how individuals should relate to one another in particular situations, to principles of conduct guiding those relationships, and to the kind of reasoning one engages in when thinking about such ideals and principles" (p. 141). He argues (1990a, 1990b) that explicating the process of decision making is a powerful means of improving ethical reasoning in educational research.

My reflections cluster around five themes: personal ethical principles; initiating the study; data collection; interpreting and reporting data; resolving the researcher/researched dilemma.

PERSONAL ETHICAL PRINCIPLES: ELUSIVE IDEALS

Like Alvin Haines, my personal ethical frame is largely drawn from conservative Christian beliefs and biblical principles. My husband, grandfather, and uncle are evangelical clergymen, and the religious heritage of my church and family is central to my world view. I consider myself a person of integrity and use the Golden Rule as a principle of daily living. In studying the "white knight" principal, however, I learned that addressing the needs of "others" who have diverse values, experiences, and opportunities is an elusive ideal.

In seeking a way to sort and articulate my priorities, I have found help in John Rawls's theory of justice. An equal allocation of power and resources to every participant in a social system is ideal; I live, however, with the practical reality of asymmetrical power relationships. Rawls (1971) argues that in an inequitable system, the flow of power and resources must benefit the least advantaged. This is the fundamental principle that guided my ethical decisions during research.

INITIATING THE STUDY: THE "WHITE KNIGHT" AS GATEKEEPER

While negotiating permission to conduct the study, I relied on three established ethical principles of fieldwork: informed consent, anonymity, and nonintervention. Alvin Haines and I first met at his office while he was still principal at Roosevelt School. He said he wanted to "size me up." Principal Haines indicated that he did not understand the techniques of qualitative research, but one of his friends, also a principal, had been the focus of an ethnographic dissertation. I promised to protect his anonymity and other participants by using code names for every proper name in the study. I also guaranteed not to intervene in the school. We agreed my role would be observing and interpreting events as they naturally occurred. Alvin Haines indicated these were adequate safeguards and agreed to the study.

As I left Roosevelt School, I was relieved. I had passed muster. The "white knight" was the gatekeeper. We both recognized that Alvin Haines was in control of this relationship. He had given permission for me to do the study, but emphasized that approval was dependent on his "OK." . . .

I felt managed, dependent. I had permission to do my study, but I knew Haines' approval could be withdrawn at any time. Alvin Haines' courage and self-confidence were impressive. (Lee, 1992, pp. 32–34)

Referring to it as a formality, Principal Haines directed me to write the assistant superintendent for personnel to gain approval. My letter reiterated the three points: informed consent, anonymity, and nonintervention. I received a two-sentence letter from the assistant superintendent: "Your request to work with Alvin Haines as part of your graduate studies has been approved. Welcome to the Riverside School District."

During initial negotiations, Principal Haines did not ask nor did I consider inviting him to critique and approve drafts. Midway through the first year, he casually mentioned that when the research was complete he would like a copy of the final report as well as copies of all my data. I assured Haines he would receive a copy of the dissertation, but I could not share fieldnotes or transcripts of interviews without violating confidentiality of other informants. The principal appeared to accept the validity of my position and never again mentioned access to data.

At the beginning of the study, it seemed unlikely that I could exploit Principal Haines. He was at the apex of his career; I was a doctoral student. After 10 years as a public school teacher, I had recently earned principal certification, but had no administrative experience.

I was interested in schools that effectively served poor and minority children. My dissertation would give me something close to administrative experience in an urban school serving children of African descent, increase my professional contacts with practicing administrators, and perhaps provide a mentor, Alvin Haines. Principal Haines was probably not expecting disinterested inquiry, but an endorsement of his success. We both assumed that the portrait I would create would support his reputation as a principal who "walked on water."

From my earliest studies of qualitative methods with Louis Smith, I had pondered the ethics of ethnography. I recognized the potential vulnerability of research subjects and was determined to avoid exploiting them. James Agee's (1939) words haunted me:

> It seems to me curious, not to say obscene and thoroughly terrifying, that it could occur to an association of human beings . . . to pry intimately into the lives of an undefended . . . group of human beings for the purpose of parading the nakedness, disadvantage and humiliation of these lives before another group of human beings. (p. 7)

Agee's words seemed not to describe my research subject. The "white knight" principal appeared powerful, well-armored, privileged, proud—more likely to exploit than to be exploited.

DATA COLLECTION: "WHOSE SIDE ARE YOU ON?"

During the 2 years of fieldwork, I attempted to be open, clear, and honest about what I was doing and why. Alvin Haines usually explained to others that I was studying him to become a principal. At the first faculty meeting, he held up an article on time management about a principal in an adjacent district. He explained that this was the kind of "study" I would be writing. I thought it was interesting that Haines knew what I would be writing since I did not yet know. Maybe he was right.

Everyone in the school seemed comfortable with my role as student principal and felt their advice would contribute to my development. I considered myself a guest in their school. They had not participated in the decision to offer me entrance, but I never observed classrooms or interviewed teachers without their consent. When teachers seemed uncomfortable with my questions, I changed direction, stopped recording, or offered them the option to conclude the interview. In the long run, I expected to earn their confidence.

At first, some teachers mistrusted me. One morning early in the study, I sat in the school's outer office observing the flow of teachers to the mailboxes, coffee pot, and copy machine, writing my impressions in fieldnotes. One of the teachers warned, "Watch out! She's writing down everything you say." I immediately took my fieldnotes to him and began reading at the top of the page so everyone could hear my benign description of their interactions. The other teachers laughed, and the tension was eased.

I was eventually able to interview every teacher at Washington School. Near the end of the study, eight female teachers developed a list of actresses they wanted to play their roles when the "book becomes a movie." The teacher who presented the list to me teased, "I don't care who plays me as long as she has big boobs. I've always wanted to see how I'd look with big boobs." We laughed together. Trust had been achieved, and the teachers never requested access to my data.

I consistently assured teachers that I would be the only one to read my notes or listen to the tapes and that code names would protect confidentiality. I was careful not to share information received from an informant with others in the school. This made it difficult to triangulate data. I could ask several informants the same question, but I chose not to try to evoke responses by quoting someone's words and asking others to respond.

Alvin Haines absolutely refused to allow me to interview parents, explaining it would needlessly raise suspicion. I was permitted to observe his interactions with parents and talk informally with them at school. When I asked permission to conduct formal interviews with two parents who regularly volunteered at Washington School, he consented.

Alvin Haines gave me free rein to interview students, but he did not want me to contact parents for permission. He said I should not "open that can of worms." I reasoned that the principle of *in loco parentis* gave him the right to make that decision. The children were, after all, informants—not subjects of my research. I developed my own guidelines for interviewing children: I would interview only students who volunteered, and I would not interfere with instruction. Instead, I engaged students in conversation in the cafeteria or on the playground, explaining that I was writing a story about their school. On one occasion, a student told me his teacher said I was learning to be a principal. Another boy responded, "Yeah, she's gonna be principal when Mr. Haines retires." A third boy laughed and said, "She can't be a principal. She's a woman. She can't hit hard enough."

The central ethical dilemma was my researcher/researched relationship with Alvin Haines. My process of questioning and critique began during the second month of the study when I first observed him paddle children.

When we arrived at Miss Yates's classroom, she was obviously disturbed, waiting at the door. Her third graders sat quietly [staring] in disbelief at the small girl standing on the third rung of the step ladder, screaming. "Who is she?" Haines asked.

"She's one of Mrs. Farley's [special education students]," Yates whispered.

Haines moved with authority across the room to the ladder. Standing behind the girl, he slipped his arm around her waist and lifted her from the ladder. Haines carried her, still screaming, arms and legs thrashing forcefully, to the hall. He gave her five quick, hard swats. Forcibly grasping her upper arm, he led her still screaming through the long hallway and up the stairs to Mrs. Farley's special education classroom.

Haines and I walked in silence toward his office, his face grim. "Mr. Haines!" Joan Smith called. "I have a couple of boys I want you to meet."

Smith and two African American boys entered the outer office. "Mr. Haines? You already know Andre. This is Orlando. He just came to Washington yesterday from the city."

"Come on in, Orlando." Haines spoke in a mock African American vernacular, "I don't know how yo' behaved at yo' other school, but yo' not gonna act like that here! Ya hear?" Orlando nodded.

"Andre! Come in." Andre started for the [principal's] door.

"May I come in, too?" I asked. Haines nodded. Andre stood between us. The uncomfortable silence seemed interminable. Finally, Haines reached for his paddle. He tapped the paddle twice on the surface of his desk. Andre understood the unspoken cue. He leaned over to place his hands where the paddle touched the desk. Haines [moved behind him], took a long, deep breath, drew back the paddle, exhaled and struck five sharp swats.

Haines placed his hand on the boy's shoulder guiding him around to face him. Andre turned, his eyes downcast. Haines placed the paddle under his chin and lifted his face until their eyes met. The man towered over the boy. My mind began to juxtapose images of Haines and Andre with scenes of masters and slaves. (Lee, 1992, pp. 98–100)

I began to ask myself Becker's (1970) question: "Whose side are you on?" When confronted with the dissymmetry of power between Principal Haines, teachers, and children, I began to realize I must side with the least advantaged, the students. I wanted to intervene, to contribute to the learning and life chances of children and adults at Washington School, but I stood by silently collecting data. I felt the frustration of conducting "inaction research" (Gentile, 1994), fiddling while Rome burned.

Early in the first year of the study, I decided it would no longer be ethical for me to simply present Alvin Haines's view of himself and the world as true and accurate. I felt compelled to constitute an image of him and his actions consistent with my own ethical principles.

As the months passed, I was increasingly disturbed by the data I was collecting. I attempted to share my concerns with the principal, but he successfully evaded my efforts. When I asked probing questions or tried to challenge him with alternative perspectives, Alvin Haines changed the subject, declined to respond, or physically walked away.

Near the end of the study, when I obtained copies of the district's corporal punishment summary reports, I felt I had the necessary data to confront him. During his first year as principal of Washington School, Haines had paddled 121 times. He used corporal punishment 97 times during his second (final) year. The "white knight's" use of corporal punishment exceeded the combined totals of all the other 13 elementary principals. Questioning him about these reports seemed especially significant since he routinely underreported his use of corporal punishment. No records were kept when special education students were paddled. When a student was paddled two or more times the same day, only one was reported. I observed Haines paddle a first-grade boy five times in one day. I asked the principal how many times the boy was paddled. He grinned and replied, "Five. Officially, once."

During the last weeks before the principal's retirement, he was frequently absent. I wondered if he were avoiding me and my questions. I carried copies of the discipline reports, looking for an opportunity to confront him. In the meantime, I uncovered evidence of other illegal and unethical behaviors. He was being investigated by the American Civil Liberties Union (ACLU) in response to parent complaints that his use of corporal punishment violated student rights. The federal Office of Civil Rights (OCR) was investigating staff reports of sexual harassment. Every time I saw him, Alvin Haines put me off, promising to clear a day on his calendar before his retirement. That day never arrived.

The "white knight" and I talked only once more, the last day of school when I gave him a mirrored horse collar that had been my late father's, and he presented me with his paddle, an ironic symbol of our 2-year relationship.

> "I don't like good-byes," I admitted.
>
> "I've had a lot of 'em in the last few years," Haines lamented. [He then shared intimate details of his troubled marriage, divorce, public humiliation at church, and attempted suicide.]
>
> "Why are you telling me this?"
>
> "I don't know. I've gotta talk ta somebody. I guess I just feel like talkin' taday. I trust you, Sharon. Maybe you should be a counselor instead of a principal. You're sensitive to problems. You're a good preacher's wife. You seek out problems 'n try to solve 'em before they explode."
>
> "I just wanted to study Alvin Haines, the principal," I explained. "I didn't want to know about your personal life. I've seen things, I've heard things that I didn't want to know. [Some people call] you a 'white knight.' I'd rather believe that because I care about you."
>
> "I know you do," Haines said. "I feel it. I'm sorry you've heard those things. Probably some of it's not true, but a lot of it probably is. I wish it wasn't. You just have ta write it like you see it." (Lee, 1992, pp. 223–226)

The principal who was so strong and confident at our first meeting was now vulnerable, even fragile. I had fresh insights regarding Agee's (1939) concern about "parading the nakedness, disadvantage and humiliation" of the researched. I decided it was not an appropriate time to confront him, but gently tried to express my concerns. Haines appeared to understand when he explained his metaphor, a "root out of a dry ground."

Although Alvin Haines's contract required that he work another month, he slipped quietly away to his childhood home in Daisy, Kentucky. My data gathering was complete, but I had a new dilemma. Who was now the least advantaged—the poor children of African descent or the aging administrator whose personal and professional life was crumbling?

INTERPRETING AND REPORTING DATA: FACING THE "DARK SIDE"

Answering my ethical question has been a long, painful process. I came to view both Principal Haines and his students as victims of the ideology he represented. I decided my research must do more to protect the identity of the researched than assigning code names. In order to avoid contributing further to their exploitation, I had to obscure certain geographical and historical characteristics of the school district, and alter the job titles of administrators, the grade levels of teachers, and their physical descriptions. Dates were deleted.

I had confronted the "dark side of the human condition" (Greenfield, 1991, p. 7). How could I ethically, accurately, compassionately, scientifically, and artfully interpret and present complex images of Principal Haines? Without understanding the implications, I had made ethical commitments based on the "comfortable but unwarranted premise that all practitioners are honorable men" (Hodgkinson, 1991, p. 11). It seemed both dangerous and dishonest to present images of the "white knight" that would be "too rational, too tidy, too aseptic . . . glossy pictures . . . that . . . ignored reality" (Halpin, 1966, p. 284). I felt the "public" had a "right to know." I hoped they would take ethical action in response to that knowledge.

As the dissertation approached closure, I reestablished contact with Alvin Haines, now retired and residing in Kentucky with his aged mother. I mailed him a preliminary draft. Haines's only response was a brief, handwritten note stating his "disapproval" of the study and threatening a lawsuit. He did not respond to my telephone calls nor to the letter which offered revisions based on his feedback.

Unexpectedly, I ran into Dr. Ruth Clay, former director of elementary education in the Riverside School District, at a conference. She read my dissertation, and we met afterwards to discuss her reactions. Clay expressed concern about both the methodology and the "highly negative" conclusions, suggesting the study reported "innuendo" rather than "fact." She recommended that the study be published only "when the person is dead, when the person can't come back at you." Clay was also concerned that participants were identifiable to readers who knew the community. Based on her feedback, I altered code names, changed physical descriptions, and deleted some sensitive information.

I also contacted Joyce Mitchell, still assistant principal at Washington School. She read a preliminary draft, and we met twice for several hours in her home going through the dissertation page by page. Mitchell made suggestions to further protect anonymity and corrected minor factual inaccuracies. She also shared a copy of a letter she had written to Professor Anita Hill after the Supreme Court confirmation of Judge Clarence Thomas. In the letter, Joyce Mitchell poignantly described her own sexual harassment during her years with Alvin Haines.

Mitchell provided a written statement verifying the accuracy of incidents reported in my study, but also expressed concern that Haines's "positive contributions and gifts of leadership" were not presented. She wrote that "the cohesion he brought to the [staff], the leadership he provided and the formal direction he sent the school on before his retirement were real despite his personal difficulties."

Joyce and I laughed and cried together. The concluding paragraph of her statement offers me hope that our shared reflections were indeed a "dialogic encounter" (Freire, 1973): "It is incredible to me now that I could have watched that paddling and thought it served any constructive purpose. This dissertation had a profound effect on me. What a sorry chapter in that book of years" (Lee, 1992, p. 291). I continue to regret that I was unable to draw Alvin Haines into this kind of critical, self-reflective inquiry.

RESOLVING THE RESEARCHER/RESEARCHED CONTRADICTION: FROM SUBJECT TO COLLABORATOR

When my colleague, anthropologist Seena Kohl, and I later team taught a course in action research, we struggled to help our students understand the complex relationship between the researcher and the researched. Eventually, we identified four ways a researcher might regard the researched: as subject, informant, participant, or collaborator.

Research *subjects* are like slides under a microscope or lab animals in an experiment. They are objects of study, unable to influence the direction of research. At the beginning of my study, I viewed Alvin Haines as subject.

Informants willingly contribute information and exert some influence on the direction of the study by offering or denying access to their knowledge and experiences. Students, parents, teachers, and administrators were informants in my ethnography; Alvin Haines was chief informant.

Participants are engaged in research by gathering or analyzing data, or both. They are offered opportunities, for example, to review and edit transcripts of taped interviews or conversations, and to examine and respond to drafts. Participants may hold the researcher accountable to present their voices and perspectives. Late in the study, I tried unsuccessfully to raise the status of my relationship with Haines to this level. I believe I achieved it in my interactions with Assistant Principal Joyce Mitchell.

Collaborators are coresearchers. Their relationship is an open, equal collaboration among colleagues that protects both from exploitation. The research design is dialogic, including shared responsibility for data collection, analysis, and reporting.

My experience studying the "white knight" principal has profoundly influenced the way I now conduct inquiry and teach research methods. The goal of educational research, I contend, must be to advance the learning and life chances of children and adults. I choose not to conduct research *on* subjects. Today, I conduct inquiry *with* participants and collaborators—who often become colleagues, friends, coresearchers, and coauthors.

Seena Kohl, Kathleen Cook, and I collaborated on an oral history project for the Missouri Historical Society focusing on school desegregation. Participants gave written permission to be interviewed, read and responded to transcripts, and provided permission for transcripts to be quoted or to become part of the museum archives. Drafts of the final report (Kohl, Lee, Cook, Bady, & Royce, 1994) were circulated for comment and approval. It was solid research which maintained appropriate ethical standards, but I had no evidence that our work influenced the desegregation program or improved the education and life chances of children.

Seena Kohl and I have also conducted action research (1993) on our team teaching of the action research course. With students we attempted to model participatory, collaborative relationships. I have also done collaborative, insider/outsider (Smith & Geoffrey, 1968) action research with teachers, administrators, and parents in the Pattonville School District (Morgan, Lee, & Gerstung, 1998; Lee, Morgan, & Gerstung, 1999). Kelly McKerrow and I (1991) collaborated with four parents to conduct action research, struggling to make rural schools comply with legal standards and meet the needs of their children with disabilities.

Collaborative research on collaborative actions has offered me ways to engage in school improvement efforts and to contribute to the learning of children, parents, and educators. An action research model empowers me as research practitioner not only to contribute knowledge, but to participate in the transformation of asymmetrical power relationships in schools and society.

In my ethnography of Principal Haines, I was uncomfortable listening to racist remarks, observing corporal punishment, collecting reports of sexual harassment, and recording instances of illegal behavior, but I had promised confidentiality and nonintervention. I kept my promise, but I still question if some form of action to protect the less powerful, children and teachers, would have been more ethical than my "inaction research" (Gentile, 1994).

A collaborative action research model, had it been possible, would have avoided these ethical dilemmas. If Principal Haines, like the four rural parents or my colleagues in Pattonville, had sought a collaborator to help him understand and improve his work, *our* study could have been critical research, provoking the "dialogic encounter" necessary to develop "critical consciousness" (Freire, 1973). It would have resolved the researcher/researched dilemma because the principal would have been the focus of his own inquiry; we both would have been practitioners, researchers, and researched (R. Anderson, 1996).

Educational inquiry, like teaching and administration, is "philosophy in action" (Hodgkinson, 1978), an "inescapably moral endeavor" (Codd, 1982).

> Whenever an administrator writes a memorandum or lifts a telephone, he or she acts on an underlying philosophy of administration, developed over time through experience and training. Reflection on the underlying assumptions and philosophy provides self-understanding and that, in turn, may provide a better administration. (Foster, 1986, p. 19)

Tragically, Alvin Haines seemed unable to abandon his "cloak of certainty" (Freire, 1973) and engage in such self-reflective inquiry.

To some extent, my ethnography of Principal Haines is autobiographical, reflecting my own development of "critical consciousness." I share my story to invite other researchers to participate in *praxis*—shared reflection and action on the world in order to transform it. We must critique our own ethical principles and practices, examining the intended and unintended consequences of our work. We must continue to question: Are the asymmetrical power relationships within schools and society perpetuated or transformed by our inquiry?

I completed the ethnography of the "white knight" acknowledging that both the researcher and the researched had fallen short of our ethical ideals. Alvin Haines and I had been unable to pull "a root out of a dry ground" without being dirtied. In contrast, action research offers my collaborators and me reciprocal critique, accountability, and empowerment.

NOTES

1. Names of people, places, and institutions in this chapter were changed to maintain the confidentiality of data agreed upon by all participants.

2. Excerpts from my original dissertation have been shortened somewhat but are otherwise verbatim.

Chapter 7

ACTION RESEARCH ON ACTION RESEARCH: EMANCIPATORY RESEARCH OR ABUSE OF POWER?

Sally Barr Ebest

As a composition specialist and Writing Program Administrator (WPA), I cannot separate my teaching, research, and administration. Consequently, when I began my first action research project, my purpose was twofold: to improve my teaching and to help my graduate teaching assistants (TAs) improve theirs. I discovered that action research is the key to both. In this essay, I describe the genesis of my project, the false starts and misdirections, and the essential role that action research can play in the professional development of teachers. Most important, I present a model for analyzing the ethical implications of making action research a requirement in university courses.

THE CONTEXT

Initially, I planned to study the writing and the behaviors of students in Teaching College Writing, the required seminar for new TAs, to note gender differences in collaborative learning. By observing my students during group work, tape-recording their interactions, and analyzing drafts of their essays, I hoped to confirm the feminist theories of socialization, which implied that women would appreciate and benefit from group work, while men would resist and continue writing as they had in their previous classes (see for example Barr Ebest, 1998; Gannett, 1993).

Fairly quickly I encountered a number of ethical issues and research guidelines I had not anticipated. The first time I tried to tape-record a peer response session, one of my two focus students said taping would make her too uncomfortable and asked me not to. Obviously, I had to honor her request, which meant that I gathered data only through observation. That incident reinforced the importance of telling students my research focus the first night of class and asking permission to tape their conversations. Because I wanted to analyze student writing, I realized I would need written permission. These requirements raised further ethical considerations. If some students refused to tape-record their group work or to grant permission to read and analyze their writing, I would need to assure them that their grades would not be affected. I resolved this dilemma by instituting portfolio grading and waiting until after the semester to analyze how collaborative learning had impacted the students' writing and revision. In the years since I began doing action research, only one student has refused permission.

At the end of that first semester, I discovered that I would have to revise my initial hypothesis because some of the women were resisting group work, while a few of the men actually liked it (Barr Ebest, 1998). This finding suggested that I would have to rethink the feminist theories about women's preferred learning styles and overcome my own feminist prejudices about the men's. Rather than disconcerting me, this led me to extend my study, to broaden my reading, and to pay closer attention to the construction of the peer response groups. At the end of the next academic year, as I began to analyze my graduate students' portfolios and listen to the tapes of their group work, I discovered that my focus on collaborative learning had been too narrow. Granted, some students found it inappropriate for the graduate classroom, but their resistance was not limited to collaboration per se. One-quarter of my graduate students, most of whom were TAs teaching composition for the first time, also resisted journaling, drafting, and writing about teaching. This finding led me to reflect upon how to make this course more relevant and productive.

In Teaching College Writing, I had assigned three essays of gradually increasing complexity. In the first, participants were to describe an ideal teacher whose qualities they wanted to emulate. These essays were usually disappointing. As graduate students, they were unused to writing narratives; as new TAs, they had not considered what made their teachers good. Indeed, because they were graduate school material, these students had excelled regardless of how their teachers performed. The second essay, "On Becoming a Teacher," was usually slightly better because it was not a narrative. Nevertheless, since these TAs were in the process of "becoming teachers," they found reflection on the topic difficult. This too could go. The third essay was equally troublesome. Hoping to move the students toward professionalism, I had designed a project that entailed analyzing professional journals and writing a researched essay about teaching, using the professional article as a model. Because the students already knew how to conduct library research, they found this essay the easiest. But did it help them reflect on their teaching?

As I thought about my students' resistance to reflective writing, I decided it was time for a change. If action research had helped me to reconceptualize my curriculum, then new TAs might also learn from this process. Based on this premise, I began to change the emphasis of my seminar's writing assignments.

I believed that engaging the students in action research was the solution, but the groundwork would have to be carefully laid. First, I added Ruth Ray's *The Practice of Theory* (1993) to the seminar's reading list, reasoning that this text would provide the necessary background. Next, I changed the end-of-semester research paper to an action research project in which data collection would begin the second week of class. When I presented this assignment, I emphasized that the students could focus on any aspect of teaching that interested or concerned them. The choice was theirs, but they would have to submit weekly research logs so I could follow their progress and offer suggestions. To start the process, I referred the students to Ray's guidelines, which asked them to "record all thoughts, questions, data, hypotheses, and conclusions related to your research project," and suggested they consider Ray's list of possible entries such as descriptions of classroom exchanges, discipline problems, and reflections, reflections, reflections (pp. 163–164).

This did not work. Although my graduate students were supposed to turn in a minimum of two pages of logs a week, few of them did so, and those I received were unfocused and undeveloped, full of questions about what they were supposed to be doing. Therefore I was not surprised that few of the final products were sufficiently documented or developed. Once again I had to reflect and change my pedagogy. Since the syllabus for Teaching College Writing already required weekly reading response journals, I decided to add weekly research questions. The first few entries asked them to write about teaching issues and to describe interesting or puzzling students. Later, the questions related to what we were reading. The students could answer them or move on to a more pertinent area, but whatever their focus, they had to generate at least two pages of fieldnotes per week. Periodically, I asked the students to reflect on their original hypotheses to see if they still held true. At midterm, I asked for a rough outline; before they began drafting, I gave them excerpts from my own work-in-progress as a model. I also asked them to develop a working bibliography drawn from the class readings and other relevant secondary sources. Later, I set aside class time so that the students could exchange first and second drafts in their peer response groups.

These papers were better; nevertheless, I could see that this preparation was still insufficient. Since the students seemed to need additional modeling, I paved their way by recasting the initial essay assignments to provide scaffolding for the action research project. For the first essay, I borrowed an idea from Madelaine Grumet's (1988) *Bitter Milk*. Grumet asks students to develop three different stories about learning experiences, to search for common threads running throughout, and to relate those elements to how they could make their own classrooms sites of successful learning. Like my original essay assignment, this one calls for narrative and reflective writing. More importantly, searching for and synthesizing the common threads would mirror the process they would follow to analyze the data in their action research projects.

The second assignment—a case study of their composing process—also draws on very specific experiences. Adapted from the writer's autobiography in Elbow and Belanoff's *A Community of Writers* (1995, pp. 447–448), my assignment asks students to compare the writing they have done in our graduate seminar to that done in the past, analyze the process exemplified in one specific piece (usually Essay 1), quote from their writing to exemplify their process, and consider the effects of peer and instructor response. Based on these data, they must determine what they do well and what elements of their composing process need improvement. This paper requires a great deal of information drawn from varied sources; students have to decide on a slant and organize their information accordingly. In sum, it is a dress rehearsal for their action research report. No matter what form it takes, their final project will follow the same steps, rely on a similarly wide variety of data, and entail the same type of analysis. Such examination also raises the students' awareness of process—that most writers have one, that process often reflects a writer's personality, and that in this regard these graduate TAs are no different from their freshman students.

In writing this case study, the TAs begin to develop feelings of identification and empathy for their student writers. Without this understanding, some TAs might ridicule or dismiss their poorer writers; without this awareness, most would be unable to help such students. After writing the case study, and as they begin assembling their action research report, the graduate students start to make connections. They begin to understand why they chose a particular student; they notice common backgrounds, similar personalities, eerie coincidences. Whatever the parallel, writing the case study of themselves helps my students to develop new insights into teaching and writing. It also results in vastly improved action research studies of student writers.

Every semester, my graduate students and I discuss the ethical dilemmas that might arise during their action research. Since they usually develop a case study of one or two students, they want to know if they should inform students that they are research subjects. If so, when? And will that knowledge affect the students' attitude or behavior? Should the TAs reward their student-participants in some way? Should these undergraduates fill out consent forms? Should the TAs share the results with the student-participants or just type up the report and turn it in?

My response to these questions is based on my own experiences with action research; it has been further informed by participating in discussions of ethics at the St. Louis Action Research Collaborative, by observing the results of previous TAs' approaches, and by my political views, which parallel Patti Lather's in *Getting Smart*. Because I believe that this research is, as Lather says, "emancipatory" for both the researcher and the student-participants, I encourage my TAs to inform their students of the project. This usually occurs during conferences, held approximately 4 weeks into the semester. Without exception, the undergraduates have been flattered by the attention and willing to devote the extra time to interviews. Because I also believe that we can learn from our students, I urge the TAs to practice "reciprocity" and share drafts of their research reports with the students (Lather, 1991, p. 57). More than once, confused over their findings, TAs have found that consulting with their student-participants has answered their questions.

Although the results of these studies are rarely published, I also suggest that the TAs have their participants sign a consent form so that the students understand that they will not be penalized for refusing to participate and that they have the option of using a pseudonym to preserve their anonymity. To this date, no one has refused and most prefer to use their real names.

Finally, with regard to rewards, participating in a case study does require extra time. The TAs and I generate a number of options, ranging from dropping an absence (since the student generally spends at least an hour being interviewed), to extra credit (raising the final grade slightly), to giving a gift certificate, or even making a donation to the participant's favorite charity. Basically, the reward should be appropriate. More important, the students should understand that their participation will not result in preferential treatment in the class.

These basic ethical guidelines, when discussed over the course of the semester, seem to have prevented any major problems. In the next section, I illustrate the potential of action research with a story of one graduate student's developing knowledge and understanding.

A STORY

Rebecca Kniest O'Malley's first teaching log was devoted to the difficulties she encountered with a shy African American student we will call "Niles." During the opening day icebreaker of interviewing and introducing a fellow student, Niles refused to participate, saying he preferred to work alone. More than once, Rebecca asked Niles to get involved, but when he continued to refuse, she finally suggested he write about himself to fulfill the exercise and invited him to stop by her office if he needed any help.[1]

Niles took this personal attention to heart. Every day he would appear in Rebecca's office to chat or to show her his latest efforts at a draft. Part of this behavior seemed to stem from his identification with Rebecca, for he had learned that she shared his love of baseball; but another part may have stemmed from his continuing refusal to participate in peer response, an essential element of the first-year writing program. As a new TA, Rebecca was frustrated not only by Niles's in-class behavior, but also by his daily visits to her office when she was trying to prepare for class. Each week her teaching log included a section devoted to Niles in which she recounted his latest behavior and asked for advice. Although I offered numerous suggestions, the situation did not improve. Indeed, by midterm, Niles had begun to reproach Rebecca if she arrived to her office late. Finally, tired of losing sleep over this student, Rebecca decided to channel her frustrations positively: she would focus on Niles for her action research project in an effort to understand his behavior.

Having made this decision, Rebecca relayed the plan to Niles and asked if he would like to participate. Not surprisingly, he agreed, for he liked Rebecca and clearly sought her attention. However, Rebecca then added a twist—in thanks for his participation, she would raise his final grade by one-third (e.g., from a C to a C+), but only if he agreed to participate in peer response during class sessions.

With Niles as her student-participant, Rebecca focused her reading on understanding his behavior. When we read Mike Rose's *Lives on the Boundary* (1989), she began to believe that Niles was a basic writer, for he certainly displayed common traits such as resistance to writing. Rebecca also assumed, because of his race and his attitude toward writing, that Niles had been a poor student in the city schools. However, as she came to know him, she learned that he had ranked second in his high school class; that threw off her basic-writing hypothesis. She was further thrown off when she noticed that Niles had begun participating in group work, chatting and exchanging ideas with his peer group members. At semester's end, when she read his final two papers and found them more competent than anything he had written previously, she did not know what to think.

When Rebecca began to draft her analysis, she returned to Niles's early journals and essays and to her research and teaching logs for clues. There she found that when Niles wrote about an unfamiliar subject or in a mode he believed beyond him, his writing became awkward and labored. But when he wrote on a topic and in a format he felt confident about, as he did in his introductory freewrite and in his final two papers—a research paper on trains and his writer's autobiography—the style changed dramatically. Reflecting on these papers, Rebecca recalled that at the beginning of the semester, Niles had told her he loved trains, but since the first assignment had been a narrative, she had discouraged him from pursuing the subject. Throughout the semester, Niles had claimed an ability to write research papers, but because of his general difficulties, she had not believed him.

After reviewing these data, Rebecca came to a number of realizations. She realized that Niles suffered from writing apprehension—when he was allowed to write on what he knew, he performed well, but when he felt constrained by the topic or the format, his feelings about writing were self-fulfilling. This realization led to others. Rebecca concluded that in addition to the differences between them in race and gender, her desire that her students like her increased her timidity. "I was afraid," she wrote, "to tell him something was inadequate or poorly done."

As a result of these reflections, Rebecca decided to increase the number of conferences she held with her students. More conferences would give her a chance to "talk about how they chose their subject, their writing process, their reader's responses, their own feelings about the paper's strengths and weaknesses. [They] would work to discourage mere mechanical revision; they would force students to think about their writing process, and to look at and consider their classmates' responses." Conferences would also help her recognize and address writing apprehension and help students overcome it by writing about what they knew. "For his first essay, [Niles] wanted to write about trains," she concluded. "I now know that if I had not dismissed it as an inappropriate topic, I might have learned something of him. He grew up watching the trains near his mother's house when she lived in Kansas. That is where *his* stories lie" (O'Malley, 1998, p. 16).

Like most TAs in our graduate program, Rebecca is a white student from a middle- to upper-middle-class literate background who excelled in school and had little or no contact with minority students. Suddenly, as a teacher of two sections of freshman composition at an urban campus, she was dealing with students whose backgrounds she could not relate to. Although our composition seminar included Mike Rose's (1989) book, an essay by Lisa Delpit (1988), and S. Barr Reagan's (1991) essay-length case study of a minority student and basic writer, these readings and discussions represented only 2 or 3 weeks of the semester, during which the TAs were dealing two or three times a week with the differences these students brought to the writing classroom.

In this regard, freshman composition presents these novice teachers with a crash course in cultural studies and raises issues of social justice and caring that often seem contradictory. Such issues cannot be dealt with in the abstract by a few readings or class discussions. Gaining an understanding of students from different cultures requires deeper study and closer examination; it necessitates communication so that their teachers begin to move beyond prejudices and misconceptions to see these students as individuals. Obviously, this will not always be possible. However, by engaging with the local problems discovered through action research, our graduate students can begin to move toward a more global understanding of students whose backgrounds seem so different from their own.

EMANCIPATORY RESEARCH OR ABUSE OF POWER?

Requiring action research projects of novice TAs raises a number of ethical issues. Is this approach empowering, or is it just a means of furthering my own research agenda? Am I imposing my own political and pedagogical views on my students, or helping to shape them as future professionals? After 5 years of documenting my own practice, I believe that action research is the most effective approach to professional development for graduate students. But is that enough? Is it ethical to mandate it?

Newman and Brown's *Applied Ethics for Program Evaluation* (1996) offers a paradigm by which to analyze this pedagogy by classifying "ethical theories into five categories based on criteria used to decide whether the behavior is right or wrong": *consequences, duty, rights, social justice,* and *ethics of care* (p. 24). Each of these criteria can be examined on two levels—the ethics of using action research to study my graduate students' professional development and the ethics of requiring my students to conduct action research.

Consequences

According to Newman and Brown (1996, pp. 24–28), using the ethical criterion of *consequences* means judging which actions lead to the greatest good for the greatest number. In conducting my own action research, I was able to reformulate my pedagogy so that it better met the needs of new TAs. During the first 5 years of the project, I asked my students to submit their portfolios at the end of the term so I could develop case studies illustrating the challenges of using nontraditional pedagogy, including action research, in the graduate classroom. (These findings are reported in *Changing the Way We Teach*, 2000.) Before I began assigning the action research project, I found that one-quarter of my graduate students resisted using journaling, drafting, and working in groups. Among this cohort, such resistance led to a concomitant refusal to try these strategies in their own classrooms. Obviously, I could not insist that they teach in this way, but after action research helped them see the effects on their students' writing, most TAs who initially balked at these strategies overcame their resistance.

Duty

Newman and Brown's (1996, pp. 28–29) second category for applied ethics is *duty*. To determine one's duty, they suggest asking, "What are the expectations and obligations in this setting based on my relationship with the client [read graduate student] and the [graduate students'] resulting expectations?" Sockett (1990, pp. 247–248) answers this question when he argues that "ethically responsible teacher education" must include opportunities for reflection and for students to behave as colleagues, instruction based on an "ethic of caring," strong role models, and an environment which fosters mutual respect and collaborative efforts. If I allowed my TAs to leave their pedagogy seminar without reflecting on their beliefs, without expecting them to act professionally, without helping them to develop a sense of professional responsibility, and without modeling such behavior, I would have failed to fulfill my ethical responsibilities toward them as a teacher educator.

In assigning action research projects, I built in the opportunity for reflection, collegiality, and mutual respect; in conducting my own action research and sharing the work-in-progress with my graduate students, I demonstrated my respect for them as researchers, provided a role model, and gave them the opportunity to collaborate with me. Almost without exception, students say that this pedagogy succeeds for them, as exemplified in comments from Fall 1998 course evaluations:

> The teaching log was most useful—especially your comments back. [The research log was] second most useful—I had some thoughts as I wrote that might not otherwise have emerged.

> I'm glad I took this course. I've learned a great deal about myself as a writer and a teacher of writing.

Rights

In assigning and conducting action research, have I violated my students' rights? In conducting action research in their own classrooms, are these inexperienced teachers and researchers in turn violating the rights of their freshman students? According to Newman and Brown (1996, pp. 29–31), *rights* refer to issues of respect, privacy, and confidentiality, as well as the right not to participate. I try to protect my graduate students' rights and, in the process, model how to protect those of their students.

In my own research, I draw on my fieldnotes of classroom interaction, written after each class meeting; on tape recordings of the students' group work; on their journals, drafts, peer response sheets, and final drafts of essays; and on their feedback when I show them drafts of my findings. As mentioned before, I inform graduate students of my research at the beginning of the semester, ask permission to tape their discussions, require that all writing be submitted in a portfolio, and distribute consent forms which preserve the students' rights to privacy and confidentiality.

As a professor, I can delay my data analysis until the summer, after grades have been submitted. But since TAs have to submit their own action research before the semester's end, they worry that a student-participant might refuse consent. Luckily, this has not yet occurred, possibly because the process of selection takes place over a period of weeks, during which classroom rapport is being developed. Indeed, at both the graduate and undergraduate level, students generally feel a sense of pride that they have been selected; they want their names to be used and ask when the findings will be published.

Social Justice

When evaluating ethics, Newman and Brown (1996, p. 32) point out that re-searchers must ascertain if *social justice* has been furthered for those "least advantaged" because of their race, class, or gender. My own research has fo-cused on gender. By learning how and why to use nontraditional teaching strate-gies, I hope that my female students will gain the confidence to maintain author-ity in a decentered classroom, and that my male students will allow the classroom to be decentered without feeling they have abdicated authority. My goal in assigning action research to TAs is to help them recognize social injus-tices possibly generated by their privileged race and class so that they can work toward justice in their diverse undergraduate classrooms. Rebecca's story sug-gests that this goal is both realistic and attainable.

Ethic of Care

Such stories also suggest that attaining these goals is related to an *ethic of care* (Newman & Brown, 1996, pp. 33–35). As Carol Gilligan (1983) and Nel Nod-dings (1995) have discussed, for most women an ethic of care focuses on devel-oping relationships; men tend to be more concerned with individual rights. While conducting my own action research, my reflections led me to see that my caring had been somewhat selective, directed more toward the accommodating graduate students and lacking toward the resistant. This realization suggested that through action research, my TAs might recognize similar tendencies, a hy-pothesis which has been confirmed. By reflecting on relationships with their students, TAs have become aware of inadvertent tendencies toward selective caring in their own classrooms.

REFLECTION

Newman and Brown (1996) remind us that teaching ethics and ethical concerns is a complex task. As Fontaine and Hunter (1998) point out, such an understanding must acknowledge "the importance of context and the value of permitting different approaches to assist in different situations" (p. 7). Rebecca's story illustrates how action research introduces graduate students to a broad range of issues and opportunities for differing approaches arising within fairly similar contexts.

By engaging in action research with my graduate students, I have been able to pass on what I have learned in the form of my graduate curriculum, in the tenor and focus of the graduate seminar, and in my expectations that my students become stronger, more reflective, and ethically aware teachers and researchers. Such an approach is not only empowering and emancipatory; it is also a key element of professional and ethical responsibility.

NOTE

1. References to a teaching assistant [R. K. O'Malley] in this chapter use her real name to recognize their contributions to my thinking. A pseudonym is used for the undergraduate student [Niles] to maintain the confidentiality agreed upon for bringing the case study to a wider audience.

Chapter 8

THE ETHICS OF ACCOUNTABILITY
IN ACTION RESEARCH

Owen van den Berg

Any discussion of the ethics and methodology of qualitative research necessarily takes as a central issue the question of the relationship between the researcher and the researched. Typically this discussion focuses on the need to "protect" those who are involved in the research from whatever harm the act of research and its publication (making it public) may do to them.

For instance, Elliott Eisner (1991) argues that, by furthering the public good through the creation of knowledge, what researchers do "can involve harming others in order to achieve that good" (p. 214). He then proceeds to raise three issues regarding the protection of the researched: informed consent; confidentiality; and whether those studied can opt out of the action or research. Similarly, Louis Smith argues (1990b, p. 260) that "the two most important principles for the protection of human subjects are informed consent and anonymity." In another variation on this theme, Yvonna Lincoln (1990, p. 279) views "privacy, anonymity and confidentiality" as the key points.

Given that the need for the protection of research subjects is widely regarded as axiomatic, most of the debate in the literature revolves not so much around the principle of protection itself, but rather around the difficulty of achieving it. In asserting that "privacy, anonymity and confidentiality" are the key issues, Lincoln continues by stating that they "are virtually impossible to guarantee in qualitative case studies that are of high fidelity" (1990, p. 279). Allow me to cite just three further examples from the literature of issues that arise from this focus on the protection of subjects.

First, there is Eisner's discussion about whether consent can ever be truly "informed." There are at least two challenges, he says, facing researchers who seek informed consent from their subjects. One has to do with how researchers can ever assure themselves that their subjects' understanding of a project is the same as their own, given that researchers have typically spent long hours and even months wrestling with the issues the research creates—Fullan's (1991) notion of "shared understanding." The other is that "the concept of informed consent implies that the researcher knows *before* the event that is to be observed what the event will be and its possible effects. Just how does one get such knowledge?" (Eisner, 1991, p. 214). Especially, one might add, in action research, where the focus of the research often changes during the period it is being undertaken.

Second, in Jennifer Mason's (1996) discussion of the problem of citing "anonymous" interview data, she wonders whether and how

> you can guarantee the confidentiality and anonymity of your interviewees, if this is what you have said you will do. You must think carefully about how you will fulfill such promises, and this can be quite difficult given the full, rich, and personal nature of the data generated from qualitative interviews. Such data can usually be recognized by the interviewee whether or not you attach the interviewee's name to them, and also they may be recognizable to other people. (p. 56)

Finally, Margot Ely (1991) points out that there might be very specific reasons why a particular class of human subjects needs to be protected:

> The very naivety of many research participants makes it more imperative that we are careful to protect them. I find that the elementary school students with whom I work prefer to have their names used if they are going to be written about. When I tell them "this is not the way it is done," they often turn to a game of making up new names for themselves and each other. . . . (p. 223)

But Ely's way of proceeding with her youthful research respondents also reveals the very definite power relations existing between the researched and the researcher. When they say they would like their real names used, she simply tells them "this is not the way it is done," and considers the matter settled!

The qualitative research community thus seems basically to have decided that the subjects of its enterprises need protecting, and that there are certain ways in which this is to be done (which apparently seldom, if ever, involve consulting the researched about the matter). Researchers, in engaging in a discourse about the protection of their human subjects, seem often to be doing so first and foremost to meet the requirements of their peers or superiors in the research enterprise—human subject review boards, for instance—rather than to advance or protect the interests of their subjects. The discourse regarding the protection of subjects takes place between researchers, not between researchers and their subjects. That would seem to suggest, particularly in such a litigious society as the United States, that the persons the researchers are particularly concerned to protect are themselves. Their decisions about protection may well be driven more by the fear of being sued, or by the fear that review boards will not allow their research to continue, than by genuine concerns for the rights of their subjects, or research coinhabitants.

The notion of protection, then, presupposes an unequal relationship between the researcher and the people she or he claims to be researching *with* (if the claim is that the work is collaborative). In such a situation, the subjects appear to be subjects rather like those of the prerevolutionary French emperors, and the relationship between researcher and researched similarly one that is feudal in form.

On the other hand, one could argue for a democratic, or at least a more democratic, notion of the relationship between all the inhabitants of the research. Miles and Huberman (1994) argue, for instance, that in certain kinds of research, there may well have to be more "democratic" approaches:

> Participants involved in action research, collaborative research, and perhaps in efforts intended to be "consciousness raising" or "empowering" may well want to be credited for their work, be recognized as inquirers who do not need, any more than the "researcher" does, the protection of anonymity. (p. 296)

What would be the argument for more democratic notions of qualitative research? I argued at the start of this paper that any discussion of the ethics and methodology of qualitative research necessarily takes as the central issue the question of the relationship between the researcher and the researched. In qualitative research generally, researchers do not consider themselves in any significant way to be accountable to the people involved in their research; if the axiomatic principles of "privacy, anonymity and confidentiality" have been unilaterally decided upon for those people, then researchers seem to believe they have met their responsibilities toward them. But this is a *choice*, a "political decision" made by researchers, and reflects their seeing themselves as members of a privileged class accountable only to other members of that privileged class. That such power relations exist does not mean that they can easily be defended in a political context that is supposedly democratic.

Regarding "insider" educational qualitative research, however, a distinguishing feature is that insiders research while they teach; they do not cease to teach in order to research. The goal of their research is to improve their practice; the goal of their teaching is to enhance the education of their students so that the students might become full democratic agents in the society. Therefore, says Altrichter (1993, p. 44), "action research should be compatible with the educational aims of the situation under research." What is more,

Action research holds that profound and lasting development of practice will only occur in collaboration with other persons concerned with the situation under research and not against their will. Thus, the research strategy must build on democratic and cooperative human relationships and contribute to their further development. (p. 44)

An equally compelling reason for arguing that insider qualitative research has to be collaborative arises from the recognition that participants hold multiple perspectives on what is occurring in social situations and what the meaning of those occurrences are. Educational innovation and research are socially complex phenomena that involve the "process of coming to grips with the multiple realities of people who are the main participants" (Fullan, 1991, p. 65). That means that there are compelling epistemological reasons for me to consider myself accountable to the inhabitants of my research, or else the work is likely to reflect my particular voice alone and not a multiplicity of perspectives. Holding oneself accountable makes democratic and epistemological sense.

THE CASE

In many parts of the world, but not in the United States, it is possible for academics to secure senior positions in schools of education without first having completed a doctoral degree. When I came to start Ph.D. studies at Washington University in St. Louis in 1992, I had been a professor for 16 years and a head of department for 10. I chose as my dissertation topic a critical reflection on some of the work I had done in an attempt to bring about innovations in the Faculty [School] of Education at the University of the Western Cape (UWC),[1] a historically Black university in Cape Town, South Africa, from 1985 onward (van den Berg, 1994).

One of those innovations was the launching of a master's program in action research in 1987. Previously all master's work at the university had been by thesis only; the "structured" program I launched offered a year of coursework to a cohort group of students, followed by a minithesis involving action research in the students' classrooms. The program was launched with the intention that it would explicitly promote educational and political transformation in South Africa, at a time when the apartheid regime still held full sway. One chapter of my dissertation dealt with the story of the "Class of '87," the nine students who enrolled as the first cohort in 1987, eight of whom were to graduate over the next five years. The chapter was developed in the following way (as I explained in a methodological excursus at the beginning of that chapter):

1. During the coursework year I made extensive notes on what was occurring, and had frequent sessions with the group about "how things were going." At the end of the year the students were requested to complete an evaluation of

the program, writings which I used extensively in preparing an end-of-year report to the faculty's higher degrees committee. Together these were the central
documents I used in writing a first draft of the chapter about the Class of '87.

Also, at the beginning of 1989 I requested Sandy Lazarus, a new faculty
member who had substantial background in action research and who had agreed
to participate in the 1989 master's program with a particular focus on evaluation,
to read my 1987 report and comment on it. In my draft chapter I specifically
cited Lazarus's comments and responded to them.

2. I did not keep extensive notes on my work with each student during the
thesis phase of their work. I did have a complete list of dates on which I had
met with the students, and dates of appointments that had been cancelled, post-
poned, or ignored.

3. By 1992, when I turned to writing the draft chapter on the basis of the
above information, I had reread all but one of the theses of the students concerned (the remaining one being reread in 1993). In the draft chapter I then
wrote a brief overview of the thesis of each student, plus reference to any comments they had made in their theses on (a) the course itself, (b) how they considered their educational practice to have changed, and (c) how they viewed action
research.

4. This done, I sought to share my writings, first with the members of my
Ph.D. committee in the United States. I consolidated their marginal comments
onto a single copy of the text in 1993, and on returning to South Africa, I shared
this text with the key nonstudents who had been involved in some or other way
with the process. These people were Wally Morrow, who had participated in the
selection of the students and in the opening weekend, had taught the metatheory
component of the coursework, and had supervised the thesis of one of the students; Sue Davidoff, who had begun to work on a funded action research project
with me during 1987 and was heavily involved in facilitating the classroom
research of several of the students; Dirk Meerkotter, who had joined the department at the beginning of 1988 and had immediately become fully involved with
me in supervising the minitheses of all but one of the students; Jan Esterhuyse
of the University of Cape Town, who had served as external examiner for the
coursework component of the program; and Peter Hunter of the University of
the Witwatersrand, who had acted as external examiner for most of the minitheses produced by the 1987 group and had subsequently served as coursework
external examiner for the next two intakes of students into the program.

5. In South Africa in 1993, I also convened a meeting of the eight students
who had graduated from the program, first by telephoning them and then by
sending them a letter of explanation and a copy of the draft chapter. (I would
have invited the other student, but he had emigrated to Australia.) I asked them
to write comments on the text of the copy sent to them and to return the annotated text to me at the meeting; to write any additional comments they might
have on separate pages; to bring with them any notes or artefacts of their experi-

ence they thought might have relevance to my writing; and to put on paper their answers to or comments on three questions:

- Do you feel that the Action Research [AR] course and thesis experience has made any permanent difference to the way you go about your work? If so, in what way(s)?
- What was your experience of the supervision you received during the minithesis phase?
- You have probably chatted with people who have done courses like the AR one at other universities as well as at UWC (e.g., the Democracy and Education course). What is your view (and please be honest) about the quality of your total experience (coursework and minithesis) compared to that of other students in similar programmes? (Letter to alumni, May 1993)

Seven of the students attended the group meeting on June 9, 1993; all provided me with their annotated copy of the draft chapter and with responses to the three questions. (The eighth student, who had had car trouble on his way to the meeting, did so by mail a few days later.) I had decided to chair the meeting, but to have its proceedings recorded by Donavon Goliath, a member of the current 1993 master's class. When Goliath provided me with a copy of his report, I circulated it to all who had attended the meeting with the request that they comment on its accuracy and adequacy as a set of minutes of the proceedings.

I had asked the students for 3 hours of their time for the meeting, and I proceeded by putting one page after another of the draft chapter on the table for discussion. I considered myself a full participant in the meeting, with a right both to conduct research and to have an opinion, a position I explained at the meeting and set out more fully in my fieldnotes written afterwards:

> I . . . did not see myself as a "passive interviewer," just capturing their views. My sense of accountability, and the process we developed in the course, made me want to explain certain things to them even at this stage, and to argue certain matters with them. After all, that was how it was set up, as a form of "triangulation"—first they were asked to write comments on the text, then to discuss these with the group (on the idea that often one has views, but these might be changed in the face of reasoned argument in a group, of which I was fully entitled to be a member). . . . This is a complex and time-consuming process, but justified on . . . democratic and epistemological grounds. . . . (van den Berg, 1994, p. 219)[2]

By the end of the meeting I felt "relieved, exalted, irritated and exhausted," according to my reflections, but now I had to await Goliath's writing of the minutes of the meeting and their circulation to all the students for approval. In due course the approved minutes were returned to me: they stated that the students were generally "happy that chapter 4 was a fair representation of the events of that year" [1987]; perhaps more important, the approved minutes also stated that "the group was in agreement that the meeting was conducted to their satisfaction" (Goliath's memorandum of 1993, cited in van den Berg, 1994, p. 220).

6. In due course I reworked the chapter to take account of all the feedback generated by the procedures. Often this reworking took the form of quoting from the respondents' written reactions to the draft and adding further comments about the issue at hand, making the text an interactive one at many points. As most of the students were Afrikaans speaking, I also submitted my translations to them to ensure that they felt I had captured their views accurately in translation. When my amended text came to be resubmitted to my Ph.D. committee, fortunately they did not ask for further changes to be made to a text that had been through such a rigorous and complicated procedure of discussion and critique. I followed basically the same processes of referral, consultation and accountability in producing chapters about the Class of '89 and the Class of '91, except that I provided these generations of students with copies of the chapter on the Class of '87 to provide background information.

Let me give one example here of the type of "interactive text" that emerged from the procedures I followed. Gill Cowan, of the Class of '89, wrote a lengthy response to my comments in the draft chapter about how Dirk Meerkotter and I had approached the supervision of the students' theses, and what our uncertainties were about our work with them. I added her response to the draft chapter by way of a long quotation:

> I note that you say in Chap. 5 p. 57 [of the draft chapter] that "by taking teacher voice seriously" you wonder if you are "short-changing your students by being too self-effacing" about your own experience, knowledge and expertise. In terms of the course, I think that the thesis supervision was actually "your time" for all those things while the rest of the course laid the groundwork for a democratic sharing of knowledge which had to be facilitated within a different set of "academic rules." (You refer to the desire to "shift the power relations between the walls of academe and its students . . . "; Chap. 5, p. 55).
>
> I think there was an intention, whether or not it was apparent at the time, to transform the role of the academic, let alone that of the student. (Cowan's personal memorandum, cited in van den Berg, 1994, p. 265)

After including the above in the next version of my chapter, I responded by saying that I felt Cowan's comments provided a "provocative and yet appropriate summative evaluation of the intentions and execution of the master's programme as a whole," but that for the reader of my text, the data and reflection contained in the previous pages provide a quarry from which to mine for an individual viewpoint on this matter (van den Berg, 1994, p. 266).

My point in providing a detailed account of how I went about preparing a written reflection on aspects of my practice over a number of years is not so much to invite a debate about the merits or demerits of the details of my particular approach, but rather to offer it as an example of an attempt to engage the major research inhabitants as fully as possible in the text arising from the research, without ceding to the other inhabitants the final say, or even the veto right, over the content of the writing. I believe that I held myself accountable to my students and the other people involved in my research, and I believe that this is the way we need to go in the future, rather than continuing to act as free agents by hiding behind notions of the protection of our subjects.

POINTS TO PONDER

In rethinking our approach to treatment of the human beings who inhabit our research, I think we would be well advised to avoid using terminology related to "subjects" or "human subjects" altogether. In what follows I shall, therefore, refer to "research inhabitants." I believe there are at least six related ethical questions that need to be pondered:

1. By denying our research inhabitants their own voice in our research, do we not *objectify* them, treating them as objects of our study rather than as (active) subjects, even as we term them our "human *subjects*"?
2. By removing their names from their work that we choose to include in our research, do we not violate their rights to intellectual property, subsuming their work into ours?
3. By requesting our research inhabitants' participation in our research at the time we commence it, but by not referring the fruits of our work back to them at the end of and during the study, do we not pay mere lip service to the ethics of informed consent? Do we not owe them a more visible, structured, and regular program of referral of our work?
4. If a fundamental ethical dimension of research is seeking after the truth, do we not violate that commitment by treating ourselves, the researchers, as the only serious voice in making sense of complex social situations in which there are, in fact, often many conflicting voices? How do we defend our work epistemologically if ours seems to be the only voice inhabiting the final research writings?
5. If the inhabitants of our research are not made party to our work in a significant way, do we not violate principles of political ethics, by denying them real participation, and so diminishing rather than enhancing their active ("political") role in events that concern and influence them deeply?

6. If, conversely, I start, as a researcher, from the assumption that my research inhabitants will be involved and named, unless particular circumstances make this unwise or impossible, then how do I deal with the implications of this position?

This opens a whole new debate. At the very least, I have had to read my research inhabitants their rights and point out that, by agreeing to be named or involved in my work, they could lose their jobs. They will very likely have to face the issue that local, state, or university administrators consider it their right to tell them what research they may do and how they may do it. If one sees action research and other forms of practitioner inquiry as attempts to improve one's practice, then they are political acts in a very significant way, and they can draw significant sanctions. As a researcher, a key criterion, for me, of my willingness to be accountable to the inhabitants of my research is the extent to which I am prepared to engage them, in an ongoing way, about the potential implications of what we are doing.

ACKNOWLEDGMENT

I wish to thank the College of Public Service at Saint Louis University for providing me with an ethics case study award in the summer of 1998. Much of the work for this paper was undertaken during that period. I also wish to thank Peter Theodore, my research assistant in terms of that award, for his help in reviewing the literature on qualitative research ethics and for our many stimulating conversations.

NOTES

1. Of course, all references to people, places, and institutions in this chapter use their real names.

2. Excerpts from my original dissertation have been shortened somewhat but are otherwise verbatim.

Chapter 9

WHEN EVALUATION TURNS SOUR: QUANDARIES OF THE INDIVIDUAL CASE

Louis M. Smith

Some years ago now, I was one of two central figures in a meeting concerning an early draft of our evaluation report, *"Difficult to Reach, Maintain, and Help" Urban Families in PAT: Issues, Dilemmas, Strategies, and Resolutions in Parent Education* (Smith & Wells, 1990). The other central figure was a member of the state-level educational establishment who was angry with our product. A number of other Parents as Teachers (PAT) staff members, including my colleague and coauthor Wilma Wells, were also present. But the "yelling match" was essentially between me and the establishment.[1]

EVALUATION AND CONFRONTATION

The story had begun several years before and has continued since, although at a reduced pace and level of emotion, at least from my perspective. Fortunately, the hours-long meeting was tape-recorded, and the transcript has enabled me to return to the events with some precision at the verbal level at that moment in time. That meeting, which culminated in a yelling match, will be the focal event of this chapter; other stories and interpretations will flow in and out. Until now, I have not written about the meeting and its meaning to me. In some fundamental sense, as I begin writing, I am not sure *what* I think about the event. My hope is that I will present a number of issues that relate to the topic of this book, ethics in action research. I also see the possibilities of discussion regarding the interplay of modernism, postmodernism, and agency.

That meeting climaxed a history of intellectual excitement with the Parents as Teachers evaluation project per se, but also frustration with the overall relationship between my role as observer-evaluator and PAT as an organization. One of the project's strengths was the inside/outside collaboration between Wilma Wells and me. She was a coordinator within PAT and an outspoken advocate of the program. After a growing professional relationship and a long series of discussions, she accepted my invitation to be a coinvestigator and coauthor of the report and later the revision that became a book (Smith & Wells, 1997). Those decisions moved the project from an ethnographic investigation to one that became more and more like a piece of action research. The decisions also make a strong ethical statement.

The Yelling Match

The meeting started with a long tirade from my adversary. As he began, I turned on the tape recorder. He continued for several minutes, actually over a full single-spaced page of typescript. In summary, and enumerated for clarity here, his criticisms of our report and some ancillary comments were these:

1. "[The report is] so difficult to read that I don't think anyone will."
2. "[It's] filled with things which, in my view, are unrelated to the issue or to the study that I thought we were undertaking. . . . "
3. "[F]rankly I can't, nor do I think our office would, ever agree to have our name on some of the content of this report."
4. "For example, the lengthy description of the political and social views of the investigators. In my view, that's not relevant and clouds the whole issue we were looking at."
5. "There's a great deal of stuff in it that I simply can't understand why it's there because it does not seem to contribute."
6. "My suggestion would be that the main body of the report be edited down. . . . "
7. "The style of the research I don't have an opinion on. We agreed, I guess, to that approach."
8. "[T]he report itself just seems to me to be not in the nature of a scholarly report, it seems more in the nature of a—novel, I guess. . . . "
9. "[M]y first reaction when I read it, and I did not read the whole thing—let me point that out quickly—I read 40–50 pages and fell into such distress I didn't even continue it."
10. "In fact, my initial reaction when I began reading it was that it looks like a trade book—ready to be submitted to the publisher and not like a research study."

11. "The second thing, I had looked forward to getting the summary, Chapter 7, Conclusions, and was expecting to see a manual, which was what we understood to be the most concise product of it. And I didn't find that either."
12. "And that last piece, the manual, is what we hoped to disseminate to all the programs in the state. And I had hoped that the executive summary on the front of it could be published and widely distributed also."

He concluded with, "Now having said all that, I'm willing to listen or to entertain arguments, discussions, or rebuttals or anything like that."

I commented, "I guess it's my place to start." He said, "OK."

As one might guess, I was mad as hell. I thought his comments were inconsistent and off the mark. Rightly or wrongly, my experience with bullies—and I thought he was one, both from comments I had heard about him beforehand, like "he pushes people around," and my feeling at the moment after his long opening shot—is that you confront, counterattack with your best arguments, and reestablish some kind of equality as an opponent. If that does not occur, bullies continue to bully. If some kind of equality is established, then later a potential standoff—if not peace—can occur, and collaboration toward an acceptable product might be possible. So I confronted and counterattacked. I still am not sure whether the gambit I chose was a wise one. This doubt seems to be at the core of the ethical issues in carrying out and reporting on our inquiry.

Some Consequences

We did, in fact, revise the report: expanded the recommendations, put them up front, and reorganized some of the substance to fit better some of the questions in the original proposal. Wilma Wells and I both thought the report was better. These activities were crowded in during my month's return to St. Louis in the midst of 3 months in Cambridge, England, where I was working on a biography of Nora Barlow, a granddaughter of Charles Darwin (Smith, 1992, in press). Carrying out two large projects simultaneously was a continuing major frustration. Little time was available for any roadblocks, large or small. Hence, the Barlow project seems an important context for understanding the yelling match and the interpretations of the present essay.

The revised final report on the PAT project was submitted in 1990 and accepted, in the sense that the bills were paid. We received no formal acknowledgment from the program or from the foundation that had funded the evaluation. No distribution was made. In effect, the report was buried, at least formally. Our ideas and conclusions, however, did get circulated. We sent copies of the report to friends and colleagues. Wilma Wells spoke to various groups around the state and the country concerning our findings. The responses were

validating about our images, ideas, and suggestions for rethinking parent educator roles and activities. I declined several invitations, which may have also been
less than wise decisions. Several colleagues who have remained in the PAT
program have used the materials in workshops and larger publication efforts.
About this time, I received a copy of a publication from the Harvard Family
Research Project, which made a half dozen citations to our report. We had made
some desultory efforts at publication, none successful until several years later
when the editor of an ethnography of schooling series read the manuscript for
publication as a book and recommended it to Hampton Press, who offered us a
contract. Until then my heart had not been in a revision effort. And I am in a
strange part of my career cycle, what has been called "transition into older
adulthood" (Levinson, Darrow, Klein, Levinson, & McKee, 1978).

By contrast, Wilma, in mid-career, was promoted in the city school district
and became even busier. Then she moved to a position as assistant to the superintendent of another district. Even more recently, she has accepted a position as
project officer with the Danforth Foundation. Until then we would have lunch
from time to time and raise lingering thoughts about PAT, the evaluation project, and the manuscript. Finally, we got our busy schedules arranged, established
meeting times, and began listing references toward a broader intellectual con-
strual of our data and findings. We did get the book, now titled *Urban Parent
Education: Dilemmas and Resolutions*, published and into the public domain in
1997. I believe that these complications, decisions, and activities are important
and underanalyzed issues in the ethics of evaluation.

Issues in the Drama

It is obvious from the brief account given here that I have little in the way of
firm conclusions. Staying close to the data and the story line—and perhaps to
my increasingly explicit values and personal perspective, if not prejudices—I
see several issues that I want entertained in the continuing discussion of the
project and the confrontation.

First, my adversary and I had major differences in what I call the logic or
structure of a recommendation. He thought recommendations grow easily and
straightforwardly from "the facts." I did not believe that then and I do not
believe that now. Recommendations have been a long-term puzzlement to me.
I believe they demand a value-laden theory, a practical theory in the Aristotelian
sense. For instance, some religious conservatives in America see programs like
Parents as Teachers as an unwelcome thrust of government into family life—us-
urping parental responsibilities. If their perspective and values differ in this way
from those of someone who views such program activities as a simple humani-
tarian effort, then the things they would recommend may also differ drastically.
Explicating the value positions of program participants, government officials,

and evaluators is very important in practical policy and action. A "good" program is not a simple judgment—in my view.

Second, PAT was the most politically laden program I have ever been involved in, and the evaluation was also, but we were supposed to stay out of the political issues. For instance, PAT was offered to all citizens in the state rather than to a selected sample based on need, high risk, or other qualifications. Considerable disagreement existed about having unmarried mothers still attending school involved in meetings in the high school itself. Church and state issues interacting with "family values" influenced the political context as governors and senators ran on particular platforms. An attempt to discuss such issues seemed important in my view of evaluation. I was terribly conflicted then and remain so. Wilma and I thought we were presenting "realistic images" of life in the program. For her as a PAT coordinator, the issues and concerns underlying the images became points of focus for changing and improving the program.

Third, in my view, the PAT organization was full of multiple interpersonal conflicts, as with many, if not most, groundbreaking organizations (Smith & Keith, 1971; Smith & Dwyer, 1979). These conflicts were to be ignored, suppressed, or not spoken about at any great length in our report. Implicitly, if not explicitly, many of our recommendations did address those issues. Our later book permitted us to enter them into the public discussion. The public's right-to-know value kept pushing me, as did the needs of adopters and adapters to have realistic views of an innovation they might want to try.

Fourth, from the earliest discussions of the contract, I was careful to avoid phrasing our activities as in any way a summative evaluation of the program's effects on the development of the children. I felt that those questions demanded an experimental or quasi-experimental study with some kind of comparison group, if not control groups. We had neither the resources nor the inclination to enter that part of the debate. This set of issues was terribly complicated. I thought then, and still believe, that the data on differential outcomes of PAT on the children's development were very limited and that the earlier evaluation data (Pfannenstiel & Seltzer, 1985) were derived from a pilot that was much more richly endowed with resources and activities than anything I saw happening in the urban program at the time of our observations. Tackling those issues would be a move toward reviewing and opening a discussion on the credibility of the entire program. Much as I thought, and still believe, that such a discussion needed to occur, I was not prepared to engage in it. That tack also would have opened an even greater confrontation with the PAT director and several members of the national board of advisors, who I thought then, and still think, are "true believers," individuals who mostly wanted testimonials to the program's beauty and importance, positive statements that could be used in enlarging and spreading the "good" program not only in our home state but to other states and countries. So, there are evaluations and evaluations, ethical decisions and ethical decisions.

Fifth, having said all this, I found this experience one of the most important and exciting pieces of inquiry and evaluation in which I have ever engaged—the "realities" of urban America, the magnitude of the difficulties and possibilities in the lives of urban parents and children, the school people trying to educate parents and children. Desperation seems not too strong a descriptor or interpretation. What do I do now as an emeritus professor, a retired educator in a university department of education? Is talking about the PAT evaluation at meetings and conferences that I still attend enough? My biggest "cause" these days seems to be helping my colleagues—school teachers and professors—learn action research and qualitative inquiry methods as a means of enhancing their own work in schools and universities and perhaps contributing to their own "liberation" and "empowerment," although these grand objectives seem to have their own puzzlements in the concrete day-to-day ways their lives get lived out. I believe that urban education (and culture) needs massive rethinking, if not critique, both from within and without its formal boundaries. The PAT data and interpretations, tentative as they are, could enter those discussions and reconstruals. Is there an ethical dimension to those thoughts?

Sixth, at the time of the evaluation and the culminating meeting, and even as I write now, my professional life remains caught up in my other large project, the biography of an extraordinary woman, Nora Barlow. Within a month of this controversial meeting, I left America for a semester sabbatical in England in order to work with the original Barlow documents now housed in the Cambridge University Library. I returned home for a month and did the final rewrite of the PAT report. It went into the mail the morning I returned to England. These complications and the malaise over the report and its reception took away both time and enthusiasm for speaking out on the program or pushing hard for publication. Now, this essay is an attempt to clear away some of the emotional underbrush. I am not sure I have the energy, the interest, or the fight left in me to move back into that discussion and debate. But my main point: I believe that the place of evaluation activities—and the ethics thereof—in the broader career serial or autobiography of the evaluator is an important but little-discussed issue. Job changes, too-busy schedules, personal frustrations, all impinge in ways independent of a simple rational analysis of the events.

Seventh, some 25 years ago, in 1972, a group of educators met at the first Cambridge Evaluation Conference at Churchill College. Malcolm Parlett, David Hamilton, and the rest of us were full of excitement and fire over *illuminative evaluation*, a qualitative, interpretive approach to understanding new curricula and educational programs. A central issue in the PAT meeting was the lack of understanding by a key educator of this genre of inquiry, which has found a place in the sun of the broader educational community. To him it wasn't "real" research or evaluation. That posed another set of practical problems in the ethics of inquiry. At a minimum, norms as to what is good and beautiful and virtuous about educational inquiry vary from group to group, organization to organization, university to university, government bureaucracy to government bureaucracy. At the farther reaches, we may be dealing with issues as fundamental as a paradigm shift from modernism to postmodernism. How and where does one enter this set of problems with all the ethical implications?

Eighth, I remain struck with the perception that powerful establishment educators who are used to defining situations and imposing their definitions on the world have great difficulty taking on alternative perspectives and seeing their possibilities. In a sense they are almost as closed minded as some of us who are university professors. This complex state of affairs seems to me both a personality problem and a problem of educational culture. Sometimes I wonder how any significant evaluation gets done or enters the dialogue where decisions are made. At a minimum, communication becomes difficult. At another extreme, standards and their legitimacy never enter into the evaluation.

These are a few of the perplexities that flow from my yelling match with a high-level administrator and my experience evaluating the Parents as Teachers program in an urban community. Politics, conflict, and agency were everywhere. Modernism, neomodernism, and postmodernism lurked under the surface. Quandaries in the ethics of evaluation were not far behind.

MAKING SENSE OF THE EXPERIENCE: AN INTERPRETIVE TURN

Ethics has to do with "rightness" or "wrongness" of human action, or, to quote from my old *Webster's Collegiate Dictionary*, "the science of ideal human character." I am left with several questions: Did I do what was right at the meeting? Was there a right way of acting? How should I think about this episode in program evaluation? What should I do next time? The individual case forces one to think at this level of analysis, decision, and action. Several items from reading over the years provide a helpful commentary toward an ethical perspective.

An Example from Literature: Steinbeck

In the PAT project I felt caught between three poles—a strong personal conviction about new ways of educational evaluation and inquiry, a strong protagonist for a conservative approach to evaluation who was part of and supported by a politically powerful educational bureaucracy, and a strong perception that local school people are often pushed around by some of the leaders. Was my decision and action to confront a "bully" a mistake? A vivid anecdote from Steinbeck's

Travels with Charley (1962) has remained with me as a source of advice—which I did not follow this time. Steinbeck writes:

> As I sat secure in the silence, a jeep scuffed to a stop on the road and good Charley left his work and roared. A young man in boots, corduroys, and a red and black checked mackinaw climbed out and strode near. He spoke in the harsh unfriendly tone a man uses when he doesn't much like what he has to do.
>
> "Don't you know that this land is posted? This is private property."
>
> Normally his tone would have sparked a tinder in me. I would have flared an ugliness of anger and he would then have been able to evict me with pleasure and good conscience. We might even have edged into a quarrel with passion and violence. This would be only normal, except that the beauty and quiet made me slow to respond with resentment, and in my hesitation I lost it. I said, "I know it must be private. I was about to look for someone to ask permission or maybe pay to rest here."
>
> "The owner don't want campers. They leave papers around and build fires."
>
> "I don't blame him. I know the mess they make."
>
> "See that sign on that tree? No trespassing, hunting, fishing, camping."
>
> "Well," I said, "that sounds as if it means business. If it's your job to throw me off, you've got to throw me off. I'll go peacefully. But I just made a pot of coffee. Do you think your boss would mind if I finished it? Would he mind if I offered you a cup? Then you could kick me off quicker."
>
> The young man grinned. "What the hell," he said. "You don't build no fires and you don't throw out trash."
>
> "I am doing worse than that. I'm trying to bribe you with a cup of coffee. It's worse than that, too. I'm suggesting a dollop of Old Granddad in the coffee."
>
> He laughed then. "What the hell!" he said. "Let me get my jeep off the road."
>
> Well, the whole pattern was broken. He squatted cross-legged in the pine needles on the ground and sipped his coffee. Charley sniffed close and let himself be touched, and that's a rare thing for Charley. (pp. 109–110)

In this short passage, it seems to me that Steinbeck's story contains a very powerful theoretical and practical stance. He solved his problem. Ethically? I did not solve mine nearly so well. Myths and dramas are everywhere for the taking and making of meaning. Did I miss one in my adversarial discussion?

Conflict: H. H. Anderson's Integrative Resolution

Although totally unconnected and written independently, the incident from *Travels with Charley* implicitly receives, I would argue, a more formal theoretical resolution in the thinking of H. H. Anderson (1937; Anderson & Brewer, 1945, 1946; Anderson, Brewer, & Reed, 1946), one of the early students of pupil-pupil and teacher-pupil interaction. Interpersonal conflict, both its origins and resolutions, was a major issue in Anderson's interpretation of classroom relationships. His most general statement, and a minimally cited one, is the 1937 work with kindergarten children. His discussion implies a causal sequence of ideas. The chain of concepts begins with difference among individuals in their needs, abilities, and goals. These differences produce conflict and incompatible actions. He argues that most group members and leaders (teachers in his analysis) respond dominatively or integratively toward the conflict. He isolates compromise as a separate action alternative. The dominative action leads to higher frequencies of submission or resistance. Integrative reactions, seeking common purposes, produce higher frequencies of creativity, spontaneity, and growth. Compromise does not remove the differences although, I would add, it frequently allows other task activities to occur. Other times it creates more problems. I have developed a pictorial miniature theoretical model of his ideas as Figure 9.1.

Much of Anderson's later work involved observational studies of teachers and children in elementary school as they worked through their daily activities. His attempts to develop observational schedules to measure dominative and integrative action gave important clarification. Ethical values were more implicit

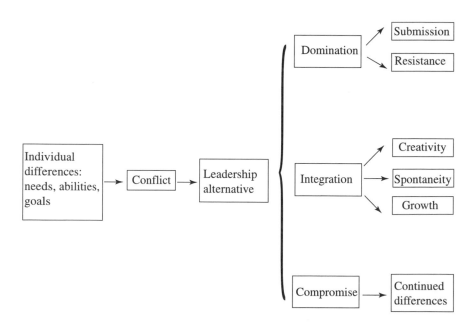

FIGURE 9.1. An Interpretation of H. H. Anderson's Early Theory of Conflict (1937)

than explicit in his research, built into the very language he used. "Integrative" and "dominative" sound very similar to Lewin, Lippitt, and White's (1939) and White and Lippitt's (1960) use of "democratic," "autocratic," and "laissez-faire." Adorno, Frenkel-Brunswick, Levinson, and Sanford (1950) continued the analytical and ethical tradition with their conception of "the authoritarian personality." One of my strongest retrospective questions is, "Why did I forget or ignore a set of ideas and ethical principles in my reaction to a bully from the educational establishment?" Thinking about—if not through—that puzzlement is a major goal of this essay.

A Curriculum and Teaching Perspective: Oliver and Shaver

In their *Teaching Public Issues in the High School* (1966), one of the most provocative curriculum and teaching books of the 1960s, Oliver and Shaver present a rationale for their new approach to secondary social studies. If our PAT project involves public issues, and I believe it does, then their position and rationale may be relevant.

Their rationale for tackling public issues suggests looking to three dimensions of a problem: (1) What definitional issues are critical for understanding and action? (2) What are the established facts in the setting? (3) What are the values latent in the discussion? I believe this approach is important for entering any ethical discussion.

My debate with the administrator involved several issues of *definition*. His conception of *research* did not include a descriptive, qualitative, interpretive, constructivist approach that accented vignettes, storytelling, and reconstruals of program activities and conceptions. Our definitions not only included these, but accented them. His conception of a *manual* was different from ours. For him a manual seemed more of a collection of dos and don'ts; to us a manual is a platform for reflective practice with no simple yeas or nays. His definition, or conception, of *audience* was more limited than ours. We wanted to speak to multiple audiences, including the state legislature and the national politics of early child care as well as school officials thinking of adopting or adapting PAT as well as teachers and parent educators implementing the program. Definitions slide into conceptual stances. Finally, though we did not talk directly to the issue, he seemed to have a technocratic modernist conception of the paradigm underlying program inquiry and evaluation. In contrast, we leaned toward a neomodern, realist perspective with a touch of postmodernism. In retrospect, I see that we erred in not having those discussions early on. We made assumptions that these were not issues. Big mistake! Oliver and Shaver, whose work we knew, should have alerted us.

Factual issues appeared throughout the discussion. The most important of these was that my opponent alleged that he had not seen the total research proposal at the beginning. Somewhere along the way between our drafting the proposal and getting bureaucratic clearance, an abbreviated version seems to have been transmitted. We had a full copy in the appendix to our report and I went to it directly—in the middle of the yelling match. That a briefer version of the proposal existed was perhaps the biggest surprise to me in the 2-hour discussion. Again, in retrospect, I see that some ethical issues could have been averted by more careful work on our part early on. Hearing that I would be meeting with a bully triggered too brief a thought as to how to deal with bullies. I still think he was and is a forceful, dominating type of individual, but knowing this fact and dealing with it in action are two separate issues. Factual issues merge with creative and less-than-creative tactics and strategies. These, too, have major ethical implications. Finally, his early comment that he had read only the first quarter of the report, some 40 to 50 pages, left me more angry than resourceful in "teaching" him about the further contents of the report. I was not thinking on my feet in a way that I usually am able to do in a class or seminar or in professional meetings and conversations.

A number of *values* seem involved in the dispute. In my view, a *recommendation* is a value-laden proposition, one that does not follow simply from "the facts." And this is an interesting mix of definitions, facts, and values. For instance, in the urban setting we studied, one of the facts is that families move frequently and often do not leave forwarding addresses. The 3-month summer hiatus in delivery of program services accents the loss of clients and increases the difficulty of finding them. Much of the parent educator activity in September and October is finding families and rebuilding case loads rather than delivering services. One recommendation is to offer the program through the summer. That increases the cost but could possibly solve the problem and improve services to the families. What are the trade-offs in values underlying the recommendation? Is PAT's service a higher priority than other activities that might be offered to urban families? The argument quickly complicates itself. Oliver and Shaver would argue that this is just the kind of discussion needed in teaching about, or working with, public issues.

To me, the authoritarianism implicit in bullying violates what Oliver and Shaver would call the broad values of human dignity and rational consent. But so do aggressive and hostile responses by an investigator!

A mix of values including investigator freedom of inquiry, the public's right to know how tax dollars are being spent, and the need for realism in viewing and reporting on a program—its warts as well as its smiles—is essential for formative evaluation that has goals of program improvement. But maintaining program integrity and community support has its priorities as well. Sorting out these issues is no small task, but that is part of Oliver and Shaver's agenda—and a major contribution, I believe, to helping with the ethical quandaries in an individual case.

CONCLUSIONS AND IMPLICATIONS

This essay presented a brief vignette of a meeting during the Parents as Teachers program evaluation, a meeting that went sour and ended up as a yelling match. Various reflections were added and three quite different lenses from the literature give both scope and power to the interpretations. Latent ethical issues were brought to the fore. Now I will offer some conclusions and implications.

Perhaps simplest—not terribly new, but often unrecognized—is my belief that any and every evaluation of a publicly supported educational program is a political event. Some educators do not believe this. Ours was a low-key political evaluation, but in my adversary's view a "rightly" done evaluation would not be political. This complicates the ethical aspects of evaluation.

We had chosen to do a qualitative, action research investigation. Copies of the proposal were seen, so we thought, by everyone before they signed off on it. As we learned in the yelling match, however, the state-level administrator reported that he had not seen the totality of the proposal. Internal slippage had occurred unbeknownst to several of us. The choice of problem, design, and method had been supported financially by a foundation and by the Parents as Teachers administration.

Further, as with much of our qualitative inquiry, we sought to create a new perspective on the program as we saw it in operation. *Reconstrual* is the term we have often used. When this kind of strategy works, it demands the best of the creativity of the investigators. And it imposes huge ethical demands upon the evaluators. In a sense the effort becomes a very personal act, a kind of action research: What can we see and how can we phrase the results and interpretations to be useful to several potential audiences? The perceptions, insights, and recommendations draw upon the large idiosyncratic reservoirs of personal experience and knowledge of a wide range of literature relevant to the problem at hand. One's personal ethical position merges with one's professional activities.

Relevance of personal experience and literature itself becomes an issue open to multiple definitions, values, and data—and discussion and debate— even among well-intentioned individuals. As broader and broader cognitive maps with interconnected elements are drawn, items that once seemed irrelevant are now brought into relationship and hence become relevant. Creativity is the watchword, in my eyes.

This line of reasoning, at least as we practiced it, led to recommendations about how the program might be changed. Again, recommendations at whatever level—local, state, or national—always, in my view, contain implicit or explicit value premises as well as definitional and factual issues. And, as different groups are favored in the recommendations, the process becomes political and ethical in another sense. Some educators, so it seems, do not believe this.

I believe that "doing science" and especially program evaluation, even a low-key one, in the human domain ultimately must confront such issues. One problem with these concluding assumptions is that they are not held universally. Differences in these beliefs lay at the heart of some of the disagreements. Unfortunately, this level and kind of discussion did not occur within the PAT program and our inquiry.

In retrospect, one of the most significant conclusions of this essay concerns the role of frustrations, emotionality, and anger on the ethical dimensions of one's activities. Why did I let that happen to me? At the time of the meeting, I was engaged in two large, frustrating, and seemingly never-ending projects: the PAT evaluation report and the Nora Barlow biography. Each step toward the end of the PAT project seemed like the blow of the woodchopper in the fairy tale where each chip produced two more to be cut. Another determinant for my emotional response was prior knowledge from several professional friends that I was meeting with a bully. This seemed to lure me toward a confrontational stance, and his initial attack corroborated this view. Steinbeck's wisdom was overruled. Further, what I had perceived to be "constructive realism" was perceived as "negative criticism." People in the program did not want to hear our tentative results or seemed afraid to entertain our stories and interpretations. In a way the public's right to know seemed denigrated. That right-to-know value and its corollary, free and open discussion toward improvement in educational practices, have been cornerstones in a long career of research, evaluation, and teaching. Educational organizations were supposed to be "centers of inquiry" inhabited by "scholar-teachers." Such were some of the complicated mix of beliefs and values. For reasons—or rationalizations—I find that I tend to have a long-term perspective, a faith that in the long run educational data and ideas will have their say and get integrated into the larger debates and practices. But in this instance I wanted our report finished, our book published, and our ideas implemented in symposium presentations and teaching efforts—*right then*. I believe all this was part of my frustration and emotionality.

In retrospect I should have listened to Steinbeck's campfire episode as he traveled with Charley, to H. H. Anderson's integrative solutions as he worked in conflictual educational settings, and to the wisdom of Oliver and Shaver as they sought to analyze public issues into dimensions of values, definitions, and facts. These seem the tentative but critical ethical lessons from our quandaries of this individual case in program evaluation.

NOTE

1. References to most people and institutions in this chapter use real names to recognize their contributions to my thinking. The state-level administrator and the school district are unnamed and some details have been fictionalized to protect privacy.

REFLECTIONS ON
UNIVERSITY-BASED RESEARCH

LOCATION

The chapters that frame this section are not truly practitioner research. Instead, Sharon Lee's piece shows the danger in the outside ethnographer stance even for a university researcher who follows the rules and tries to behave ethically. Lee's experience convinced her to focus her research agenda on fully collaborative inquiries. Lou Smith suggests some limits to her solution. Although his study was fully collaborative, leading to publications with a school employee, in his role as evaluator he had to choose between the public's right to know and the sponsoring district's reputation. These chapters show that inquiries conforming to all university research guidelines can turn sour over reporting "bad news" about schools.

Another danger for university faculty is that their position of expertise may mask their own cultural limitations. People of color are minimally represented in higher education. Lisa Delpit (1995) has described the "silenced dialogue" experienced by Black educators in the schools when they try to communicate with White academics. Ironically, Lee and Smith ran into conflicts with White administrators, but they also repeatedly questioned their own perspectives as White researchers in urban education. (See also Harris, Lowenstein, & Scott in Part III.)

Sally Barr Ebest and Owen van den Berg are action researchers who document and reflect on their practice as university teacher educators. Their roles have a second layer of complexity because the teachers in their graduate programs are required to conduct their own inquiries. Barr Ebest offers a rationale for action research as a core process of ethical teacher development. Van den

Berg sees his graduate students as the first audience to whom he must submit his research. Both explore the ethical choices they made in an effort to model and support emancipatory teaching.

What this section does not include is work by college faculty who teach about action research but never do it themselves. Would it not be an ethical violation to teach computer science if one had never programmed a computer, or fiction writing if one had never written a story?

RELATIONSHIPS

School-based researchers tend to agree that their ultimate responsibility is to the children; teacher educators who do action research may wonder to whom they are responsible. Is it to their own students, who are K–12 teachers? To the children those teachers teach? To the research community of their colleagues at the university? (Lee's dilemma came because she believed her responsibility to the children, to the least powerful, outweighed her loyalty to the school where she was a guest.)

Although action researchers at the university may encounter some disruption in relationships on campus, they are less likely than school-based researchers to find their colleagues threatened and suspicious. Instead, they are seen to be doing low-status, marginalized work. If they are isolated on a faculty where the norm is experimental or survey research, they may turn for their professional community to the seminars of K–12 teacher-researchers (the flip side of the process described by Linda Hajj).

University faculty also need to dialogue with peers doing practitioner research. In St. Louis, we are fortunate to have a monthly teacher educator seminar through the Action Research Collaborative. But the data from university-based participants in the International Conference on Teacher Research and in the XTAR on-line conference suggest that such support is rare.

INTERPRETATION/DEFINITION

Working as a consultant in the schools or teaching action research in the university raises dilemmas of interpretation. Whose reality will be portrayed? Whose interpretive frameworks? Whose language? The university-based authors in this volume are conscious that the language they choose may invite or exclude the stakeholders who have a right to critique their work.

In a consulting relationship with an insider, the university partner often plays the major role in analyzing the data. Both Lee and Smith realized too late

that "informed consent" did not ensure that school people shared their definitions of such concepts as *research* or *evaluation.*

By contrast, van den Berg refers his interpretations back to the graduates
of the program he is evaluating. He sees the issue not so much as informed
consent or confidentiality, but as *accountability* to the people whose work we
document. Their remarks (both written and oral) are incorporated into his text,
often with further explanations, rebuttals, and reflections. Barr Ebest, too, gath-
ers her TAs' interpretations of her work at the same time that she serves as
mentor to their initial efforts at researching their own practice.

Such approaches are ideal, but require a foundation of trust. Though van
den Berg and Barr Ebest postpone their analysis until coursework is finished
and they no longer hold the power of the grade, they do retain some status
among their former students. Part III will explore some fully collaborative projects.

INSTITUTIONALIZATION AND PUBLICATION

For university faculty, I believe the key ethical issue is the institutionalization
of research and publication. Published research is mandated by universities, reg-
ulated by institutional review boards, and rewarded by tenure. (I recall a few
years ago trying to tell my neighbor about my writing. "Will you get a lot of
money when you publish this book?" she asked. "No," I laughed, "but I'll lose
my job if I don't!")

Universities have traditionally seen applied research as lower in status than
pure or theoretical science. Schools of education tend to rank low, and within
them, practitioner research ranks lower than quantitative studies using the methods of natural science. If new professors hope to focus their careers on research
with practitioners in the schools, we must change the way this work is rewarded
on campus.

In 1997 I served on a committee that rewrote the tenure guidelines for the
School (now College) of Education at the University of Missouri at St. Louis.
As these excerpts show, we defined research broadly in order not to penalize
faculty who work in the schools:

> *Modes of Scholarly Inquiry.* The School of Education . . . values high quality re-
> search that is diverse in mode, audience, and authorship. . . . The following list is
> neither exhaustive nor hierarchical:
>> *Quantitative research*, including . . . experimental design, quasi-experimental de-
>> sign, and survey research
>> *Qualitative research*, including . . . case studies, ethnographies, and narrative
>> modes, supported by descriptive and interpretive data from the field

> *Action research*, including . . . studies of the researcher's own teaching, program
> portfolios, and studies in collaboration with practitioners who ordinarily retain
> ownership and direction of the inquiry
> *Varied Audiences.* Communication is the primary value; therefore the audience
> guides the level of academic style. Traditional academic prose directed to scholars
> and a direct style accessible to practitioners are both valued. (*Guidelines for Ap-*
> *pointments, Promotion, and Tenure,* 1997, University of Missouri at St. Louis,
> School of Education, pp. 2–3.)

Our document's stress on practitioner ownership and clear writing supports the
ethical principle of accountability. I believe this is one step toward a reconstrual
of research in education.

We as university teacher-researchers naturally hope to induct our own students into a culture of inquiry. We must then face some institutional and legal
dilemmas. What about permission forms, human subjects, and guidelines that
can apply to any research? Clearly, we must inform our students of the regulations and guide their theses and dissertations through the university's IRB. (For
example, the Epilogue, "A Guide to Ethical Decision Making for Insider Research.") We must help students evaluate their own situations; the practitioner
should decide whether to follow the conventional wisdom of anonymity to "protect" colleagues and students, or whether to choose accountability (as van den
Berg argues), with real names and credit for their "simple gifts" (Anderson,
1998).

More problematic is the brief case study or analysis of classroom data often
assigned in a semester course. With a short time frame and inexperienced students, it is unrealistic to expect a proposal and IRB clearance for every assignment. Some of us monitor such inquiries ourselves and keep a tight control of
the papers, limiting the audience to the seminar group. For example, my student
teachers are required in their field journals to cite their colleagues as "CT1" or
"CT2" (cooperating teachers) and their students using initials or codes. The
university considers their brief (4-week) case study a more focused piece of the
journal; the goal is simply to develop a richer understanding of one student's
learning. Early in the semester, I send a letter to each school principal, enclose
a copy of the student teaching journal and case study assignments, and offer to
make any modifications needed to follow district policy.

Gordon Wells has dealt with similar issues in his graduate courses at the
Ontario Institute for Studies in Education. In a letter to the Associate Director
of Research, he acknowledges that his M.Ed. action research projects involve
"human subjects," but explains that since topics are "emergent rather than decided in advance," a focused question may not become clear to the novice researcher until midsemester. He proposes that

> such practitioner action research in the context of a taught course should
> not require each class member to go through the ethical review procedure.

Instead, I suggest that a form of written approval be given to the course it-self. . . .

Wells adds that course members will be given a model letter to request informed consent. Because "there is no possibility of maintaining the anonymity of the practitioner" or of the research setting, he suggests that teachers, students, or their parents be given "the option to be named and take credit for their contributions." (Wells, personal communication, 1999).

CONCLUSION

University-based researchers have tended to see ethical issues more in terms of institutional regulations than in terms of sound pedagogy and respect for persons in the schools. These chapters challenge such assumptions and suggest some alternatives.

Part III

COLLABORATIVE SCHOOL-UNIVERSITY RESEARCH

Chapter 10

THE ETHICS OF CULTURAL INVISIBILITY

*Jane Zeni and Myrtho Prophete, with
Nancy Cason and Minnie Phillips*

Action research is a powerful way for us as teachers to improve our own practice. But when we try to address a problem, most often we start by looking at methods. We ask questions like "Does cooperative learning help my students learn X?" or "What kind of talk do my students use in cooperative groups as they learn X?" Sometimes the question focuses on specific groups of learners: "How do my female biology students engage in problem solving?" or "What revision strategies work best for my African American writers?" The trouble with these questions is that they make the teacher invisible, a sort of gender-free, culture-free technician, a person-of-no-color.

Perhaps the question behind the question should be more personal: "How can I, Jane Zeni, as a bookish White female, learn the perspective of Bob, who is African American, male, and producing nothing in my class?" When I work as consultant with action researchers, I watch them struggle to put themselves into the question, to see their own identities as problematic. Geertz (1988) deplores "the pretense" by some researchers that they are capable "of looking at the world directly, as though through a one-way screen, seeing others as they really are" (p. 141). Action researchers cannot observe a scene without affecting whoever is there. And a teacher's race, class, gender, age, and temperament are far from invisible to students.

When we, as teacher-researchers, do not locate ourselves and our own cultures in the research we do, our fieldnotes may simply reveal the old stereotypes. This is especially true when we describe students from groups that historically have been less successful in the school system. Teacher-researchers may see children of color as "at risk" or "learning disabled," suffering from "low self-esteem" or "family problems" or "lack of motivation." Would an observer closer to the student's culture see the same picture?

WHO IS CULTURALLY INVISIBLE?

I would like to suggest that cultural invisibility—our students' and our own—is a key ethical problem in doing action research. The two vignettes that follow were written by teachers who took a closer look, then consciously changed their instinctive response to students whose cultures differed from their own.

A decade ago, in the St. Louis suburb of Webster Groves, secondary teachers Joan Krater, Nancy Cason, and Minnie Phillips helped launch a research team.[1] Initially, they saw their goal as finding more effective ways to improve the writing of their African American male students in this majority White (75%) district. A key text in changing their perspective was this passage from Ralph Ellison's *Invisible Man* (1952):

> I am an invisible man. No, I am not a spook like those who haunted Edgar Allan Poe; nor am I one of your Hollywood-movie ectoplasms. I am a man of substance, of flesh and bones, fiber and liquids—and I might even be said to possess a mind. I am invisible, understand, simply because people refuse to see me. Like the bodiless heads you see sometimes in circus sideshows, it is as though I have been surrounded by mirrors of hard, distorting glass. When they approach me, they see only my surroundings, themselves, or figments of their imagination—indeed, everything and anything except me. (p. 3)

Ellison's words suggested the title eventually chosen for the team's action research book, *Mirror Images: Teaching Writing in Black and White* (Krater et al., 1994). White teachers on the team realized that "when we looked at Black male students in our classrooms, what we saw at first was a reflection of our own assumptions, fears, and frustrations—along with the masks the kids themselves put up for protection" (p. 43). As the team's university member, I saw the goal reconceptualized through 5 years of monthly meetings, fieldnotes, essays, and collaborative reports. Instead of "fixing" students' deficiencies, the teachers began to talk of creating classrooms where Black as well as White students would feel culturally welcome. As they learned to see "other people's children" more clearly (Delpit, 1995), most of those children learned to improve their writing.

Seeing "Other People's Children" 1

In this vignette from *Mirror Images*, Nancy Cason describes a confrontation with a seventh grader and how she saw past the mask:

I told Wilson to remove his hat in the classroom. He took a defensive and rebellious attitude, I tensed up—and we had a stand-off. For at least two weeks, there was no work from Wilson. He sat in class scowling.

Thankfully this happened early in the year, for I had time to undo the damage. After class one day I spoke to Wilson. I apologized for being curt and abrupt with him, adding that I wouldn't expect him to talk to me the way I had talked to him. I dropped that authoritative "teacher" role and approached him on a person-to-person level.

Wilson listened without saying anything, then smiled tentatively. I had offered friendship, and he had accepted. The next day he entered class and took out paper and pen with the air of a dedicated student. From that day he became my champion, scolding others who were talking or not on task.

As the holidays approached, my teammate and I took a group of students to *A Christmas Carol*. My teammate did not want to take Wilson because the scowling, nasty attitude that I had seen from him was ever present in her class. I assumed responsibility for the decision and he went. He enjoyed the play tremendously. He hushed the talking students, held doors open for "little old ladies," and smiled the entire day. The other teacher's faith began to build and Wilson's attitude changed in her class, too.

Across the board, in all four core classes that quarter, we saw more improvement in grades from Wilson than from any of the other one hundred students on team. . . .

Wilson and I had a second confrontation later in the year. He had headphones and a cassette player on as he entered class. I smiled (very important) reassuringly, held my hand out, and requested he give them to me to be returned after school. For a moment, Wilson assumed the same defensive body language and demeanor that he showed in the beginning of the year. His gut reaction was defiance. Suddenly, he returned my smile, his body relaxed, and he handed the prize over to me. (*Mirror Images*, p. 168)

Nancy catches herself in an attitude that will only play into the stereotypical interaction of White female teacher with Black male student. She takes the risk of showing her humanness and inviting the same from Wilson. Most important, she reflects on their relationship, recognizing her power to change the mode of cross-cultural communication.

Seeing "Other People's Children" 2

The ethical imperative to see culture in our classroom relationships is, of course, not limited to White teachers. Myrtho Prophete gathered and led a multiyear action research team in her elementary school in the affluent suburb of Rockwood, Missouri. All her teammates (like the great majority of their students) were White, and most Black students were bused from St. Louis. Myrtho, who is African American, describes a confrontation with a White student who challenged her:

As I was passing out information about the life of Martin Luther King Jr., I observed a sour look from one of my fifth graders. Then he crumpled up the sheet before I could distribute the rest of the papers. Anger boiling at the back of my throat, I decided to ignore the behavior. I had daily conflicts with Johnny and wanted to avoid another.

Johnny whined, "What do we have to learn about him for?"

I knew the retort I was thinking was bound to come leaping out of my mouth. I wanted to ask him to leave the room. (I felt insulted; how dare he question the importance of Dr. King?) After all, this was the first African-American topic I had taught since the new year of 1996. It wasn't as if I had started the daily diet of Black History Month curriculum. I wanted to say, "How do you think *we* (meaning African Americans) feel living in a White society daily?"

I decided to explain why I was upset. Maybe Johnny was just parroting ideas he had heard elsewhere. Why was I assuming he was personally insulting me? (Well, he did have a demeaning tone!)

I said I was upset because my feelings were hurt. (This was the first time I shared such feelings with my class.) I said I felt hurt because I am Black and he was rejecting a Black person. "Yeah!" chimed in several other students. Some looked relieved that they had found a way to express that they did not share his attitude. As an African American teacher in a district with an 85% White enrollment, I welcomed their support.

As calmly as I could, I began to explain that we had studied many historic Americans at school. "For Social Studies projects you had your choice to study Amelia Earhart, Theodore Roosevelt, Annie Oakley, Benjamin Franklin, or some other person. Dr. King is an American, too. His birthday is a national holiday. He made significant contributions to our country. That is why we study his life."

"Oh," said Johnny in an effort to change the subject. "I didn't know we could do Theodore Roosevelt."

Later, I shared the incident with my colleagues at our action research seminar. Sponsored by the Gateway Writing Project, we were a racially diverse group of teachers from many districts. That day we were discussing "Factors that Hinder the Education of Black Children in Predominantly White Schools" (1990) by local African American teacher William Jenkins. I remarked that *my* problem was with a White child. When I told my story, one of our consultants, Jane Zeni, commented that European American students often shut down when confronted with the history of slavery and racism:

"Many kids today don't know that Black and White students worked together in the 1960s fighting for Civil Rights. Today they see it as a 'Black thing.'" Jane cited Joel Spring's (1995, pp. 90–91) discussion of "White Guilt."

We concluded that it may be difficult to avoid a sense of overpowering guilt by association. I wondered, "Do my students know and identify with White people who helped in the Civil Rights struggle? Maybe if they did, they wouldn't be so resistent to hearing the facts."

So I brought such stories into my classroom. I pointed out White clergy in marches, the trio of Civil Rights workers (two White, one Black) killed in Mississippi, a White man brutally beaten for participating in the freedom rides, and others in the struggle.

Next, I selected *Days of Courage: The Little Rock Story* by Richard Kelso for literature study by the entire class. This book was an excellent choice because it keeps to the facts. All the words in quotations are the actual words spoken by the participants. Kelso describes some White people as segregationist, others as integrationist. Their actions, detailed from the first day, range from the kind White girl inviting a Black girl to lunch to the angry mob outside protesting the integration of Central High School.

Journal writing gave my students a daily opportunity to express their feelings and reactions to the novel:

"It was sad when the mob was trying to beat up the newscasters."

"I thought it was a bad idea that they wanted to hang somebody."

"I'm glad that some of the White children were nice to the nine children."

"I can't believe some of the police officers threw down their badges and joined the mob!"

These dialogue journals, and my own responses, were a great asset to my understanding.

I also showed a video, *America's Civil Rights Movement* (1989), from the Teaching Tolerance Project of the Southern Poverty Law Center. This film led to a fabulous discussion. Astra Cherry, another teacher-consultant, had modelled a Socratic seminar for our group. Using the Socratic method (Letts, 1994), I posed open-ended questions and allowed the students to talk, basing their responses on facts from the documentary. My role was facilitator. I tried to stay nonjudgmental and let students come to their own conclusions.

A few weeks later, during an interdisciplinary project that included an African American research paper, I shared some pictures of African Americans [for the students] to color. Johnny chose a picture of Thurgood Marshall. He didn't scribble over it as I feared. Instead, he colored it carefully. He stepped up to my desk to whisper, "Shouldn't the cloak be black? It says he was a judge." I sensed he wanted to do an excellent job.

My action research did not turn Johnny into a model student. He continued to challenge me on many occasions. But the strategies seemed to give him some new insight, and the experience gave me some insight into him. My students needed a vehicle to express their thoughts—through the dialogue journal, the video, the Socratic seminar, and literature that helped them identify with historical events that are still relevant today. I think these strategies can help children learn tolerance and develop respect for issues from more than just the obvious opposing perspectives.

Finally, the action research was a tremendous lesson for me. I found out what was on my students' minds. This experience was a strong reminder that student input is crucial to learning. Students have valuable things to say. I need to listen and learn. (Prophete, 1996; rev. 1999)

Myrtho, like Nancy, was determined to look beyond her ingrained cultural reactions and assumptions to see what might be going on inside a "difficult" kid. I believe this willingness to listen and learn, to study our students, is an ethical principle for doing action research in culturally diverse classrooms.

Of course, all classrooms are "culturally diverse" if the notion of culture is not reduced to race. Even in an apparently homogeneous classroom, the teacher will differ from students in many dimensions of culture, such as gender, social class, religion, and certainly age.

"SECOND-SIGHT"

I believe that any teacher-researcher who is committed to listen, observe, and document life in the classroom must work to become at least somewhat fluent in other cultures. The insights of four African American scholars suggest ways we can learn to cross over, to take on another perspective.

In 1903, W. E. B. DuBois described Black people as "gifted with second-sight in this American world," meaning that they are raised in the African American culture but also exposed to and shaped by the dominant White culture. The result is "this double-consciousness, this sense of always looking at one's self through the eyes of others" (1903/ 1982, p. 45). DuBois emphasizes the pain of this position—but he also calls it a "gift."

Feminist theory suggests another kind of second-sight. According to Patricia Hill Collins (1991), women see the world, and themselves, from two perspectives—through the dominant male culture as well as through their own female experience. Can the concept of second-sight be applied to practitioner research?

James Banks (1998) proposes a "typology of crosscultural researchers" with four categories based on the ways people in a pluralistic society are socialized (p. 7). Of particular interest in this discussion are Banks's two middle categories. The "indigenous-outsider" has grown up within a marginalized community but assimilated into the dominant culture; the "external-insider" was socialized in the dominant culture but became an "adopted" member of another community (p. 8).

Anthropologist Janice Hale-Benson (1986) suggests that people who have learned to live in two worlds can play some powerful educational roles. According to her categories, "cultural translators" are minority group members "who have been successful at dual socialization. They share their own experiences in negotiating the intricacies of the majority culture and convey ways to meet the society's demands without compromising ethnic values." "Cultural mediators" are people "from mainstream culture who can serve as guides for minority persons"—including teachers and counselors, but also informal mentors (p. 190).

When I read DuBois, Collins, Banks, and Hale-Benson, I think of the "second-sight" that we as teacher-researchers need if we hope to understand *any* of our students and to reflect on our own roles in the community inside and outside the school. Gradually, we can stretch the boundaries of our own socialization enough to see our students in a more authentic way.

OUR STUDENTS, OURSELVES

If action research is to be ethical, if we are to avoid projecting our own biases on the students we study, we must also observe ourselves and the culture we bring to the classroom. A few years into the project, the Webster Groves team began to write cultural self-portraits. These autobiographical pieces, which appear between the chapters in *Mirror Images* (Krater et al., 1994), proved essential to the team's research. Two examples follow.

Seeing My Own Culture 1

Minnie Phillips teaches basic and college prep classes at Webster Groves High School. Like Myrtho, she is an African American working in a majority White school. But Minnie's research led her to examine her relationships with her Black students. When she wrote about her own childhood for *Mirror Images*, she discovered a theme of cultural "repression."

Minnie had grown up in a small, segregated town where poetry recitals, dramatic performances, and skills in oral expression were features of African American life:

> Language facility meant adeptness in speech and rhetoric—at emotional persuasion and comic jabs (playing the dozens, quick rejoinders, and embellished folktales)— homespun entertainment which offset the "Jim Crow" humiliation and subjugation imposed by the world outside. (From *Mirror Images*, p. 9)

At 16, Minnie left her rural home to enter the University of Missouri. There she immersed herself in the artifacts of European American culture. "I resolved to alter my dialect (a kind of self-taught Eliza Doolittle)," she wrote, "and since I was minoring in speech and drama, stage speech seemed properly elevated." After college, she began teaching in a newly integrated school where Black students were second-class citizens:

> Running away from my culture, I had run into it, but this time I had to choose, I thought, between students or the institution. I was, after all, hired to teach standard English, I insisted to myself, and I set about ferreting out "nonstandard English" with a passion (although I'm horrified to think of the bodies I left behind . . .). I included a few Black writers and social activists in the curriculum but with such traditional standards that Black students often stared in amazement to see if I was

"for real." Less charitable ones dismissed me as "Oreo"—Black on the outside, White on the inside. What they didn't know was not only was I Black, but my overgrown cultural roots still lay in the cotton fields. I had the scars to prove it. I didn't want to be White. I wanted them to be educated. I had just come to think that the "White way" was the only way to the prosperity they coveted. (From *Mirror Images*, pp. 8–9)

Through her years of action research, Minnie began to reach more of her Black students by drawing on the African American culture they shared—hers rural, theirs urban:

> I realized the extent to which I had denied my own cultural background when I began to connect with Black students and my own children as listener, advisor, and interested reader of their writing. The writing project helped me make those connections systematic. I try especially to interweave examples from my personal background into the lessons and works we study, and invite students to share their examples. . . . It's important that we feel connected, freeing ourselves to learn from our cultural pasts as well as each other. (Adapted from *Mirror Images*, p. 9)

By acknowledging her own roots, Minnie showed her students that they could connect with majority culture without losing their own. She sees herself as a cultural translator for her Black students and a cultural mediator for her White students.

Seeing My Own Culture 2

As a consultant and member of the Webster Groves team, I too wrote my cultural profile for *Mirror Images*. Through writing, I discovered a thread running through my story. It is a theme I call "cultural adoption," my willingness to adopt—or be adopted by—people who differed from me. Despite the naive "we're really all the same under the skin" attitude of my early years of teaching, I had repeatedly sought out cultural diversity.

My formal education began at a parochial school where I was a loner, immersed in classical music and incompetent at jump rope. Then,

> entering the 1960s and public high school, I found a peer group where I belonged—girls who scorned makeup and the top forty in favor of poetry, politics, and folk music. Nearly all of my crowd was Jewish. At Teaneck High, if you were Black or Catholic, you got married after graduation; if you were Jewish, you went to college. I suppose school showed me the difference between ancestry and culture. Ancestry is a given, but culture can be adopted. . . .
>
> College was a heady time of idealism, crisis, and assassination. I moved on the fringes of the civil rights and antiwar movements. I'd march, carrying candles and singing "We shall overcome," but I wasn't about to occupy buildings or get thrown

in jail. During the next ten years, I taught Black and White students at a Philadelphia alternative school, then Pueblo, Hispanic, and Anglo students in New Mexico. . . .

My sons were adopted as babies in Santa Fe. Though my husband and I had talked of choosing an interracial family, the growing racial polarization of the 1970s made us hesitate. After much soul-searching, and with more bravado than confidence, we filled out the adoption forms stating "no preference" under "race or ethnic group." Adam Pablo is Hispanic; Mark Hosteen is Navajo and African. Going for adoption—regardless of what "people" might say—was the best crazy decision I've ever made. . . .

Today both my sons have developed a multicultural identity. They learned African American communication style with neighborhood kids, codeshift fluently, and date across racial lines. Adam joined a Black fraternity and now prefers his middle name, Pablo. Perhaps it is my own cultural past—my tentative belonging in Catholic, Jewish, and Anglo circles—that tells me it's OK. I've learned that integration is no magic solution to racism and that White people can't drop out because we're all in this together. (Adapted from *Mirror Images*, pp. 290–293)

This writing brought me unexpected insight into a problem in my practice as a university teacher. In English Methods, I often encounter resistance from preservice teachers to topics of diversity. Like me, most of my students are White, but their response baffled and troubled me. When Myrtho shared her dilemma, I immediately thought of "White Guilt" because I was reading Spring's book in an attempt to make sense of my own situation.

Could Myrtho's fifth grader be expressing more blatantly what was really going on with my college seniors and graduate students? I suspect that many preservice teachers tacitly believe:

1. "I don't really have a culture."
2. "I don't have any prejudices."
3. "When I teach, I will treat all my students equally."

My responsibility is to help them grow beyond this stage of taking their own cultural neutrality for granted—to help them problematize their own cultures before they begin teaching.

Perhaps my own cultural past as a college student of the 1960s in Boston had left me prejudiced against my midwestern students, most of them born after the major struggles for civil rights. When they yawned at my enthusiasm for multicultural curricula, I bristled. As I realized that I could be a cultural translator instead of a judge, I decided to take action with an assignment that has become a mainstay of my course.

For several weeks, my students begin class with 15 minutes to freewrite their own cultural profile in nine dimensions: gender, race, age, region, religion, ethnic heritage, education, class, and family. I guide them through each dimension with questions to recreate in their memories the experiences that taught them what it meant to be, for example, male or female. Finally, they reflect on the "dimensions" log to write an essay, "The Culture I Bring to the Classroom." Imaginatively re-seeing their own past prepares them to see more clearly what happens in the classrooms where they observe and teach.

For years I had exhorted future teachers to value cultural diversity, but failed to suggest that they start by studying their own cultures. The "dimensions of culture" lesson has helped me appreciate the diversity (in age, religion, family, ethnicity, and so forth) that actually exists among my White midwestern students. And as they recognize and share the richness of their own stories, they find it easier to connect with different stories. In the process, I hope they will replace a legalistic ethic of fairness ("treating all my students equally") with a more relational ethic of commitment, authenticity, and awareness of self and others.

BECOMING VISIBLE

Minnie Phillips explains how action research and attention to cross-cultural communication help her connect with her students:

> Education is fundamentally a personal experience. In the classroom, we teach along with content who we are and what we believe. Similarly, our students bring to the classroom their views of the world as well as their perceptions of relatedness to others. "Reading" the world through the eyes of student writers, hearing voices through the words of writers we teach, and incorporating a variety of teaching approaches compel not only an openness to cultural differences but to learning itself. (Phillips memo, 1999)

As teacher-researchers, we must beware the mask of cultural invisibility. Instead, we can choose to let ourselves be seen, to include the dimensions of our own cultures in our classroom data, and to let our relationships with students challenge our cultural assumptions. In this way, we reduce the ethical risk of presuming to give voice to others while we are merely rewriting our own worlds.

As I read published research, I often want to ask the author, "Who are you? Who is writing this story? What experiences have forged your research tools (two eyes and one brain)? What communities have taught you how to see the world?"

Perhaps one mark of ethically responsible action research is that our readers will know something of who we are.

NOTE

1. References to all adults and institutions in this chapter use real names to recognize their contributions to our thinking. Names of children were changed to protect their privacy.

Chapter 11

INSIDERS AND OUTSIDERS: PERSPECTIVES ON URBAN ACTION RESEARCH

Jacquelyn C. Harris, Michael Lowenstein,
and Rosalynde Scott

The three of us started working together on the Urban Sites Writing Network (USWN) in 1991. USWN was a National Writing Project (NWP) initiative that enabled eight St. Louis teachers to conduct inquiries in their own classrooms. Rosalynde Scott, a St. Louis Public Schools (SLPS) teacher, and Michael Lowenstein, a professor at Harris-Stowe State College, were the program's St. Louis codirectors. Jacquelyn Harris (Jackie), formerly coordinator of the SLPS writing enrichment labs, was the district administrator with whom the codirectors worked most closely. For us as participants, Urban Sites raised challenging ethical dilemmas centering on trust, race, power, control, accountability, and divided loyalties. In the following conversation, we talk frankly about these issues for the first time since the program ended in 1994.[1]

WHAT EXPERIENCES DID EACH OF US BRING
TO THE PROJECT IN 1991?

JH: I had been an employee of the St. Louis Public Schools for over 25 years—first an elementary classroom teacher, then a reading specialist, an enrichment writing lab teacher, an administrative assistant, and, at the time of Urban Sites, coordinator of the Enrichment/Extended Learning Lab Program, a court-mandated desegregation program. My responsibilities included supervision and monitoring of writing and science classes in racially isolated schools. I had also worked as an adjunct at a local college and presented many workshops and in-service sessions. When Urban Sites began, I was about a year into my 4-year term as president of the National Council of Teachers of English (NCTE) Black Caucus. Later I chaired NCTE's advisory committee on the affairs of people of color.

RS: What did all those experiences do for you?

JH: Well, they taught me the value of exploring new techniques and finding the best educational practices for our students. I have a problem with people who have tunnel vision and are not able to see that the world of education changes along with everything else. We must explore, experiment, and produce results. We must make a difference in the lives of our children.

ML: Would you say the St. Louis Public Schools supported your interest in trying innovative techniques?

JH: The St. Louis Public Schools tend to be traditional and "name"-oriented with a top-down mentality. So it's very difficult for workers in the fields and vineyards to get an audience with the powers that be to introduce or discuss new ideas, techniques, or strategies. My interest in action research was driven by my own values and beliefs.

RS: Did you go to segregated schools when you were young?

JH: I attended segregated elementary schools, started high school in an all-Black facility, then was transferred to a mixed-race school. I was unaware of the negative stereotyping of Black students by White teachers in integrated schools. We were taught to achieve no matter where we were by the teachers in our all-Black schools and by our families. Michael, what about your background?

ML: Before Urban Sites, I had been teaching at Harris-Stowe State College since 1969. When I began there, I came under the influence of innovative educators such as James Herndon, John Holt, Jonathan Kozol, and Herbert Kohl. Many of their ideas stayed with me and still defined my values and practices as a teacher when Urban Sites began. I believed in sharing power and giving students control over what and how they learned, and in participatory classrooms that allowed every student the opportunity to be heard. The more diverse my students, the better. My role was to help students be active learners.

I was uncomfortable with hierarchic, top-down, teacher-dominated classrooms in which most of the talking was done by the teacher and students were there mainly to absorb and restate what others said in textbooks or lectures. I saw teaching less as reporting in class what I had learned elsewhere than as an opportunity for the teacher to join students in learning about self, subject matter, and the dynamics of classroom life.

JH: Do you have teaching experience at another level?

ML: No, I went right from graduate school into college teaching and relied for most of my knowledge of other levels on books, conversations with teachers, classroom observations—and, of course, my own experiences as a student (at schools that were largely all-White, I might add).

JH: I believe in shared power and student-centered learning but wonder how this was demonstrated in your classroom.

ML: Over the years—I've been teaching now for over 30 years—my understanding of how to do this has evolved, and I'm still learning. Essentially, I guess it comes down to creating classroom environments that allow students room to respond actively. Like other instructors, I have used teacherless groups, performance activities, writing, open-ended inquiry, and other active learning techniques, all of which work well in the subjects I teach—composition and literature.

RS: Harris-Stowe is predominantly African American, which means you were and are in the White minority. How did you feel working in such an environment?

ML: I came to Harris-Stowe originally—and have stayed there—because I very much enjoy working in the urban setting, which means among other things teaching classes that are always predominantly African American (as well as female and, for that matter, Christian—so I have been in the minority there by virtue of my being male, Jewish, *and* White). Teaching in classes where my students are different from me, at least on the surface, probably helped me see that I had a lot to learn from my students— through writing and reading together and, later, through classroom inquiry. Seeing teaching as learning (rather than as being learned) has made minority status a privilege and an opportunity for me. Rosalynde, what did you bring to the program?

RS: By 1991, I had been teaching for 25 years in the St. Louis Public Schools. I began as a special education teacher. After 2 years of that, I taught in the regular classroom for about 14 years. In 1980, my school became a middle school. I remained and became the enrichment writing lab instructor there in the program Jackie was coordinating.

ML: You've really taught in lots of different settings.

RS: Yes, and I developed the same philosophy as you, Michael, about teaching and students as active learners. When I was young, I used to learn poems and recite them at church teas. As a teacher, I stressed that same thing—self-expression—both my own and my students'. With my EMH students, I created plays and other active opportunities for them to build their esteem and confidence. Then, as an enrichment writing lab teacher, I adapted to working without designated books. I gathered my materials from all sources and had the freedom to create my own writing lessons. Watching students develop their writing styles, I believed every child could learn. Teaching writing was exciting and engaging.

ML: Obviously you were already learning from your students!

RS: Yes, but I had also been very influenced by the origin-pawn theory of Richard DeCharms. He trained a group of us SLPS teachers to reverse our roles as bearers of knowledge to fill our students' empty cups, and he helped me put more emphasis on giving my students opportunities to be active learners with greater control over their own learning.

JH: How did your experience with process writing fit in?

RS: When I accepted the enrichment lab job, I was responsible for purchasing everything and for planning and organizing the instruction. Then, after all that, suppose that my writing lessons weren't up to par? That's when I attended the Missouri Writing Project summer institute—around 1981 or 1982—and returned to the middle school to utilize the writing process in my lab. My students began winning citywide writing contests. Five years later, writing process was introduced in the district. Jackie, you invited me to present some of my methods at an NCTE convention. I also presented at the University of Missouri at St. Louis (UMSL) administrators' workshop for Jane Zeni.

ML: How did you see the culture of the St. Louis Public Schools in 1991?

RS: I felt the St. Louis Public Schools's culture was pretty much like other school cultures. Teachers could take risks in their own classrooms. But the principals pretty much set the tone and limited what could or could not be done inside and outside of the classroom. Generally, a good teacher was one who could keep her class quiet.

ML: Were you a risk taker?

RS: Yes, I would step out and dare to do many things different from the status quo. For instance, I displayed my students' writings about "How to Prevent Teenage Pregnancy." The subject was so controversial that Jackie's boss asked me to remove some of the writings from my display.

ML: Wow!

RS: Amidst much criticism from my colleagues, I also took a group of seventh graders on an overnight trip to the Space Camp in Huntsville, Alabama, in the 1970s. Then, I was the first to be involved in the city-county/Channel 2 partnership by having my students write public service announcements to air on TV. Finally, teaching the Gateway Writing Project (GWP) summer institute and codirecting St. Louis's Urban Sites program were both risks. It was one thing to give a workshop, but another to teach my colleagues every day for a month.

ML: What was your initial response to being asked to be an Urban Sites coordinator?

RS: I did not believe that Urban Sites could hire me to work part-time for them. The two national directors of Urban Sites were White men, and I thought they were just talking when they asked me to be one of the coordinators. At the same time, I thought the SLPS would not allow me to work for the district half-time so I could be an Urban Sites codirector. When it happened—probably for the first time during my years as an SLPS teacher—I believed that anything could happen there. I realized that Jackie and her superior were open to change in allowing me this opportunity.

HOW DID WE ALL RESPOND INITIALLY TO ACTION RESEARCH AND URBAN SITES?

JH: "Action research in the SLPS? What is it? Who's going to do it? How will it affect our students and teachers, and how will it be used? In what schools are they going to do it? When will they publish their findings?" I asked those and all the other "who, what, why, when, where, and how" questions that should be asked when approaching any project that affects teaching and learning. Yes, teachers should look at their own classroom practices and use their findings to improve teaching, but I know how others can use reports either for or against. I don't believe in sugarcoating, but I do believe that many factors must be included when discussing topics like "inner city," "at risk," "those kids," "transfer students"—terms that I and other concerned educators do not use due to the negative connotations. Teachers looking at their own practices—fine—*if* that research is used by teachers as driving forces to improve teaching and learning.

ML: And it hadn't always been used that way?

JH: No. In the past, university professors had used their research to say that city public school classroom teachers lacked the ability to instruct students in ways they, the higher echelon, felt all students should be instructed. So I only agreed to assist with Urban Sites when assured that teachers would be looking at their own classroom practices and their impact on the students they teach.

As the St. Louis conduit for the program, I arranged a meeting for you, Michael and Jane Zeni—as directors of the Gateway Writing Project—with my immediate supervisor. I was skeptical, but because of my belief in the teachers, I put on a false front and introduced the proposed plan. During the initial meeting, I was basically an observer with few comments as I had provided my supervisor with some background information about action research prior to the meeting.

ML: Obviously you didn't feel you were part of the program.

JH: I was not integrally involved, but since some of our writing lab teachers were involved, it was part of my job description. I proceeded as directed. Following the meeting and other discussions, I was informed that I was to provide oversight for the SLPS, monitoring and reporting on Urban Sites. When my supervisor spelled out my tasks, this oversight monitoring and reporting took on a new meaning. I kept time and effort logs, sign-in sheets and reporting forms. I was the off-site data collection agent.

ML: I didn't realize at the time that your supervisor asked you to keep logs and monitor the program. How did you feel about that role?

JH: I had to remain neutral due to my job classification and my responsibilities in the district. I wanted to be loyal to the teachers and committed to improving classroom practices, but I also had to follow the guidelines and practices of the district, as represented by my supervisor.

ML: Was this fence-straddling difficult?

JH: It was very difficult for me because I have some strong beliefs about teachers' rights to teach and students' rights to the best teaching practices, including action research. As an employee of the district, my beliefs are often secondary to the realities.

RS: Did it make a difference that the professors introducing this program were White and from Harris-Stowe and UMSL?

JH: Somewhat, due to the negative response expressed by teachers who had been involved in a previous program. The SLPS had been used as "guinea pigs" to validate the findings of some professors that students and teachers from all-Black urban schools were "at risk." I believe our working relationships would have been better if we had honestly addressed these concerns at the beginning, when we should have been included.

ML: I agree. I wish we could have talked about this as fully then, but we had no relationship of trust to build on.

RS: I saw you, Jackie, as a conduit *and* as my supervisor. Sometimes you seemed to be in my corner and at other times I was skeptical about your intentions. I understand your position now, whereas then I often wondered why you reacted as you did. I knew you were my supervisor, and I believed you had the power to make or break me in the SLPS. At the beginning of this project, I was supposed to keep you informed on its progress; this included letting you know if Jane and Michael reported negatively on the practices of SLPS teachers.

ML: I see why you might have mistrusted action research, Jackie, but my view of it was different. In fact, the more I learned about it, the more it seemed to fit neatly within the power-sharing philosophy I had developed as an educator.

RS: In what way?

ML: First, action research seemed to sum up just what I believed in: making meaning from one's experience; creating classrooms where everyone learns, including the teacher; emphasizing self-study, reflection, and collaboration; and making a commitment to diversity and multiple voices. Urban Sites wanted to put teachers at the center and to give them voice and power, just as I wanted to do with my students. Urban Sites also seemed to oppose hierarchical, authoritarian school bureaucracies, just as I did in the classroom. I thought the program had tremendous promise for reforming the status quo in the direction in which I had tried to move my own teaching.

JH: How did you feel we were responding to action research when you first approached us?

ML: I think I most remember something between doubt about and resistance to the project. I didn't really understand what was going on until now, and the need I felt to be diplomatic and polite prevented me from asking you directly or expressing my confusion. Eventually, your reservations about a "research" project headed up by White higher ed. professors became clear. Of course, I now wish that we could have talked through these concerns then, as we are doing now, and cleared the air, but apparently we weren't ready for that, or at least I wasn't. I didn't want to do or say anything that would offend you or your office, which I now see was ironic, since we'd already inadvertently done a number of things that had had that effect. Obviously, Jackie, I didn't know very much then about how you were reacting to Urban Sites or why. What about you, Rosalynde? What was your response to the project?

RS: At first I really did not know anything about action research—like a lot of teachers today. In 1991, I received a call from Jane. She invited me to coteach, with Michael, a special Gateway Writing Project summer institute for city teachers. Eight of the teachers were later to be selected for Urban Sites and trained in action research. As a risk taker, I consented and secured my place as one of the teachers to be trained.

Later, during and after the summer institute, I realized that Michael and Jane, two White university professors, might have had a problem leading an institute entitled "Teaching Writing in the Urban Classroom." I believe I was hired because I was an African American who was writing-process trained and had experience teaching writing in the urban classroom.

ML: You're right—plus, no NWP site would ever have had two professors teaching the institute.

JH: Rosalynde, you and the Urban Sites teachers were trained in action research at the Chauncey Conference Center in Princeton. How did you see the goals of the project at that point?

RS: Urban Sites wanted to use action research to document excellent teaching practices in urban areas. At Chauncey, we were supposed to learn about action research and share our work-in-progress with teachers from the other sites. After everybody's action research projects were finished, the results were to be distributed throughout the United States.

ML: I wonder whether we might have had more of that dissemination here if there'd been better communication among us.

WHAT WERE SOME OF THE ISSUES AND PROBLEMS THAT CAME OUT DURING THE PROGRAM?

ML: One of the major program issues for me emerged in the fall of 1992, during the first full semester of the teachers' research and following our initial summer training at Chauncey. Part of our agreement with SLPS was that the teachers were to be released from their teaching on eight Fridays during the 1992–1993 school year. The teachers were to use those days to review and write fieldnotes and reports, organize data, and reflect on their work, and to do so at whatever location they chose—home, library, school, or anywhere else workable.

RS: What happened?

ML: I soon realized that my sense of this agreement was different from the district's. State and Federal Programs—where you worked, Jackie—told Rosalynde and me that while the office would help find and pay for substitutes on the released days, they would not approve of the teachers doing their inquiry work unmonitored. Instead, the teachers were to be required to spend each Friday at the State and Federal office working on their projects. I remember being very upset at this demand.

JH: And now?

ML: Now I see what pressure you were under, Jackie, to monitor the program—and how readily I read the conflict in terms of my values and biases as an educator. I saw SLPS's reluctance to allow the teachers to work on their projects without signing in or reporting as a lack of trust in teachers on the part of a top-down educational bureaucracy. Weren't SLPS's demands directly in opposition to the values that Urban Sites, action research, and I stood for: putting teachers at the center, viewing them as experts on teaching and learning, supporting and trusting their authority? Wasn't this a classic conflict between innovation and tradition, change and the status quo?

RS: I knew you and Jane were upset, but the teachers and I never really thought the free released time would happen.

ML: Yes, I was mad. I asked myself: How could I continue to advocate my cherished values and yet make sure the program survived in the SLPS? Who, in fact, was running the program? How could I retain the trust of the program's teachers, whom we had assured of free Fridays (even though they were skeptical, as you say, Rosalynde)?And what about SLPS's critical support—and yours in particular, Jackie?

For all my dedication to power sharing, I don't recall that we and SLPS had worked out procedures for resolving conflicts such as this one. We talked about it—delicately and diplomatically, as most of our talking was—and finally eased into a kind of compromise: The teachers were to sign in and report back in the beginning, but as the year passed, they were to be allowed more freedom and latitude in their Friday work.

RS: Do you think the SLPS and the teachers thought of you as the great White father demanding the teachers' manumission from the eye of SLPS?

ML: Hmmm. Was I seen as the Abraham Lincoln of Urban Sites? I've never thought about it that way, but I guess a part of me did see myself as bringing both Black and White teachers—through Gateway Writing Project and Urban Sites—the chance to free themselves from the restraints and limitations of an educational bureaucracy. But did they see me (or themselves) that way? I don't know. That was another instance of hard talk about race, gender, and power that I wish we'd had more of.

JH: My issues and concerns dealt with getting the program approved by the SLPS "higher-ups". We, the SLPS, were not included in the original planning or proposal, but only contacted when teachers and funding were needed from my particular program and division. This appears to be a pattern that was a real issue for me and others. As I recall, the proposal was submitted by UMSL and Harris-Stowe, and they do have a right to submit a proposal, but how genuine is action research if force-fed without inclusion and questioning?

ML: True, although I think part of our problem as SLPS outsiders was not knowing exactly whom to talk with in SLPS during the short lead time we had for developing the proposal.

JH: The SLPS administrators are very traditional, conservative, and careful. My division administrator during Urban Sites was precise and thorough. He believed in keeping a paper trail of everything connected with the division. He reported to an associate superintendent who reported to the superintendent. So a lot of paperwork and explaining was needed to get that released time for eight Fridays for teachers to work in unknown places on a project that no one in the SLPS knew anything about and to pay for substitutes for something not really connected to the SLPS. We approved the request for released time, but as I've said, my administrator and I still needed a paper trail for our follow-up and monitoring.

ML: I see.

JH: That's why teachers were asked to sign in and indicate their location for the day—and why I went from heroine to villain with the teachers.

RS: Do you think your effort to give teachers exposure to action research was a worthwhile risk or a mistake? Who benefited from it?

JH: I believe it was a worthwhile risk, and I hope it benefited the teachers and the students. We broke new ground and planted the seed that allowed us to grow.

RS: Even though you did not mention power as an issue, who did you think had the power in this situation?

JH: The power should have been shared throughout. Once the program started, SLPS gained power because we were granting the released time for the teachers.

RS: Well, I didn't think I had much power, but I certainly had too much responsibility. I felt overwhelmed with the demands of three different titles.

JH: Three?

RS: Yes. In the fall of 1992, I was teaching two and a half days for the SLPS and working for Urban Sites for two and a half days. At the same time, I became the codirector of the Gateway Writing Project. That position, I believed, was to insure my loyalty to GWP and to add diversity to the GWP leadership.

ML: Having a GWP codirector from SLPS was pretty well established by then.

RS: Well, had I known that I would be thrust into three totally new positions, I may not have accepted the position of Urban Sites coordinator. Another issue for me involved documentation of the teachers' action research work, especially their group meetings. Although I was supposed to be vigilant about negative reporting by Jane and Michael, I did not want the teachers to think that I was an SLPS spy recording their discussions. Trust and integrity were important to me because I didn't fully understand the philosophy or process of action research. I don't think most people do until they complete the process.

JH: Was the released time an issue?

RS: That was not a concern for me or the teachers at first. As I said, we knew that SLPS would not allow this type of freedom, and we thought Michael and Jane were naive to think they would. As time passed and tension developed around this issue, we began to resent the idea of restrictions on released time because we felt we were loyal employees.

ML: What about trust issues?

RS: Trust became a concern many times. I first realized that trust was an issue for some African American teachers in the 1991 summer institute. Because of the less structured culture of the Writing Project, many teachers were skeptical about the assignments and how they were going to be graded. They had to trust that I knew what was going on and that they could succeed in the class.

ML: And during Urban Sites?

RS: The trust issue resurfaced when I did not fully understand why and how I had replaced Jane as Urban Sites codirector even though she had written the St. Louis proposal. I wasn't quite sure how she felt about relinquishing her position. I finally told her I felt like Nurse Evers, an African American nurse who found out that White doctors had deceived her about treating the syphilis of African American men who were being sacrificed in the name of science.

ML: Like Jackie, you thought the program might put teachers in jeopardy.

RS: Yes. I was concerned with the defamation of SLPS teachers or any other devious plot to use us as specimens for data. It wasn't until I was asked to sit on the national Urban Sites board and found out how decisions were made that I decided there wasn't a plot. But, boy, had I taken a risk! This time the risk did not involve just me, but my colleagues as well.

That's why I refused to document our biweekly group meetings—I didn't want to mislead the teachers who were still going to be my colleagues after Urban Sites. I didn't want them to think they were being used to further my career. Moreover, I believed that the teachers began to trust me during the summer institute. Before our meetings, I alerted them that Jane and Michael might be taking notes on the process to report later. I knew the teachers, too, depended on me to tell them if their data and classroom observations were being reported negatively.

JH: If you thought Jane and Michael were using you as a token, why didn't you voice your frustration?

RS: I did voice my frustration when I told Jane I was Nurse Evers. This got her attention. Later she told me she was stunned and hurt, but she realized how serious my concerns and the pressures I felt were.

WHAT HAVE WE LEARNED FROM OUR
EXPERIENCE THAT MIGHT HELP OTHERS?

JH: Stakeholders need to be involved from the beginning in program planning and decision making. SLPS administrators should have been part of the conversation with those who wrote St. Louis's Urban Sites proposal so we could have seen and influenced how our teachers and funds were going to be used.

RS: When people know what is being planned for them and have an opportunity to participate in the planning, problems get discussed earlier, and there is less confusion and misunderstanding.

ML: Relatedly, I think the program planners need to find ways to talk early on about their experiences, expectations, and biases. Getting these out into the open can promote better listening and understanding and establish patterns of trust and candor.

JH: Then there needs to be open communication during the program itself. Conflicts can be avoided and misunderstandings cleared up if there are discussions of the process.

ML: Yes, I agree. Program participants can approach the implementing of the program as action researchers, asking questions, gathering and looking together at data, reflecting on their practice as program leaders or participants, articulating what they are learning and what is still problematic, and going beneath the formal or polite surface to get at the complexities of people's real concerns and conflicts. Such matters as decision-making procedures and lines of authority need to be looked at often.

RS: Participants need to be ready to address issues of race and culture in programs like ours that have participants who are diverse culturally or racially.

ML: Race can get involved whenever participants are discussing questions of power and equity—who's doing what, who's in charge, who has control, how are resources being allocated, and so on. The program needs a system—and probably special training sessions in communication skills—for approaching these difficult issues, bringing them to the surface and talking them through.

JH: So, throughout the program, from beginning to end, communication is the key.

RS: To urban teachers who are participating in collaborative action research, I would say: Be aware that you may be assuming conflicting positions or roles in the program and finding yourself caught in the midst of divided loyalties. This happened to me when I found myself codirecting a program for teachers that was initiated by outsiders and at some points was in conflict with my district superior.

But I would also say to urban teachers that collaborative classroom research can offer unique opportunities for exploring new teaching strategies and for moving into leadership roles. During the last 8 years, Urban Sites teachers have gone on to become instructional coordinators in SLPS and active members of St. Louis's Action Research Collaborative.

JH: I would say to urban school administrators who might get involved in collaborative research with outsiders, be able to mediate between the new program and the school system when their priorities conflict, as they did for me over the issue of released time for the teachers. This was my own version of divided loyalties.

I would also encourage administrators to investigate the program's focus on their own. In Urban Sites, I did this concerning action research. Become knowledgeable and inform yourself; don't rely only on program leaders or participants.

ML: To higher education faculty who might get involved in research in which they are both insiders and outsiders, I would say: Start with questions, not answers. Work collaboratively, and try to get into the habit of looking at participants' beliefs, values, intentions, and past experiences and determining how these are affecting each person's response to the program. Assume that you don't know what's going on in or what's best for someone else's professional world—whether a classroom or a whole district.

And to all involved in collaborative research—have conversations of the kind the three of us have had here.

NOTE

1. References to people, places, and institutions in this chapter use real names to recognize their contributions to our thinking.

Chapter 12

NEGOTIATING TWO WORLDS: CONDUCTING ACTION RESEARCH WITHIN A SCHOOL-UNIVERSITY PARTNERSHIP

Marilyn M. Cohn and Suzanne Kirkpatrick

For 7 years, Washington University's Department of Education and Kirkwood High School have been engaged in a growing professional development school relationship with a focus on the development of inquiry-oriented teachers.[1] All student teachers are required to complete an action research study, and all cooperating teachers are encouraged either to collaborate with their student teachers or to conduct their own action research project simultaneously. Further, a teacher-led seminar now provides support for any teacher who wants to pursue action research for district or university credit. Every May, student and experienced teachers publicly share their findings at a miniconference. All reports are published in bulletins available to district personnel, and some are submitted for publication in a state-supported action research on-line journal.

As coleaders of this partnership, we have encountered three ethical issues, which we examine in this chapter: (1) the tension between university human subjects protection policies and the school-community culture; (2) the challenge of helping student teachers tell authentic stories that respect the rights of the experienced teachers in the setting; and (3) the complexities that arise in assessing the quality and validity of the written reports. We do not, however, offer definitive solutions; rather, we provide some explication of the issues themselves, describe the actions taken to address the issues, and share some lessons learned along the way. In short, our search for solutions to ethical dilemmas in practitioner research is very much a work-in-progress. Before we explore these issues, we offer some background on the contexts in which we work.

HISTORICAL CONTEXT AND INSTITUTIONAL DEMOGRAPHICS

Our formal partnership was built upon a strong informal relationship that began in 1983 when Suzanne Kirkpatrick, Chair of Kirkwood High School's English Department, and Marilyn Cohn, Director of Teacher Education at Washington University, first worked together in the Danforth Improvement of Instruction Project. After a decade of continuous growth, Kirkwood High School and Washington University became one of three founding formal partnerships of the St. Louis Professional Development School Collaborative, and Suzanne and Marilyn became its coleaders.

Kirkwood is a suburban public school district serving over 5,000 students from a broad socioeconomic range. African American enrollment, half from the community and half bused from the city, is approximately 25%. Free or reduced lunch is provided for 21% of all students and a similar number receive special services. Average daily attendance for the district is consistently above 92% and achievement scores exceed state and national averages. Eighty percent of Kirkwood graduates go on to postsecondary education. The high school's 1,500 students work with 110 faculty and counselors and five principals, most with graduate degrees and years of experience. Parents are generally involved and supportive; for example, over 1,000 parents attend the PTO open house at the high school each fall.

Washington University is a private, highly selective research institution with a small Department of Education situated within the College of Arts and Sciences. The university attracts a predominately White student body, a growing percentage of Black students, and a significant international population. Nearly 87% of the approximately 12,000 full-time students come from outside of Missouri. The Department of Education offers preservice teacher certification for undergraduates and graduates, an Educational Studies major for undergraduates, a master's program for experienced teachers, and a small Ph.D. program. During 1998–1999, there were approximately 100 students and 12 full-time faculty, 6 tenured or tenure-track and 6 with clinical appointments.

Each fall, 12 to 22 university students are placed at the high school for a practicum of a minimum of 5 hours a week. In the spring, students generally continue with the same teacher for student teaching. Concurrent with student teaching, students attend methods courses at the university where they learn about designing and implementing action research projects, data collection and analysis, and writing final reports. Cooperating teachers learn action research either from university classes or from the seminar led by Suzanne Kirkpatrick.

During the years of formal collaboration, the focus on action research has significantly affected the partnership; correspondingly, the fact that the research focus was embedded in a strong school-university partnership has greatly enhanced its development. In effect, we have learned to do action research by doing it together. In the doing, curricular, pedagogical, and ethical issues have been confronted in a continuous cycle of learning. What follows is an explication of three key ethical issues.

THE TENSION BETWEEN UNIVERSITY HUMAN SUBJECTS POLICIES AND THE SCHOOL-COMMUNITY CULTURE

The Problem

One of the most challenging aspects of making action research a centerpiece of our partnership is the difference in the perspectives that school and university personnel hold on the protection of those participating in research. Washington University, with its strong research agenda, has set stringent guidelines to ensure that human subjects are fully protected, and expects all departments to follow the rules meticulously. Any staff, faculty, or students planning funded or unfunded research involving people must obtain prior approval from the Committee on the Use of Human Subjects. While we are pleased that the university thoroughly reviews proposals to protect human subjects, it is clear that the current policy and process do not fit the way we frame action research in our courses.

For example, in presenting action research to teachers, we stress that the research objective is always secondary to the teaching objective. Thus, if a teacher designs a study to encourage students to participate more actively in groups, and later concludes that it is not working or that something more significant has emerged for study, we encourage the teacher to change the strategy or the focus of the project. An approval process which assumes a project will remain the same throughout the research period is not well suited to the dynamic nature of action research.

Further, since the committee has neither the capacity nor the desire to review proposals from each student in each course in each department in which human subjects are involved, the committee has certain categorical exemptions. For instance, research projects within a course can be exempt from committee review if: (1) they follow guidelines for receiving assent and informed consent; (2) they maintain the subjects' anonymity and confidentiality; and (3) the results remain within the confines of the course. Unfortunately, each of these conditions for exemption poses problems for action research conducted during student teaching in a school-university partnership.

Receiving Assent and Informed Consent. If student teachers were to follow the university guidelines, they would have to seek permission from parents before they could begin their action research. In effect, they would present their projects for acceptance or rejection to parents as activities above and beyond what normally transpires in the teaching-learning process. Experienced teachers in our partnership generally believe that such a practice is both unnecessary and unwise. In their view, when teachers are focusing upon the improvement of their own practices, using strategies with and collecting data from an entire class, the rights of individual students are not at risk. Both the Kirkwood Assistant Superintendent for Curriculum and Instruction and university methods instructors agree and believe that, in many cases, this approval seeking could prove detrimental to the overall classroom learning environment by raising undesirable barriers. The research projects of student teachers are designed to be an integral part of the instructional process toward the end of improving high school student behavior and learning. They focus on basic questions such as these:

- Can teachers help students become active readers?
- What strategies are needed to turn low level math students into Wally Cleaver?
- How do positive relationships between parents and teachers affect student performance?

Seeking permission to address these questions means risking the possibility that some parents might veto their adolescent's opportunity to benefit from the teacher's effort to improve instruction in domains that clearly fall under the teacher's authority.

If, as these titles suggest, action research projects target increased understanding of what teachers can do to facilitate student learning, both school and university personnel believe they should remain the prerogative of the preservice or in-service teacher, not the parent. However, since the word *research* carries a connotation of *experiment* and can easily be misunderstood by those not familiar with how action research differs from the traditional quantitative model with its control and experimental groups, parents could understandably object, simply on the grounds that they do not want their children to become "experimental subjects."

Maintaining Confidentiality and Anonymity. At one level, confidentiality and anonymity are easily handled. Student and experienced teachers are given explicit directions to code the identities of participants and settings, and reports are carefully monitored for compliance. At another level, however, since the names of the student teacher, cooperating teacher, school, and community are common knowledge, someone could technically track down a specific class or student. To our knowledge, this has never occurred—but, of course, it could.

Keeping the Results Confined to the Course. This condition is troubling to school and university faculty alike because both are committed to sharing classroom research with a larger educational audience. This public sharing takes place each year in early May at Kirkwood High School. Principal Franklin Mc-Callie signals his strong support by planning assembly programs for students so that teachers who either want to present their research or learn from the research of others are free to attend. Student teachers and experienced teachers present side by side, and then the audience raises questions, often to clarify how the findings might apply to the questioner. The value of this exchange was recently acknowledged by Deborah Holmes, Assistant Superintendent for Curriculum and Instruction, who began her reflections on the conference by saying, "This is my favorite day of the school year!" (Cohn, fieldnotes, May 7, 1999).

Compliance with the university condition of course containment would mean elimination of the Celebration of Learning Mini-Conference, and that seems too high a price to pay. The evaluations from every segment of the audience have been consistently positive, and the comments from parents have been particularly gratifying because they express appreciation (rather than concern) for classroom research to improve teacher practice and student achievement. Further, we believe that collaboration is essential to action research, and that public exchange and dialogue are critical outcomes.

Thus, while the conditions for exception from a formal and extensive committee review may be reasonable in many cases, they do not fit the nature of what we are doing (action research), the place where we are doing it (an open school-university partnership), or the purposes for which we are doing it (improving teacher practice and student learning, constructing a common knowledge base, and developing a community of learners).

Our Response to the Problem

To address the tension arising from the university's legitimate need to have a stringent set of protections for human subjects in traditional research projects, and our partnership's legitimate need to empower preservice and in-service teachers to implement action research projects without needless barriers, we have devised a three-level response.

Our first step was to develop a shared conception of action research in our partnership. Our deliberations led us to conclude that action research as we practice it is more akin to teaching or reflective practice than it is to research. It is, in effect, teaching in a reflective way that involves a conscious effort to improve some aspect of one's instruction for the benefit of students, the systematic collection of data on that effort from multiple sources, an analysis process, *and* a sharing of the findings with colleagues. Thus, teaching is an ongoing cycle of planning, acting, inquiring, and new planning; action research is a process that makes the teaching cycle more reflective, systematic, and collaborative.

Second, with this conception in mind, we then considered what precautions are needed to protect the students whose learning we document. Our conclusion was to require student teachers to submit both a draft and final proposal to course instructors after consultation with their cooperating teachers, university supervisor, and peers. The proposal is to be no more than two pages but must adequately state the question and rationale for the study, specify the actions to be taken, identify the sources of data to be collected, and explain the steps taken to protect human subjects. Course instructors then provide written feedback on the draft and final proposals, especially on project design and protection of participants, and give final approval. Student teachers who significantly change their project along the way are required to submit a revised proposal.

In our view this proposal provides enough information to determine if reasonable protections are in place. For example, some student teachers may identify one or two students for sustained individual attention to effect some behavioral or academic change. If we think that this effort goes beyond the ordinary assistance one might give to a student, we recommend that parental permission be sought and formally recorded. After 2 years of using these guidelines, we are highly satisfied with the results and have never heard a parental concern.

Our third and most challenging response is in process. We are attempting to formally negotiate an agreement with the university human subjects committee to recognize action research as a special case that deserves a relaxation of the current policies. We will present our shared conception of action research and our existing guidelines. Further, we will try to make the case for sharing the results of action research in our miniconference by conceptualizing the course research requirement as an integral part of an existing partnership dedicated to producing inquiry-oriented teachers. In this way, all of the Kirkwood and Washington University participants are members of a single learning community hearing the results of their fellow members. In short, we will argue for a broadening of the course audience to the partnership audience because we have enlarged and extended our reach through our formal collaboration.

AUTHENTIC STORIES AND RESPECT FOR OTHERS

The Problem

Picture this: A small audience is gathered in the band room at Kirkwood High School during the Year I miniconference. In the back of the room, amidst scattered chairs and music stands, a university instructor guides a video camera to capture the proceedings. Near the front, in two rows of chairs tightly arranged in a semicircle, sit 15 people, including student teachers, cooperating teachers, a principal, two central office administrators, a parent, and teacher educators from other universities. Two student teachers have already presented, and now an earnest-looking young man steps to the podium. His scraggly beard, rumpled jeans, and casual stance evoke memories of the protesters of the 1960s. As one listens closely, one can actually hear a protest of sorts. Robert is explaining why his action research focuses on disciplining students in a respectful way, but his words are highly critical of several teachers. According to his story, faculty routinely gather in a lounge to relax; sometimes their conversation includes put-downs or sarcastic remarks about students. Angered about how some teachers talk about and to students, he is determined to be different. Several members of the audience seem uncomfortable as they listen, but when he is finished, no one comments upon his negative statements about faculty members.

Now it is time for the last student teacher, a tall and robust-looking young woman, neatly dressed in a long print skirt and a well-pressed white blouse. Nancy's long, straight blond hair and her large tortoise shell glasses convey a sense of seriousness and professionalism. However, halfway through her presentation, she, unprofessionally, contrasts her effectiveness in reaching a group of students who had failed the prior quarter with the ineffectiveness of her cooperating teacher. Although her teacher was not in the audience, the critique was heard by his colleagues, none of whom commented publicly. However, at the conclusion of the session, one of the central office administrators moved quickly to catch the facilitator and asked if he could have the videotape of the session. Both the facilitator and the university "camera man" expressed regret that negative comments about teachers had arisen in this public forum, but also complied with the wishes of the administrator. As word spread quickly among university and school faculty, fears were expressed about what the administrator might do with the tape and how it might affect our partnership.

All who had worked on the conference were shocked by the negative comments, but in retrospect we probably should not have been. In class as well as during supervisory visits, we occasionally heard negative student judgments about various faculty members and school policies, but we always dealt with them on the spot. Never did we think that any of these would find their way into a public forum, let alone one in which a high-level district administrator was in attendance. How naive and inattentive to the political as well as the ethical ramifications we were! While we were worrying about protection of the high school students as human subjects of the studies, the rights of teachers who had nothing to do with the studies were clearly at risk.

Our Response to the Problem

The first action we took following the conference was to assess how much damage had been done. To our relief, the impact was negligible. The central office administrator and some cooperating teachers were clearly not pleased at hearing blame being publicly placed on faculty; however, they seemed to understand that these undergraduates were young and oblivious of the implications of their remarks. In grateful response, we assured them that the students' written reports would carry none of the blaming that surfaced in the conference and that we would prevent any future occurrences.

Marilyn then informed the students of the stir their remarks had made and why. She introduced the notion of protecting the rights of colleagues and alerted them to the political sensitivity required as one works in any school community. Their initial response was one of surprise and defensiveness. From their perspective, they were simply accurately describing what they had observed. While Marilyn acknowledged their desire to tell it as they saw it, she also cautioned that they saw it from a limited perspective. Ultimately, both acknowledged the problem and wrote authentic reports, without laying any blame on Kirkwood faculty members.

With the immediate situation under control, we then considered longer range steps. Ultimately, we concluded that future student teachers would have to turn in a full draft of their report to their instructors prior to the conference and rehearse their presentation in class to receive feedback. We also added the following written criterion for an effective action research study: *The tone of the report is professionally respectful to colleagues in the program or school.* The descriptor of this criterion explains: "The tone is professionally respectful to colleagues if it does not make its point by criticizing or negatively presenting one's colleagues. The focus of the report is a study of the actions of the researcher, not the actions of one's colleagues" (Cohn, 1997, p. 4).

Since taking these measures, we have had no further embarrassing and unethical commentary by student teachers. On the other hand, we have had student teachers directly share their struggle with language to convey negative situations they encounter that seem relevant to their study in a truthful and professionally respectful way. In those instances, we have successfully brainstormed a variety of ways to describe a possibly negative situation in a more neutral, and therefore more professional, tone.

ASSESSING ACTION RESEARCH

The Student Teacher Problem

Most of our student teachers take their action research assignment very seriously, although a few, particularly science majors, may question whether action research is "real" research. All, however, find it a struggle to collect consistently and systematically the data they need to analyze their effort and write about it. Being faithful recorders of observations and reflections is genuinely difficult for such busy people during such a high-stress period. Further, many students have successfully completed college courses by doing much of the reading and writing at the end of the semester. Thus, some honestly believe that they will be able to pull off their action research project after student teaching, when the immediate pressures of classroom performance are over. Along the way, they know they need to keep a better set of notes, but some of them just don't.

Imagine their frustration, at the end of the semester, when they realize they do not possess the documentation, in the form of actual notes and transcripts, to go along with their recollections of key events and insights. As high-achieving students, they do their best to recall what occurred and write a coherent report, but often without sufficient supporting evidence. The problem is exacerbated when an instructor reads the draft and writes comments such as these: "Could you provide concrete examples from your notes to justify this positive conclusion?" "Do you have any transcripts that actually show how students responded to your higher-order questions?" "Did you record any students' comments that show their changing attitude toward group work?" Although some students will honestly admit that such data are lacking, others submit final drafts with the examples requested, along with new references to fieldnotes. In these cases, university faculty often sense that these new data are the result of partial recall and partial invention by well-meaning students for the purposes of pleasing the instructors and earning a high grade.

Our Response to the Student Teacher Problem

To address this problem of "invented" data, we have increased the monitoring of the action research process throughout student teaching, with a focus on data collection. At the beginning of the spring 1999 semester, Marilyn laid the groundwork for this new emphasis by announcing to student teachers that there would be sessions when they needed to bring data to class and that when they turned in their action research drafts, they would be expected to turn in their data as well. That sent an initial message that data collection was something that could not wait until the end. During the semester, university faculty met with groups of six or seven student teachers on three occasions after school, where the assignment was to "bring some data you are collecting and some preliminary attempts at analysis." Each student teacher then shared data from journals, student or parent surveys, classroom videos, student work, or tests. At these sessions students got an image of what was expected in the way of developing interpretations based on data and developed some skills in the process. In some cases, as a result of feedback from peers or faculty, students realized they needed a different focus or a different source of data. In the end, most drafts featured well-supported interpretations, and all students submitted voluminous packets of data.

The Experienced Teacher Problem

While Marilyn and her university colleagues were grappling with the written reports of student teachers, Suzanne was facing related issues with her experienced teacher group. Ironically, the biggest issue arose as a result of great progress, the district's willingness to offer credit on the salary schedule for teachers completing action research projects. First, a bit of history.

The Kirkwood faculty's involvement with action research began when Washington University faculty decided to require it of student teachers. A Danforth Foundation grant made stipends available to cooperating teachers who conducted research either with or alongside the preservice teachers. During spring 1993, several English teachers committed to doing a collaborative project on student homework. Although teachers now realize that this initial study was short on teacher action, it began a long journey toward greater understanding of the nature and power of action research.

At the same time, the university and school were (and are) part of the St. Louis Professional Development School Collaborative (PDSC) and the Action Research Collaborative (ARC). During PDSC meetings, our partnership chose as a goal the improvement of the quality of action research conducted at Kirkwood High School. As we increasingly saw the value of action research, we realized that it should not be limited to cooperating teachers; rather, all teachers should be encouraged to conduct action research for professional development. But recognizing the heavy time commitment and the absence of grant money for stipends, we searched for another incentive. Suzanne decided to ask the district to allow credit on the salary schedule for teachers who successfully completed an action research project. District administrators saw the potential for professional growth and quickly granted the request. Now, the district accepts action research for credit on the salary schedule and as fulfilling the research requirement in masters-plus work for faculty at all grade levels. Suzanne also convinced the School Improvement Team to use action research to evaluate North Central accreditation goals; teachers who agreed to do an action research study for a goal area were given some released time.

As the number of teacher-researchers in the district increased, a Kirkwood Action Research (KAR) seminar was initiated by Marilyn and Suzanne with the support of the Action Research Collaborative. ARC offered funds to train teachers as facilitators and Marilyn was paid as the trainer for one year while Suzanne was paid as a trainee. Now Suzanne and two colleagues are regularly supported by the Kirkwood Professional Development Committee to serve as KAR facilitators. Unfortunately, this success story has also created a problem for Suzanne and her cofacilitators.

When Suzanne first began as a KAR facilitator, district credit was not an option, and the teachers were basically peers. The participants were intrinsically motivated to learn, and the role of the facilitators was simply to ask questions, make suggestions, and offer support. Once credit became possible, and a facilitator had to decide whether a colleague's work was worth three hours of credit, the dynamic shifted.

One problem was the change in atmosphere at the bimonthly meetings. Some new participants were not very involved in their own research and seemed to be attending primarily for the credit. The warmth, the excitement, the synergy suffered—and it was all the more frustrating because the negative change in the atmosphere began as a wonderful professional opportunity provided by the district.

The next problem came with assessing the written reports. Since Suzanne and her cofacilitators had struggled with their initial attempts with action research, they knew full well that reports that are sincerely done, but with flaws, are great starting points for learning. They were therefore not looking for perfection. But the most difficult challenge to their standards appeared 3 years ago when a colleague handed in a report that was painfully thin. To add to the problem, it appeared that almost no action had been taken and that data had been invented. At KAR meetings, participants had offered suggestion after suggestion to the researcher, who had rejected them all. Still, the facilitators assumed that some genuine effort would be evident in the final report. But the final product, handed in just before the deadline for assigning credit, was poor. This is a hard situation even for teachers dealing with K–12 students, but teachers have some experience in this role. The facilitators were not prepared, however, to be arbiters of the quality of their colleagues' work; they saw themselves as peers, with some special training and skill, who enjoyed learning professionally with others. This role conflict caused much pain to Suzanne, the facilitator responsible for assigning credit. As an ethical dilemma, it has even caused her to question whether to continue as a district leader for action research. Without question, KAR has thrived because Suzanne and her colleagues *believe* in action research. It has been a rewarding form of professional development for them, and they want it available for others—but not if it is viewed as easy credit rather than as a growth opportunity.

Our Response to the Experienced Teacher Problem

For now, Suzanne remains committed to KAR, for she has concluded that most teachers who seemed to join only for the credit did, in fact, conduct research of benefit to them, despite their original motives. However, Suzanne and her cofacilitators have also instituted three simple policies to minimize future problems: (1) Participants are now required to bring data to bimonthly sessions; (2) two drafts are required, the second one after input from a facilitator; (3) deadlines have been moved forward to allow more time for feedback and revision. The great value and pleasure that most KAR teachers have experienced from conducting and sharing their research have been dominant in the facilitators' decision to continue. However, if Suzanne ever receives another report like the highly questionable one described above, she is not sure of her future with KAR.

CONCLUSION

Clearly, the decision to make action research a focus of our partnership has generated a number of challenging ethical issues, some from quite unexpected sources.

The difficulty we anticipated most—objections from parents—has yet to materialize. By constructing our own conceptions of action research and of what constitutes a "course" and by developing guidelines and processes to examine proposals and monitor projects, we have created internal ethical standards that protect the rights of students and researchers. Further, this approach has been validated by parents who consistently tell us formally and informally that they appreciate the efforts of student and experienced teachers to improve their practice for the sake of their children. The next challenge is to publicly present our case to the university for their external validation.

At the same time, we were surprised to find that while we were concerned about the rights of students as research subjects, the actual risks that developed within the partnership involved teachers who were not even part of the studies. Moreover, the actions that troubled us most tended to be ethical violations in reporting—in the way that teachers talk and write about their studies—rather than in the research process itself.

Finally, as we examine our various responses to these issues, we now realize that pursuing action research in an ethical manner in a school-university partnership requires enormous vigilance. Almost every action we have taken has involved putting more time into the process. To address the risk to students as subjects, we required two written proposals, following newly developed guidelines. To address the risk to teachers from negative reporting, we required of student teachers a full written draft and a rehearsal before the miniconference. To address the problem of inventing data, we required that data be brought to several class sessions and turned in with student teachers' final reports. Similarly, experienced teachers, who may be motivated more by district credit than genuine research questions, are now expected to turn in data and two drafts, one of which is critiqued by a facilitator. In our view, all of these developments are moving us in the right direction, but each comes at great cost of faculty and facilitator time and energy.

In short, conducting action research in a school-university partnership in an ethical manner can be exhausting and expensive. Fortunately, in our case, partnership evaluations (Cohn & Kirkpatrick, 1997, 1998, 1999), action research studies (Cohn, Balcerzak, Capasso, Copley, Holmes, & Kirkpatrick, 1998), and daily experiences reveal that it can also be exhilarating and illuminating. In our view, it is definitely worth the cost.

NOTE

1. In this chapter, references to school and university faculty, administrators, and programs use real names to recognize their contributions to our work. Names of under-graduate students were changed and descriptions fictionalized to protect their privacy.

REFLECTIONS ON
COLLABORATIVE RESEARCH

LOCATION AND RELATIONSHIPS

Practitioner research may cross institutional roles and borders: between school and university, between teacher, student, and administrator. When successful, such collaboration makes for rich, authentic research with multiple perspectives and voices.

Chapter 10 weaves stories by three teacher-researchers with my own personal and classroom experience; two of us are Black and two are White. Our collage essay illustrates the importance of seeing our cultural differences as legitimate areas of inquiry. But long-term collaborative research is a major challenge.

The dialogue by Harris, Lowenstein, and Scott vividly portrays the struggles of people in different institutions and roles to overcome layers of suspicion in order to lead a joint project. Five years later, they came together again to write the most truly collaborative piece in the book. The three met for several long sessions, which they taped and reviewed. Each drafted a personal response to four organizing questions they had identified. The university member took major responsibility for weaving the statements into a script, but all authors reviewed many drafts and met for a final session to recapture the conversational voice.

INTERPRETATION AND PUBLICATION

The strength of collaboration is the likelihood of multiple perspectives. In Kirkwood, preservice and in-service teachers pursue their inquiries side-by-side and present at a joint conference. How can we ensure that the dialogue is not silenced when collaborative research is reported to a wider public?

Sandra Hollingsworth (1994) has devised an intriguing process in her research with K–12 teachers. Participants brought a variety of documentation to a team meeting. Hollingsworth taped and transcribed the discussions, organized a text, referred the drafts back to her collaborators, and incorporated their parenthetical comments. She continued this process through the preparation of their book manuscript. At this point, the research team held a retreat in the mountains where they all read the whole work. Using colored pens, teacher-researchers wrote through the text, and again she incorporated their voices.

Recently her groups have turned to computer technology, using digital cameras to produce a collaborative "video document." She finds that this process supports multivoiced interpretations that quickly develop into exciting presentations. Realizing that most K–12 teachers do not see themselves as writers, Hollingsworth has devised alternative ways to make her coresearchers' voices heard (personal communication, 1999).

Perhaps because I work with K–12 teachers in the National Writing Project, I have found coauthorship natural to action research. The Webster Groves team (Chapter 10) wrote a 515-page book, *Mirror Images* (Krater, Zeni, Cason, & the Webster Groves Action Research Team, 1994). My two coauthors were secondary teachers, three served as in-house reviewers, and nine more contributed fieldnotes and reports.

For 5 years, this team met for monthly study sessions. Each June every member wrote a summary of her fieldnotes organized by our emerging principles for culturally inclusive teaching. Reports were shared in an intense, 3-day seminar. Initially I then drafted a "team synthesis" which was distributed to all teachers for feedback; in 2 years, the team leader took over this responsibility; eventually, most teachers participated.

When we began to write a book, there was a consensus that the central chapters should develop the team's eight principles, giving us our macro-organization. For each chapter, one coauthor was charged with drafting, but all three shared in planning and revising. We would meet after school to "launch" a chapter. Each of us first reread the topic in the synthesis reports and came with ideas for a focus and key stories. We talked through the chapter over popcorn if all went smoothly, over dinner if we struggled. Drafts then circulated; when we three were satisfied, a draft went to the in-house reviewers—a crucial check for authenticity and clarity. Although this collaborative process was exhausting, I believe it led to a very rich, nuanced text.

In 1968, Lou Smith and William Geoffrey published a classic of collaborative school-university research. Unlike Smith's evaluation that "turned sour" (see Chapter 9), *Complexities of an Urban Classroom* brought "a resolution of a number of difficult ethical choices in a manner that was as ideal as any project

I have done since" (Smith, 1990b, p. 260). The study was launched when a seventh-grade teacher, then a graduate student, invited Smith to visit his classroom "to see what 'it was really like' in an urban school." Formal permission was sought from the principal and the district; Smith was introduced to staff and children as a professor who wanted to understand teaching and learning, but he did not interfere in the classroom and probably seemed "sort of like a student teacher" (p. 262). Outside of class, professor and teacher shared in the interpretive dialogue.

One issue seems more problematic today, 30 years later. Smith promised that "every proper name in the story would be coded for anonymity" so "no harm could come to anyone. . . . The most difficult decision involved coding the teacher" (p. 262). Though the coauthors split the royalties evenly, and the teacher pursued a successful career as a school principal and superintendent, "William Geoffrey" is not his real name. Using a pseudonym for school-based partners was once seen as a given; now it is an ethical choice. However, to choose wisely, researchers must try to foresee long-term as well as current risks and benefits.

When collaborative work is published, the university partner may face a related dilemma. Coauthored publications receive limited credit at most institutions. Authors must state the percentage each has contributed, an incentive for professors to overstate their own contributions. The real problem is the reduction of a long-term relationship to a percent; the whole is greater than the sum of its parts. Suppose the university member plays the leading role in research design and writing, school members are chiefly responsible for research questions and data collection, and all share the work of cointerpretation. Any calculation will punish a professor who collaborates ethically.

At the University of Missouri at St. Louis, our new guidelines for tenure begin to address this issue:

> *Varied Authorship.* Research in education may involve critical decisions about authorship and credit that cannot be reduced to a percentage. Alternative approaches may be equally valued if individuals clearly describe their contribution to the work: [A list follows, including] collaborative authorship by a university faculty member with educators and other professionals in the field. . . . (*Guidelines for Appointments, Promotion, and Tenure*, 1997, p. 3)

A school-based researcher who is immersed in collaborative inquiry, publication, and leadership may find all this empowerment draining. Rosalynde Scott (Chapter 11) was overwhelmed as she tried to codirect a Writing Project, lead an action research team, and continue teaching half-time. This concern was raised by several research teams at a symposium on "Teacher-Led Inquiry" sponsored by the Office of Educational Research and Improvement (OERI,

1994, p. 26). Most of the team leaders and codirectors with whom I have worked eventually sought leaves from the classroom, were promoted into leadership roles, or took early retirement. The ethics of collaboration must include protection for the long-term health and sanity of teacher-researchers.

INSTITUTIONALIZATION

Four chapters in this volume describe school districts with institutional support for action research; those in Part I contract for some university services, but those in Part III have designed joint research programs with higher education. We can examine Chapter 11, from St. Louis City/Harris-Stowe State College (Harris, Lowenstein, & Scott), alongside Chapter 12 from suburban Kirkwood/ Washington University (Cohn & Kirkpatrick).

The first was a shaky urban partnership based on a grant written by college and university faculty; although the St. Louis Public Schools had had many joint ventures with higher education, the individuals who wound up collaborating on the Urban Sites project had not known one another. As a bit player in the tense drama of 1991, I am still amazed (and grateful) that the main characters came together to reflect on the experience for this book.

The Kirkwood partnership is a model for school-university action research, and the authors address many problems raised earlier in this book. The idea was based on years of informal collaboration by faculty in both institutions, who later wrote grants. Preservice teachers, experienced teachers, and program leaders all conduct research. As the program grew, it grappled with anonymity, public audiences, and the institutional review board. The decision-making process resembles that used by the district teams in Fairfax County, Virginia (Chapter 1), and in Clayton, Missouri (Chapter 5). What is striking is that this dialogue extends to university decisions on student teaching, credit, and review.

CONCLUSION

My reflections on each set of chapters have no doubt raised more ethical questions than they have resolved. After living with this project for many months, I am convinced that practitioner research must approach ethical decisions through ongoing dialogue. I hope that the Epilogue may stimulate such a dialogue.

Epilogue

A GUIDE TO ETHICAL DECISION
MAKING FOR INSIDER RESEARCH

Jane Zeni

Practitioner research has become a major mode of inquiry in American education. As classroom teachers discover the intellectual excitement of studying their
own practice and the power of collaborative action research with other insiders,
many decide to pursue their inquiries through grant proposals, publications, or
graduate theses. At this point, however, many are bewildered by the advice on
"research ethics" dispensed by various colleagues and institutions.

Most universities and school districts have an institutional review board
(IRB) that monitors research proposals using questions designed for traditional
scientific experiments. Researchers are asked if their tests are dangerous, if their
subjects will be given drugs, if the treatment will be traumatic. Researchers are
asked to state precisely which data they will collect, which techniques they will
use. But research by insiders—which may be called "practitioner inquiry," "action research," "teacher research," or "classroom ethnography"—does not fit the
IRB's model. Action researchers pursue a question through an often meandering
route, finding appropriate data sources along the way. When researchers investigate their own practice, many of the traditional guidelines collapse. Yet practitioner research raises its own, often sticky, ethical issues, which may never be
addressed by review boards.

In my graduate classes, I find that teachers see the issues more clearly by
locating action research on a matrix of research methods (see Figure E.1). Action research draws on the qualitative methods and multiple perspectives of
educational ethnography. When challenged, those of us who do action research
take pains to distinguish our work from traditional *quantitative* research: We
explain that we do not deal with big numbers, random samples, or manipulated

QUANTITATIVE	QUALITATIVE

Traditional Research

Outsider: Researcher investigating a teacher's practice

Classic experiment   Classic ethnography
(techniques of   or case study
natural science,   (techniques of
agriculture)   anthropology)

Goal: To change/improve/document someone else's teaching/learning

Action Research

Insider: Teachers documenting their own practice

"Small-n" statistics   Classroom
(test scores; surveys;   ethnography; case
word counts; syntax   study; autobiography;
measures)   curriculum development
                            and field testing

Goal: To change/improve/document one's own teaching/learning

FIGURE E.1. Educational Research: A Methodological Matrix

variables, but with the human drama as lived by self-conscious actors. Perhaps it is just as important to distinguish action research from traditional *qualitative* research: We aren't outsiders peering from the shadows into the classroom, but insiders responsible to the students whose learning we document.

Figure E.1 illustrates modes of research across two dimensions: qualitative/quantitative and insider/outsider. Action research usually falls in the lower right quadrant of the matrix: qualitative research by insiders.

Such insiders may be preschool teachers, assistant principals, reading specialists, high school math teachers, curriculum coordinators, coaches, university professors—any of us who study our own practice as educators. We find the ethical safeguards of the outsider doing quantitative, experimental research (random selection, control groups, removing the personal influence of the researcher) either irrelevant or problematic for us as insiders. In the same way, the ethical safeguards of the outsider doing qualitative research (anonymous informants, disguised settings) are subverted as soon as the inside author is named; in addition, anonymity may defeat the insider's goal of open communication with students, colleagues, and parents. Ethical guidelines need to be rethought for the special case of research by practitioners in their own workplaces.

When does good teaching become research? The line is hard to draw until a study is underway. Research tends to involve:

1. more systematic documentation and data gathering
2. more self-reflection in writing
3. more audience (collaboration, presentation, publication)

It is this third feature that most often brings ethical dilemmas. If our journals remain private and our videotapes are not played, we can inquire with equanimity. But though we document our own practice, we rarely work in isolation. We draw energy and insight from colleagues, seminars, outside researchers. From this informal sharing, we may reach out to wider audiences at conferences or in print. Dilemmas of responsibility and ownership arise, and the academic codes of conduct are silent.

AN ALTERNATIVE HUMAN SUBJECTS REVIEW?

This guide emerged from discussions in the Teacher Educator Seminar of the Action Research Collaborative in St. Louis, Missouri. We meet monthly, a dozen or more faculty from several colleges and the Gateway Writing Project, to share our own action research and to discuss issues in facilitating teachers' work. As some teacher inquiries led to proposals for grants and dissertations, I found myself struggling with the language and assumptions of the mandated human subjects review (see P. V. Anderson, 1996). "Human" in contrast to what? Rodent? And "subjects"? How can this impersonal term identify the relationship between teacher and student? I raised the issue of ethics at the seminar and found that others had similar concerns. Could we, perhaps, revise the university IRB process to make it appropriate for action research?

An ARC committee examined human subjects reviews and ethics policies from local universities and from the American Anthropological Association, the Oral History Association, and the American Educational Research Association. I began writing the guide, bringing drafts to ARC seminars for discussion. Feedback came from a wider audience of teachers and administrators in conferences, graduate courses, and teacher research groups.

What at first seemed a rather straightforward exercise in translation proved a formidable task. The more I tried to address the different contexts and communities in which practitioners do research, the more convoluted our ethical guidelines became. As teacher educators, we began to see that a "new paradigm code of ethics" would itself become "procrustean" (Gregory, 1990, p. 166). I finally abandoned the goal of an alternative human subjects review. Even if an adequate ethical code could be written, having it enforced by administrators who were not grounded in action research might do more harm than good. How, then, could we protect the rights of students without inhibiting the rights of teachers to gather and reflect on data from their own classrooms?

The document contained in this chapter supports what Jennifer Mason (1996) calls an "active and self-questioning" approach (p. 167):

> It is because of the complexities of research ethics, and because there is unlikely ever to be one clear ethical solution, that a practical approach to ethics which involves asking yourself difficult questions—and pushing yourself hard to answer them—is particularly appropriate. (p. 29)

The guide offers a set of questions as a heuristic for reflection. A research team or dissertation committee can work through the guide with anyone who is planning a project. Most questions ask the researcher to discuss a potential ethical problem, to consider alternative actions, and to explain his or her choices.

The following "Questions for Review and Reflection" use the categories of a typical IRB ethics review only as a point of departure. Part I requests an overview of the project. Part II examines the role and location of the researcher within the research setting. Part III asks about methods, and whether the research falls within the everyday decisions of a teacher or whether there is some further intervention. Part IV examines what the IRB calls subjects and the impact of the research on relationships with students, colleagues, and administrators. Part V considers the consequences of the research for participants and ways to reduce risks either through informed consent *or* through openness, dialogue, and acknowledgment. Part VI deals with publication and the issues of credit, privacy, voice, and multiple perspectives. Part VII poses some questions that have been generally ignored in IRB documents, but have been especially problematic for researchers studying their own practice.

QUESTIONS FOR REVIEW AND REFLECTION

I. Overview of the Study

1. Briefly describe your project as you see it today.

2. What is your time frame? Is this a one-shot project or do you anticipate several cycles? Have you done a preliminary study?
3. What problem does your research address? Is it a problem in your own practice? Or is it a problem with your students or with your administrators? Who owns the problem?
4. What (initial) action will you take? What do you hope to accomplish?
5. List your research questions as they appear at this time.
(Questions will be revised or refocused during your project.)

Comments. This section can help beginners grasp the mind-set of action research, recognizing that their study will not provide simple "yes" or "no" answers, that each cycle of research will lead them to a deeper inquiry, and that the questions themselves are likely to change. They may need to redefine their initial problem so that they "own" it and can therefore take action to address it. Hubbard and Power (1993) portray this initial phase of research:

As Glenda Bissex writes, "A teacher-researcher may start out not with a hypothesis to test, but with a wondering to pursue" (1987, p. 3). All teachers have wonderings worth pursuing. Transforming wonderings into questions is the start of teacher research. (pp. 1–2)

II. Location

1. Are you, the researcher, also a participant in the setting where this research will take place? Specify your role (teacher, supervisor, principal, counselor, social worker, and so forth).
2. Map your position on such dimensions of culture as gender, race, age, region, ethnic heritage, education, class, and family.

Comments. Practitioner research is inquiry into one's own practice. Therefore we begin by looking at ourselves and what we bring to the research— personally, culturally, and professionally (see Chapter 10 in this volume). Traditional experimental research sees the ideal researcher as neutral, unbiased, and objective, but as teachers we are personally involved in our classrooms. Instead of trying to distance ourselves, we need to articulate our own position and analyze how it differs from that of other participants in the research.

As Gesa Kirsch (1999) explains, "The goal of situating ourselves in our work and acknowledging our limited perspectives is not to overcome these limits—an impossible task—but to reveal to readers . . . what factors have shaped the research" (p. 14).

III. Methods

1. For this research, will you gather data on your normal educational practice and on changes in curriculum, instruction, and assessment that you could make in your role according to your own professional judgment?
2. List the kinds of data you plan to collect (e.g., fieldnotes, taped interviews, writing samples).
3. How is this plan different from the way you normally document your practice? Consider two or three alternative ways you could gather data for this project. What are the ethical implications of choosing your preferred method?
4. At this time in your research, what do you aim to understand? What do you aim to change?

Comments. Traditional research in education is conducted by outsiders who intervene in the instructional process to answer questions that may benefit themselves or the profession in general. While the goal may be to improve instruction, rarely do the teachers or students in the study benefit directly.

In practitioner research, insiders study their own professional practice and frame their own questions with an immediate goal to assess, develop, or improve their practice. Such research belongs to the daily process of good teaching, to what has been called the "zone of accepted practice."

This concept has been used to determine whether research requires a formal proposal to an institutional review board (IRB). Answering "yes" to question 1 made a project exempt from full review by a university or district IRB. Most practitioner research would thus be exempt.

In 1995, the Office for Protection from Research Risks tightened its regulations, directing that all research, even in the zone of accepted practice, must be reviewed (P. V. Anderson, 1998). This directive poses an ethical dilemma for educational institutions that want to encourage teacher research. One solution is an expedited review of projects conducted within an established seminar or professional development partnership (see Chapters 1, 5, and 12 in this volume). Another is a reviewer who understands qualitative research and is designated by the IRB to offer quick, appropriate feedback to practitioners.

Beyond the institutional regulations, research in the zone of accepted practice may involve genuine risks to participants. Practitioner research should be discussed with a principal, supervisor, or other school-based mentor and often with parents. It must, of course, conform to local school policy. A research team based in the school, district, or university, with advice from a professor or team leader, can help members work through the ethical dilemmas that may surface during the research.

Question 4 takes a closer look at purpose as well as methods. Traditionally, subjects were not considered at risk if the research was merely unobtrusive observation of behavior not "caused" by the researcher. But a teacher inevitably tries to cause some outcome (such as learning); action research involves taking some action and observing what happens.

"Understanding," however, is a valid goal for practitioner research. We may cause more harm than good by trying out new methods to solve an alleged problem we have never taken the time to understand, document, and analyze. The first cycles of action research might well aim simply to understand the problem; later cycles might involve specific changes designed to address it.

IV. Subjects, Subjectivity, and Relationships

1. Describe the individuals, groups, or communities you expect will be touched by your project. List their roles (student, parent, resource teacher, and so forth). Which participants are minors?
2. Analyze the power relations in this group. Which people (e.g., students, parents) do you have some power over? Which people (e.g., principals, professors) have some power over you?
3. What shared understandings do you have with these people? Do you have personal bonds, professional commitments? Will your research strengthen this trust or perhaps abuse it?
4. Will your study attempt to read and interpret the experience of people who differ from you in race, class, gender, ethnicity, sexual orientation, or other cultural dimensions? How have you prepared yourself to share the perspective of the "other" (coursework, experiences, other sources of insight)?
5. Will an insider review your questionnaires or teaching materials for cultural bias? Have you provided for consultation by adult members of the community? How will you reduce or correct for your misreading of populations who differ from you?
6. Does your inquiry focus on people with less power than you? Children in classrooms are always vulnerable—especially if their families have little money or education. ("Where are the ethnographies of corporate boardrooms?" asks House, 1990, p. 162.) How does your project demonstrate mutual respect and justice?
7. What negative or embarrassing data can you anticipate emerging from this research? Who might be harmed (personally, professionally, financially)? What precautions have you taken?
8. Might your research lead to knowledge of sensitive matters such as illegal activities, drug and alcohol use, or sexual behavior of participants? How do you plan to handle such information?

Comments. We must examine the impact of our research on the people whose lives we document. A classroom teacher may write fieldnotes in order to improve her own practice. But what if her notes focus on certain members of the class ("at risk," "Black males," "learning disabled")? These questions suggest a closer look at the power the researcher may have over students and staff (see Chapters 3, 7, and 8 in this volume).

Our students and colleagues are more than "subjects." Sharon Lee and Seena Kohl (see Chapter 6) suggest these distinctions:

Subject: Observed by researcher; no active participation (Not suited to action research)
Informant: Knowingly gives information to researcher
Participant: More involved; perspective considered in research
Collaborator: Fully involved in planning and interpretation

We should also examine the impact of the study on ourselves. Becoming a researcher changes a teacher's professional status. Relationships with colleagues, administrators, and students may be threatened or enhanced. (See Chapters 2, 3, 4, and 11 in this volume.)

Since I cannot be a fly on the wall in my own classroom, I must deal with my emotional and interpersonal responses as part of my data. Hammersley and Atkinson (1983) call this the principle of "reflexivity." Teacher research is engaged and committed. Its "findings" should include the relationships among participants.

V. Consequences

1. Describe the possible benefits of your research—to students, teachers, or other participants; to society or to the profession.
2. Describe any risks to participants. For example, might your current students be disadvantaged for the possible benefit of future students? What steps are you taking to minimize risks?
3. Explain how you will protect the people from whom you collect data through surveys, interviews, or observations.
4. Describe how you will obtain informed consent. Do you need permission from students, parents, or both? How will you work with any students who refuse to be interviewed or to allow their materials to be quoted?
5. Are different kinds of consent needed at different stages in the project? (a) A blanket *consent to participate* from all students at the start of each year (with parent signatures of minors). (b) An individual *consent to publish* from selected students, giving you access to writing samples, videotapes, photographs, or fieldnotes that describe recognizable people.

6. Do you wish to protect the anonymity of students, teachers, parents, and other participants? If so, it is wise to use pseudonyms even in your fieldnotes. If your report is eventually published, you can also interchange physical description, grade level, gender, and so forth or develop composite rather than individual portraits. What are the gains and losses of anonymity?

7. On the other hand, instead of anonymity, it may be wiser to seek full participation and credit for students and colleagues. Research by an educator in his or her own classroom is rarely anonymous. Even if names are changed, students can be recognized in a well-written case study or classroom scene. What are the gains and losses of open acknowledgment?

Comments. These questions deal with the welfare of students and colleagues. Informed consent should be viewed as a process rather than a single gesture (see Chapter 5 in this volume). According to the AERA's Qualitative Research SIG (1993), "Informed consent is granted at the initiation of the study and codified in signed consent forms. . . . Informants may withdraw at any time, [so] informed consent is ongoing, continual negotiation" (Mathison, Ross, & Cornett, p. 3).

But how "informed" is informed consent? Traditionally, participants have been considered free from risk *if* the following conditions are met:

- They are first informed. They must know the general nature of the study and what is expected of them.
- They give informed consent.
- They can refuse to participate, and they can withdraw without penalty after beginning the research.
- Anonymity of persons or confidentiality of data, or both, are protected *if appropriate*.

On the other hand, Lou Smith argues that "field research is so different from the usual experimental approaches that many individuals, even responsible professional educators, do not understand what . . . they are getting themselves into" (1990a, p. 151). He stresses the need for dialogue, moving beyond "contract" relationships to "covenants" of trust (pp. 149–150). In this volume, Chapters 6 and 9 portray the misunderstandings that can occur in the absence of this dialogue.

Qualitative researchers have long considered anonymity the norm, essential to protect "informants." Concepts from outsider social science spilled over into guidelines for teacher research (e.g., Hubbard & Power, 1993, pp. 60–61). Today some researchers, especially those working in collaborative and feminist modes, are challenging the assumptions. Why should a teacher quote published writers with credit and citations, but quote her own student writers under pseudonyms? Can anonymity conflict with intellectual property rights?

Yvonna Lincoln (1990, pp. 279–280) agrees that "privacy, confidentiality, and anonymity regulations were written under assumptions that are ill suited" to qualitative research. She suggests that colleagues, administrators, and parents participate "as full, cooperative agents," our coresearchers.

Recent models of consent forms by the National Council of Teachers of English (see P. V. Anderson, 1998, pp. 84–86) and by Hubbard and Power (1999, p. 62) give students their choice of anonymity or personal credit; a parent must approve the choice of a minor. When teacher-researchers have used this approach, most students have chosen to be named (see Chapters 7 and 8 in this volume).

VI. Publication

1. What data will be contributed by others? Will you record student writing, oral histories, or other documents that may be considered someone's intellectual property? How have you arranged with colleagues or students for credit in your manuscript?

2. If your study is collaborative, how are you negotiating authorship and ownership? University researchers, colleagues, students, and parents may interpret their stake in the research in quite different ways. Who owns the videotape of a classroom writing group, the dialogue journal between teacher and mentor, the transcription of talk by teacher-researchers in a college seminar?

3. Who is responsible for what is said in the final report? Will other stakeholders (teacher, principal, school board) review your report in draft? Will this (a) improve your accuracy or (b) compromise your candor? Which participants (students, colleagues) might be embarrassed if they were to read your report?

4. You will inevitably gather more data than you "need." Consider why you choose some data to report to a wider audience and why some is left in your files. (On what basis do you select?) Consider the politics of the way you focus your story.

5. How will your report recognize the perspectives of participants who disagree with some of your interpretations? For example, you may revise your views, quote their objections and tell why you maintain your original view, or invite them to state alternative views in an appendix.

6. Have you decided on anonymity or on full acknowledgment of other participants in your report? Perhaps you will identify teachers but use pseudonyms for students. If you began your study with a blanket consent

form, have you now requested consent to publish specific material from specific people?

Comments. Publication brings out ethical dilemmas that may lie dormant during a study. Recent discussions (P. V. Anderson, 1998) call into question the practice of relying on a general "consent to participate" when colleagues or students are to be quoted in an eventual publication. For example, students should be shown not only the samples of their work that will be published but also the passages in which they will be quoted. (This practice may lead researchers to edit such comments as "John, a low-skilled B.D. male, produced the following garbled response.")

Action research can support democratic, student-centered pedagogy when teachers periodically share their drafts with students or colleagues. Lather (1991) sees "the submission of a preliminary description of the data to the scrutiny of the researched" (p. 53) as an emancipatory approach to inquiry and a source of "face validity" (p. 67).

A growing trend in practitioner research is "multivoiced" publication, incorporating not only the perspectives but also the texts of colleagues, students, and others. Sometimes these reports take the form of a script or simulated dialogue (Chapter 11 in this volume); sometimes they weave together several authors' statements on a common topic (Chapter 10); sometimes they use quotations and layers of feedback (Chapter 8). Incorporating other voices, especially when their views differ from that of the researcher, can make a report richer, more nuanced, more authentic (McCarthy & Fishman, 1996).

VII. Ethical Questions Specific to Insider Research

1. Does your district have a formal review procedure for research? If you are collaborating with people at a university or research institute, you may need approval from the institutional review board (IRB) in both settings.
2. Which participants at your school or college have read your research proposal? Which ones have been informed of the research orally in some detail? Which ones know little or nothing of this project? Reflect on the decisions behind your answers.
3. What do your students know of your research? Who told them? What are the risks to them or their families of their knowing (or not knowing) what you write or collect?
4. How do your school administrators view your work? Is action research under suspicion or is it mandated from the top in a drive for organizational quality control? How safe do you feel in this institutional setting

pursuing this research? Would you be free to report your findings and interpretations to a wider audience?

5. Who is sponsoring this research through grants, contracts, released time, course credit, and so forth? Will you evaluate the sponsor's program, textbook, or method? Do you anticipate pressure to report what the sponsor wants to hear?

6. Does your study evaluate your own effectiveness or a method to which you are committed? How will you handle the temptation to see what you hope to see? How will you obtain other perspectives—for example, classroom observation or analysis of student work by people who do not share your assumptions?

CONCLUSION

Practitioner-researchers who have worked through this guide may be unnerved by the sheer range of ethical concerns. It seems that three major tasks are facing us. First is to know the Federal and institutional regulations that may apply to our work. Second is to educate the people charged with enforcing those regulations so that they do not force us to mimic an inappropriate mode of inquiry. Third is to continue developing our own professional discourse about ethics.

Paul Anderson (1998) calls for an ethical standard "beyond the Federal regulation" (p. 72). Along with obtaining whatever consent is legally required, we must protect our relationships of trust with those vulnerable to exploitation, especially students.

Marian Mohr states it this way: "Teacher-researchers are teachers first. They respect those with whom they work, openly sharing information about their research. While they seek understanding and knowledge, they also nurture the well-being of others, both students and professional colleagues" (Chapter 1 in this volume). Whenever possible, parents, students, and colleagues should be knowingly involved in the work from the start, with time to ask their own questions and make suggestions (see Chapters 5 and 12).

Collaboration and communication are the best guides to preventing the ethical dilemmas of practitioner research.

ACKNOWLEDGMENT

An earlier version of this chapter was published in 1998 under the title "A Guide to Ethical Issues and Action Research," in *Educational Action Research*, vol. 6, no. 1, pp. 9–19.

The guide was originally prepared for the St. Louis Action Research Collaborative (ARC) and the Gateway Writing Project, the local site of the National Writing Project. The topics addressed reflect the suggestions and experiences of the ARC's Teacher Educators' Seminar, especially Lou Smith (Washington University), Sharon Lee (Webster University), Kathryn Mitchell Pierce (Clayton (Missouri) Public Schools), Sunny Pervil (Maryville University), and Mike McGrath, Jori Martinez, and Owen van den Berg (National-Louis University). Douglas Wartzok (University of Missouri at St. Louis) also gave helpful feedback.

REFERENCES

Abbey, T., Connor, D., & Squires, A. (1995, April). *Sustaining whole school change.* Presentation at the annual meeting of the International Conference on Teacher Research, Davis, CA.

Adorno, T. W., Frenkel-Brunswick, E., Levinson, D. J., & Sanford, R. N. (1950). *The Authoritarian Personality.* New York: Harper & Brothers.

Agee, J. (1939). *Let us now praise famous men.* Boston: Houghton Mifflin.

Altrichter, H. (1993). The concept of quality in action research: Giving practitioners a voice in educational research. In M. Schratz (Ed.), *Qualitative voices in educational research.* London: Falmer Press.

Anderson, H. H. (1937). An experimental study of dominative and integrative behavior in children of preschool age. *Journal of Social Psychology, 8,* 335–345.

Anderson, H. H., & Brewer, H. (1945). Studies of teachers' classroom personalities. I: Dominative and socially integrative behavior of kindergarten teachers. *Applied Psychology Monographs, 6.*

Anderson, H. H., & Brewer, J. (1946). Studies of teachers' classroom personalities. II: Effects of teachers' dominative and integrative contacts on children's classroom behavior. *Applied Psychology Monographs, 8.*

Anderson, H. H., Brewer, J., & Reed, M. (1946). Studies of teachers' classroom personalities. III: Follow-up studies of the effects of dominative and integrative contacts on children's behavior. *Applied Psychology Monographs, 11.*

Anderson, P. V. (1996). Ethics, institutional review boards, and the involvement of human participants in composition research. In P. Mortensen & G. E. Kirsch (Eds.), *Ethics and representation in qualitative studies of literacy* (pp. 260–285). Urbana, IL: National Council of Teachers of English.

Anderson, P. V. (1998). Simple gifts: Ethical issues in the conduct of person-based composition research. *College Composition and Communication, 49*(1), 63–89.

Anderson, R. (1996). *Study of curriculum reform.* Washington, DC: U.S. Department of Education.

Banks, J. (1998). The lives and values of researchers: Implications for educating citizens in a multicultural society. *Educational Researcher, 27*(7), 4–17.

Barr Ebest, S. (1998). Going against nature? Graduate students' resistance to collaborative learning. In E. Peck & J. Mink (Eds.), *Common ground: Feminist collaboration in the academy* (pp. 227–248). Albany: State University of New York Press.

Barr Ebest, S. (1999). Preparing the next generation of WPAs: A survey of graduate programs in composition/rhetoric. *Writing Program Administration, 22*(3), 65–84.

Barr Ebest, S. (2000). *Changing the way we teach*. Manuscript in preparation.

Barr Reagan, S. (1991). Warning! Basic writers at risk: The case of Javier. *Journal of Basic Writing, 10*(2), 99–115.

Beauchamp, T., Faden, R., Wallace, R., Jr., & Walters, L. (Eds.) (1982). *Ethical issues in social science research*. Baltimore: Johns Hopkins University Press.

Becker, H. (1970). *Sociological work: Method and substance*. Chicago: Aldine.

Belenky, M., Clinchy, B., Goldberger, N., & Tarule, J. (1986). *Women's ways of knowing*. New York: Basic Books.

Bissex, G. L. (1987). What is a teacher-researcher? In G. L. Bissex & R. H. Bullock (Eds.), *Seeing for ourselves: Case study research by teachers of writing* (pp. 3–5). Portsmouth, NH: Heinemann.

Burgess, R. G. (1989). *The ethics of educational research*. London: Falmer Press.

Carr, W., & Kemmis, S. (1986). *Becoming critical: Education, knowledge and action research*. London: Falmer Press.

Clay, W. C. (1998). *The evolution of an instructional coordinator's role: Action research for school improvement* (Doctoral dissertation, University of Missouri at St. Louis). *Dissertation Abstracts International, 59*(03), 0711A. (University Microfilms No. 98-28891)

Cochran-Smith, M., & Lytle, S. (1993). *Inside/outside: Teacher research and knowledge*. New York: Teachers College Press.

Cochran-Smith, M., & Lytle, S. (1999). The teacher research movement: A decade later. *Educational Researcher, 28*(7),15–25.

Codd, J. (1982). Some ethical problems in special education. *Australian Journal of Special Education, 6*, 8–14.

Cohn, M. M. (1997). Qualities of an effective action research report. In M. Cohn (Chair), *Report guide for the Show Me Action Research Online Journal* (pp. 3–4). St. Louis, MO: Action Research Evaluation Committee. Also available online: http://info.csd.org/www/resources/arc/arcdata/html

Cohn, M. M., Balcerzak, P., Capasso, M., Copley, C., Holmes, D., & Kirkpatrick, S. (1998, April). *Incorporating action research into the culture of school systems and university teacher education programs: A five-year case study*. Paper presented at the annual meeting of the American Educational Research Association, San Diego, CA.

Cohn, M. M., & Kirkpatrick, S. (1997). *Evaluation of Kirkwood–Washington University Partnership, 1996–1997*. Unpublished manuscript, Washington University, Department of Education, St. Louis, MO.

Cohn, M. M., & Kirkpatrick, S. (1998). *Evaluation of Kirkwood–Washington University Partnership, 1997–1998*. Unpublished manuscript, Washington University, Department of Education, St. Louis, MO.

Cohn, M. M., & Kirkpatrick, S. (1999). *Evaluation of Kirkwood–Washington University Partnership, 1998–1999*. Unpublished manuscript, Washington University, Department of Education, St. Louis, MO.

Collins, P. H. (1991). Learning from the outsider within: The sociological significance of Black feminist thought. In M. M. Fonow & J. A. Cook (Eds.), *Beyond methodology:*

Feminist scholarship as lived research (pp. 35–59). Bloomington: Indiana University Press.

Davidoff, S., & van den Berg, O. (1990). *Changing your teaching: The challenge of the classroom*. Pietermaritzberg, South Africa: Centaur Publications/University of the Western Cape.

Delpit, L. (1988). The silenced dialogue: Power and pedagogy in educating other people's children. *Harvard Educational Review, 58*(3), 280–298.

Delpit, L. (1995). *Other people's children: Cultural conflict in the classroom*. New York: The New Press.

DuBois, W. E. B. (1982). *The souls of black folk*. New York: Penguin. (Original work published 1903)

Eisner, E. W. (1991). *The enlightened eye*. New York: MacMillan.

Eisner, E. W., & Peshkin, A. (Eds.) (1990). *Qualitative inquiry in education*. New York: Teachers College Press.

Elbow, P., & Belanoff, P. (1995). *A community of writers* (Rev. ed.). New York: McGraw Hill.

Elliott, J. (1991). *Action research for educational change*. Milton Keynes, U.K.: Open University Press.

Ellison, R. (1952). *Invisible man*. New York: HarperCollins.

Ely, M. (with Anzul, M., Friedman, T., Garner, D., & Steinmetz, A. M.). (1991). *Doing qualitative research: Circles within circles*. Philadelphia: Falmer Press.

Fontaine, S., & Hunter, S. M. (1998). Ethical awareness: A process of inquiry. In S. Fontaine & S. M. Hunter (Eds.), *Foregrounding ethical awareness in composition and English studies* (pp. 1–11). Portsmouth, NH: Boynton/Cook.

Foster, W. (1986). *Paradigms and promises: New approaches to educational administration*. Buffalo, NY: Prometheus.

Freire, P. (1973). *Pedagogy of the oppressed*. New York: Seabury.

Freire, P. (1993). *Pedagogy of the city*. New York: Continuum.

Fullan, M. J. (1991). *The new meaning of educational change*. New York: Teachers College Press.

Gannett, C. (1993). *Gender and the journal*. Albany: State University of New York Press.

Geertz, C. (1988). *Works and lives: The anthropologist as author*. Stanford, CA: Stanford University Press.

Gentile, J. (1994). Inaction research: A superior and cheaper alternative for educational researchers. *Educational Researcher, 22*(5), 30–32.

Gilligan, C. (1983). *In a different voice*. Cambridge, MA: Harvard University Press.

Greenfield, T. (1991). Foreword. In C. Hodgkinson, *Educational leadership: The moral art* (pp. 3–9). Albany: State University of New York Press.

Gregory, T. B. (1990). Discussion on ethics. In E. Guba (Ed.), *The paradigm dialog* (pp. 165–166). Newbury Park, CA: Sage.

Grumet, M. (1988). *Bitter milk*. Amherst: University of Massachusetts Press.

Guba, E. (Ed.). (1990). *The paradigm dialog*. Newbury Park, CA: Sage.

Guidelines for Appointments, Promotion, and Tenure. (1997). University of Missouri at St. Louis, School of Education.

Hale-Benson, J. (1986). *Black children: Their roots, culture and learning styles* (Rev. ed.). Baltimore: Johns Hopkins University Press.

Halpin, A. (1966). *Theory and research in administration*. New York: MacMillan.

Hammersley, M., & Atkinson, P. (1983). *Ethnography: Principles in practice*. London: Routledge.

Hodgkinson, C. (1978). *Towards a philosophy of administration*. Oxford: Blackwell.

Hodgkinson, C. (1991). *Educational leadership: The moral art*. Albany: State University of New York Press.

Hollingsworth, S. (1994). *Teacher research and urban literacy education: Lessons and conversations in a feminist key*. New York: Teachers College Press.

Hollingsworth, S., Teel, K., & Minarik, L. (1992). Learning to teach Aaron: A beginning teacher's story of literacy instruction in an urban classroom. *Journal of Teacher Education, 43*(2), 116–127.

House, E. R. (1990). An ethics of qualitative field studies. In E. Guba (Ed.), *The paradigm dialog* (pp. 158–164). Newbury Park, CA: Sage.

Hubbard, R. S., & Power, B. M. (1993). *The art of classroom inquiry*. Portsmouth, NH: Heinemann.

Hubbard, R. S., & Power, B. M. (1999). *Living the questions: A guide for teacher-researchers*. York, ME: Stenhouse.

Jenkins, W. (1990). *Educating the Black child*. St. Louis, MO: Parkway Schools.

Kelso, R. (1993). *Days of courage: The Little Rock story*. New York: Steck-Vaughn.

Kimmel, A. J. (1988). *Ethics and values in applied social research*. Newbury Park, CA: Sage.

Kirsch, G. (1999). *Ethical dilemmas in feminist research: The politics of location, interpretation, and publication*. Albany: State University of New York Press.

Kohl, S., & Lee, S. (1993). *A case study in teaching and learning*. Paper presented at the national conference of the Society for Applied Sociology, St. Louis, MO.

Kohl, S., Lee, S., Cook, K., Bady, A., & Royce, A. (1994). *Experiences in the voluntary integration programs at St. Louis cultural and educational institutions*. St. Louis: Missouri Historical Society.

Krater, J., Zeni, J., Cason, N., & the Webster Groves Action Research Team (1994). *Mirror images: Teaching writing in Black and White*. Portsmouth, NH: Heinemann.

Lather, P. (1991). *Getting smart: Feminist research and pedagogy with/in the postmodern*. New York: Routledge.

Lee, S. (1992). *Hegemony in an elementary school: The principal as organic intellectual* (Doctoral dissertation, University of Missouri at St. Louis). *Dissertation Abstracts International, 53*(04), 1008A. (University Microfilms No. 92-24760)

Lee, S. (in press). *Unmasking the white knight: Emerging perspectives and images of the principalship*. New York: Hampton.

Lee, S., Morgan, T., & Gerstung, M. (1999). Strengthening the learning culture: The Pattonville Heights vertical team story. In J. Machell (Ed.), *Enhancing school culture to improve student achievement: The Missouri vertical team project*. Jefferson City: Missouri Department of Elementary and Secondary Education.

Letts, N. (1994, April). Socrates in your classroom. *Teaching K–8*, pp. 48–49.

Levinson, D., Darrow, C. N., Klein, E. B., Levinson, M. H., & McKee, D. (1978). *The seasons of a man's life*. New York: Knopf.

Lewin, K., Lippitt, R., & White, R. (1939). Patterns of aggressive behavior in experimentally created social climates. *Journal of social psychology, 10*, 271–279.

Lincoln, Y. S. (1990). Toward a categorical imperative for qualitative research. In E. W. Eisner & A. Peshkin (Eds.), *Qualitative inquiry in education* (pp. 277–295). New York: Teachers College Press.

Lincoln, Y. S. (1995, April). Emerging criteria for naturalistic research. Paper presented at the annual meeting of the American Educational Research Association in San Francisco.

MacLean, M. S., & Mohr, M. M. (1999). *Teacher-researchers at work*. Berkeley: University of California, National Writing Project.

Mason, J. (1996). *Qualitative researching*. Thousand Oaks, CA: Sage.

Mathison, S., Ross, E. W., & Cornett, J. (Eds.). (1993). *A casebook for teaching about ethical issues in qualitative research*. Washington, DC: Qualitative Research SIG, American Educational Research Association.

McCarthy, L., & Fishman, S. (1996). A text for many voices: Representing diversity in reports of naturalistic research. In P. Mortensen & G. E. Kirsch (Eds.), *Ethics and representation in qualitative studies of literacy* (pp. 155–176). Urbana, IL: National Council of Teachers of English.

McKerrow, K., & Lee, S. (1991, April). *Case study of hegemonic confrontation in a rural school district*. Paper presented at the annual meeting of the American Educational Research Association in Chicago. (ERIC Document Reproduction Service No. ED334036)

Miles, M. B., & Huberman, A. M. (1994). *Qualitative data analysis*. Thousand Oaks, CA: Sage.

Minarik, L., & Lock, R. S. (1997). Gender equity in an elementary classroom: The power of praxis in action research. In S. Hollingsworth (Ed.), *International action research: A casebook for education reform* (pp. 179–189). London: Falmer Press.

Mohr, M. M. (1996). Ethics and standards for teacher research: Drafts and decisions. In *Research in language and learning: Reports from a teacher-researcher seminar*. Fairfax, VA: George Mason University, Northern Virginia Writing Project.

Morgan, T., Lee, S., & Gerstung, M. (1998). Advancing student learning: Pattonville's vertical team story. In B. Monk (Ed.), *Vertical teaming: Toward coherence in education*. Austin, TX: Texas Leadership Center.

Nelson, D. (1999, April). *Inner and outer voices: Private and public uses of teacher research and writing*. Presentation at the International Conference on Teacher Research, Quebec, Canada.

Newman, D. L., & Brown, R. D. (1996). *Applied ethics for program evaluation*. Thousand Oaks, CA: Sage.

Noddings, N. (1995). *Philosophy of education*. Boulder, CO: Westview.

Noffke, S. (1997). Professional, personal, and political dimensions of action research. *Review of Research in Education, 22*, 305–343 (M. W. Apple, Vol. Ed.).

Noffke, S. E., & Stevenson, R. B. (Eds.). (1995). *Educational action research: Becoming practically critical*. New York: Teachers College Press.

Office of Educational Research and Improvement [OERI]. U.S. Office of Education (1994). The rich possibilities of teacher-led inquiry for transforming teaching and learning. In *Proceedings of the Teacher-Led Inquiry Conference*, prepared by A. Ashburn. Washington, DC: OERI.

Oliver, D., & Shaver, J. (1966). *Teaching public issues in the high school.* Boston: Houghton Mifflin.

O'Malley, R. K. (1998). *The case of the recalcitrant student: Gender and race in the writing classroom.* Unpublished paper, English 489, University of Missouri at St. Louis.

Pfannenstiel, J., & Seltzer, D. (1985). *Evaluation report: New Parents as Teachers project.* Jefferson City: Missouri Department of Elementary and Secondary Education.

Prophete, M. (1996). "What do we have to learn about him for?"—Dr. King in Black and White. Unpublished essay, University of Missouri at St. Louis, Gateway Writing Project.

Rawls, J. (1971). *A theory of justice.* Cambridge, MA: Harvard University Press.

Ray, R. (1993). *The practice of theory.* Urbana, IL: National Council of Teachers of English.

Rose, M. (1989). *Lives on the boundary.* New York: Penguin.

Rosow, L. V. (1995). *In forsaken hands: How theory empowers literacy learners.* Portsmouth, NH: Heinemann.

Schlechty, P. (1990). *Schools for the twenty-first century.* San Francisco: Jossey-Bass.

Schubert, W. H., & Ayers, W. C. (1999). *Teacher lore: Learning from our own experience.* Troy, NY: Educator's International Press.

Shannon, P. (1992). *Becoming political: Readings and writings in the politics of literacy education.* Portsmouth, NH: Heinemann.

Shannon, P. (1995). Kissing and telling, teaching and writing. *The Reading Teacher, 48,* 464–466.

Smith, L. M. (1990a). Ethics, field studies, and the paradigm crisis. In E. Guba (Ed.), *The paradigm dialog* (pp. 139–157). Newbury Park, CA: Sage.

Smith, L. M. (1990b). Ethics in qualitative field research: An individual perspective. In E. W. Eisner & A. Peshkin (Eds.), *Qualitative inquiry in education* (pp. 258–276). New York: Teachers College Press.

Smith, L. M. (1992). *Doing ethnographic biography: A reflective practitioner at work during a spring in Cambridge.* Unpublished manuscript, Washington University, St. Louis, MO.

Smith, L. M. (in press). *Nora Barlow and the Darwin legacy.* Manuscript in preparation.

Smith, L. M., & Dwyer, D. (1979). *Federal policy in action: A case study of an urban education project.* Washington, DC: The National Institute of Education.

Smith, L. M., & Geoffrey, W. (1968). *The complexities of an urban classroom: An analysis toward a general theory of teaching.* New York: Holt, Rinehart & Winston.

Smith, L. M., & Keith, P. (1971). *Anatomy of educational innovation.* New York: Wiley.

Smith, L. M., & Wells, W. (1990). *"Difficult to reach, maintain and help" urban families in PAT: Issues, dilemmas, strategies, and resolutions in parent education* (Final Report). Westport, CT: Smith-Richardson Foundation.

Smith, L. M., & Wells, W. (1997). *Urban parent education: Dilemmas and resolutions.* Cresskill, NJ: Hampton Press.

Sockett, H. (1990). Accountability, trust, and ethical codes of practice. In J. I. Goodlad, R. Soder, & K. A. Sirotnik (Eds.), *The moral dimensions of teaching* (pp. 224–250). San Francisco: Jossey-Bass.

Sockett, H. (1993). *The moral base for teacher professionalism.* New York: Teachers College Press.

Soltis, J. F. (1990). The ethics of qualitative research. In E. W. Eisner & A. Peshkin (Eds.), *Qualitative inquiry in education* (pp. 247–257). New York: Teachers College Press.

Spring, J. (1995). *Intersection of cultures: Multicultural education in the United States.* New York: McGraw-Hill.

Steinbeck, J. (1962). *Travels with Charley.* New York: Viking Press.

Teaching Tolerance Project (1989). *America's Civil Rights movement* [Videotape]. Montgomery, AL: Southern Poverty Law Center.

Urban Sites Network of the National Writing Project (1996). *Cityscapes: Eight views from the urban classroom.* Berkeley: University of California, National Writing Project.

van den Berg, O. C. (1994). *Innovation under apartheid: Collaborative action research in a South African university* (Doctoral dissertation, Washington University, St. Louis, MO). *Dissertation Abstracts International, 55*(08), 2351A. (University Microfilms No. 94-33549)

White, R., & Lippitt, R. (1960). *Autocracy and democracy.* New York: Harper.

Wilson, S. M. (1995). Not tension but intention: A response to Wong's analysis of the researcher/teacher. *Educational Researcher, 24*(8), 19–21.

Wong, E. D. (1995). Challenges confronting the researcher/teacher: Conflicts of purpose and conduct. *Educational Researcher, 24*(3), 22–28.

Zeni, J. (1990). *WritingLands: Composing with old and new writing tools.* Urbana, IL: National Council of Teachers of English.

Zeni, J. (1996). A picaresque tale from the land of kidwatching: Teacher research and ethical dilemmas. *The Quarterly of the National Writing Project, 18*(1), 30–35.

Zeni, J. (1998). A guide to ethical issues and action research. *Educational Action Research, 6*(1), 9–19.

ABOUT THE EDITOR
AND CONTRIBUTORS

Sally Barr Ebest is Director of Composition and Associate Professor of English at the University of Missouri at St. Louis. She has published on writing program administration and training teaching assistants in the *WPA Journal* and in *Writing With: Research in Collaborative Teaching, Learning, and Research* (1994), which she coedited with David Bleich and Tom Fox; she also coauthored *Writing From A to Z* (2000). At the present time, Sally is completing work on *Changing the Way We Teach*, a longitudinal study of graduate students' teaching and learning. She is also conducting a nationwide study of graduate students' professional preparation in composition and rhetoric.

Nancy Cason taught middle and high school Spanish and English for 19 years. She was a participant and team leader in a 6-year action research project to create a climate for cultural diversity and to improve student writing with a focus on African American males; she coauthored *Mirror Images: Teaching Writing in Black and White* (1994) with Joan Krater and Jane Zeni. Nancy has served as director of the Gateway Writing Project and consultant to several teacher action research groups—a 3-year project on mathematics and two writing-across-the-curriculum projects. She also loves to investigate whether the crappie are biting in the Lake of the Ozarks.

Wanda C. Clay taught secondary English and public speaking in the St. Louis Public Schools before being named to the new position of instructional coordinator (IC). Her dissertation was a 3-year action research study of her own evolution in this role. Having served as IC at a comprehensive senior high, she currently holds that position at McKinley Classical Junior Academy, a magnet middle school for students identified as gifted. She coordinates an annual project sponsored by the NSF, "A World in Motion," in collaboration with Boeing engineers. Wanda has taught courses in research methods and in curriculum and instruction for the gifted at Maryville University.

Clayton (Missouri) Research Review Team includes teachers and administrators in varied roles in this suburban district. **Cathy Beck** is a language arts teacher at Wydown Middle School who also teaches writing process, adolescent literature, and action research for the areawide Gateway Writing Project. **Laura DuPont** is principal of Glenridge Elementary School; during the past 25 years, she has taught children from preschool through grade 6 and has conducted research as a teacher and a principal. **Lori Geismar-Ryan** coordinates Clayton's early childhood program and action research collaborative, a support group for educators studying issues at the classroom and building levels. **Linda Henke**, assistant superintendent, has focused her practice and her publishing on literacy education, curriculum as inquiry, and teacher leadership. **Kathryn Mitchell Pierce** is a multiage primary classroom teacher at Glenridge Elementary; long involved in teacher research and study groups, she has also served on a university human subjects review committee. **Catherine Von Hatten** is Clayton's professional development director; she is responsible for supporting teacher research and for helping identify ways to embed research in the teaching and learning work of the district. All six members of the team have been engaged in action research and in sharing and publishing what they learn.

Marilyn M. Cohn is Director of Teacher Education at Washington University in St. Louis, where for a decade she has helped preservice and in-service teachers, teacher-leaders, and administrators develop as action researchers. Her publications include *To Be a Teacher: Cases, Concepts, and Observation Guides* (Cohn, Kottkamp, & Provenzo, 1987) and *Teachers: The Missing Voice in Education* (Cohn & Kottkamp, 1993). Marilyn was a founder of St. Louis's Action Research Collaborative and Professional Development School Collaborative, as well as the *SHOW-ME Action Research On-Line Journal*. A fellow in the Carnegie Academy for the Scholarship of Teaching and Learning, she is now conducting a study of her own practice in teaching action research to student teachers.

Linda Hajj has been an educator for the last 23 years, both international and stateside schools. She is currently a reading teacher in the Fairfax County (Virginia) Public Schools, near Washington, D.C. Linda has been involved in teacher research since completing her master's degree, both in her own classrooms and as a reading specialist. An active member of the Fairfax County Teacher Research Network, she has cochaired their annual conference for the last 2 years.

Jacquelyn C. Harris is currently an instructional coordinator at Normandy Senior High School near St. Louis. For 35 years she was employed in the St. Louis Public Schools, serving as teacher, reading specialist, administrator, and program coordinator for various programs. After retiring, she resumed her career in education with the Normandy School District. She was selected by the NCTE as a consultant for the Intercontinental Staff Development Program in South

Africa. Her other NCTE roles include president of the Black Caucus and chair of the Advisory Council on the Affairs of People of Color.

Suzanne Kirkpatrick has taught English for 30 years, mostly at Kirkwood High School in Kirkwood, Missouri. Her formal introduction to action research came through her school's partnership with Washington University in St. Louis. When student teachers were required to conduct action research, she volunteered to conduct a project alongside her student teacher. After feeling the value of the process, she proposed that her district offer credit for teacher-researchers. For the past 6 years, Suzanne has facilitated Kirkwood Action Research (KAR), whose members present at conferences sponsored by the partnership and by the areawide Action Research Collaborative.

Sharon Shockley Lee, Associate Professor of Education at Webster University in St. Louis, teaches preservice and in-service teachers and administrators. A practitioner and advocate of action research, she received the Kemper and the Emerson Electric awards for teaching excellence. She coordinates a professional development schools partnership with Pattonville School District. The central themes of Sharon's work are social justice, equity, leadership, and collaboration. Recent publications (Lee, Morgan, & Gerstung, 1999; Morgan, Lee, & Gerstung, 1998) focus on building collaborative cultures in classrooms and schools. She is now completing *Unmasking the White Knight: Emerging Perspectives and Images of the Principalship* for Hampton Press.

Michael Lowenstein is a professor of English at Harris-Stowe State College in St. Louis and a codirector of the Gateway Writing Project, the St. Louis site of the National Writing Project. He has been a leader in NWP's Urban Sites Writing Network and in the areawide Action Research Collaborative. He has worked with prospective and active teachers in a variety of settings at Harris-Stowe and through Gateway, with a particular interest in teacher inquiry and inquiry-based instruction in culturally diverse classrooms. Michael's current research interests include British higher education and the jazz community in St. Louis, the latter an outgrowth of his avocation of jazz saxophonist.

Leslie Turner Minarik has taught primary grades in a large, urban, culturally diverse district in northern California for 13 years. Active in a teacher-research collaborative, she has made presentations at AERA meetings, published articles, and contributed to *Teacher Research and Urban Literacy Education* (Hollingsworth, 1994). She coauthored "Gender Equity in an Elementary Classroom: The Power of Praxis in Action Research" for *International Action Research* (Hollingsworth, 1997). Her other research has dealt with grouping for reading, multiple literacies, and the impact of power in the classroom on student achievement. Leslie is currently teaching second grade and training new teachers.

Marian M. Mohr was a high school English teacher for over 20 years in the Fairfax County (Virginia) Public Schools, and she currently assists schools in establishing, coordinating, and maintaining teacher research groups. She has served as the codirector of the Northern Virginia Writing Project, a member of the board of the National Writing Project, and a trustee of the National Council of Teachers of English Research Foundation. Her publications include articles about teacher research and the teaching of writing as well as three books: *Revision: The Rhythm of Meaning* (1984) and, with Marion S. MacLean, *Working Together: A Guide for Teacher-Researchers* (1987) and *Teacher-Researchers at Work* (1999).

Minnie Phillips teaches English at Webster Groves High School, a suburban school of 1,300 students near St. Louis. She was a founding member of the Webster Groves Writing Project in 1987 and a contributing writer for *Mirror Images: Teaching Writing in Black and White* (Krater, Zeni, & Cason, 1994). She also served as district staff development coordinator and high school writing-across-the-curriculum director. Currently she is writing a fictional biography of Samuel Chapman Armstrong, founder of Virginia's Hampton Normal School and Agricultural Institute, a training school for ex-slaves following the American Civil War.

Myrtho Prophete is currently a first-grade teacher at the Ralph Blevins Elementary School in Rockwood, Missouri, a growing suburban school district. The daughter of Haitian immigrants, she was born and raised in St. Louis, where she has been an educator since 1980. Her action research has dealt with such issues as using small group instruction to improve math performance among fifth graders. She has been a mentor for teachers doing action research through the Developing Leadership in Action Research (DLAR) project and a consultant for teachers of writing through the Gateway Writing Project. In addition, Myrtho is interested in African dancing and drumming.

Rosalynde Scott has been an educator in the St. Louis Public Schools for 34 years. She was a writing enrichment lab teacher in elementary and middle schools, a second-grade teacher at a magnet school for math, science, and technology, and codirector of the Gateway Writing Project. From 1991 to 1993, she conducted her own action research while serving as St. Louis coordinator of the Urban Sites Writing Network. She is now instructional coordinator at Meramec Accelerated School, where she and her teachers are using an inquiry process to prepare for Missouri's performance-based assessment. Rosalynde enjoys oral performance of poetry and hopes to publish some of her writing after she retires.

Louis M. Smith is a professor emeritus at Washington University in St. Louis, where he taught educational psychology, qualitative research, and educational evaluation for 40 years. He has coauthored several books of collaborative research, including *The Complexities of an Urban Classroom* (with William Geoffrey, 1968), *Anatomy of Educational Innovation* (with Pat Keith, 1971), and *Urban Parent Education: Dilemmas and Resolutions* (with Wilma Wells, 1997). He is currently working on a biography of Nora Barlow, an early geneticist and historian of science in Victorian and Edwardian England and granddaughter of Charles Darwin. Lou has been a mentor to two generations of practitioner-researchers.

Owen van den Berg is a native of South Africa, where he established a master's program in action research at the University of the Western Cape in 1987. He has published in the areas of curriculum, politics of education, history teaching, and early childhood education. Since 1995 he has been living in St. Louis, Missouri, where his major work has focused on supporting teachers doing action research, both in the DLAR project and in his teaching at Maryville University and National-Louis University (NLU). He is currently associate professor in the National College of Education at NLU.

Jane Zeni is an associate professor of English Education at the University of Missouri at St. Louis, where she works with preservice and in-service teachers. She directed the Gateway Writing Project from its founding in 1978 until 1997. Previously, she taught diverse middle and high school students in Philadelphia and in Santa Fe. Jane has collaborated with many teacher-led inquiry groups; she has also worked to incorporate action research in her courses without destroying teacher ownership. Her publications include *WritingLands: Composing with Old and New Writing Tools* (1990) and *Mirror Images: Teaching Writing in Black and White* (Krater, Zeni, & Cason, 1994).

INDEX

Abbey, T., 20
Accountability in action research, 83–91, 107
  collaboration with subjects and, 87–91
  insider educational qualitative research,
    85–86
  master's program in action research, 86–90
  power relations and, 84–85
Action research
  defined, xiv, 25
  experienced teachers in, 145–147
  researcher/researched contradiction in,
    69–71
  student teachers in, 143–145. *See also* Prac-
    titioner research
Action Research Collaborative, xi, xii, xx, 76,
    106, 134, 145, 155
Adorno, T. W., 101
Advocacy for students, 18
African Americans
  cultural invisibility and, 114–120
  "white knight" as gatekeeper project, 62–71
Agee, James, 64, 67
Altricther, H., 85–86
American Anthropological Association, 155
American Civil Liberties Union (ACLU), 67
American Educational Research Association
  (AERA), xiv, xix, xv, 5–7, 22, 155,
    161
Anderson, H. H., 99–101, 104
Anderson, Paul V., xvi, xvii, 22, 108, 155,
    158, 162, 163, 164
Anderson, R., 71
Anonymity, 83, 84, 85, 139, 161–162
Applied Ethics for Program Evaluation (New-
    man and Brown), 79–82
ARC Teacher Educator Seminar, xx
Assent, 138–139
Atkinson, P., 160–161
Atwell, Nancie, 36
Au, Kathryn, 36
Authentic stories, 141–143
Ayers, William C., 38–39

Bady, A., 70
Balcerzak, P., 148

Banks, James, 118–119
Barlow, Nora, 94, 97, 104
Barr Ebest, Sally, 72–82, 73, 105–106, 107
Barr Reagan, S., 78
Beauchamp, T., xvi
Beck, Cathy, 45–54
Becker, H., 66
Belanoff, P., 75
Bissex, Glenda, 157
Bitter Milk (Grumet), 75
Brewer, J., 99
Brown, R. D., xv, xvi, 79–82
Burgess, R. G., xvi
Byers, Lisa, 8

Calkins, Lucy, 36
Campbell, Jane, 8
Capasso, M., 148
Career development, 52
Carr, W., 33–34
*Casebook for Teaching about Ethical Issues in
    Qualitative Research, A* (Mathison et al.),
    xv
Cason, Nancy, xii–xiii, 113–122, 114–115,
    119, 150
Changing the Way We Teach (Barr Ebest), 79
Classroom-level reform, 20–21
Clay, Wanda C., 24–34, 27–29, 30–33, 55, 56,
    58
Clayton Action Research Collaborative, 46–54
Clayton (Missouri) Research Review Team,
    45–54, 55
Clayton Writing Project, 46
Cochran-Smith, Marilyn, xiv, xx, 36, 56
Codd, J., 71
Cohn, Marilyn M., 136–148, 137, 140, 143,
    148, 152
Collaborative Action Research Network, xiv
Collaborative research, 70, 87–91, 161–162.
    See also School-university partnerships
College Composition and Communication (jour-
    nal), xvii
Collins, Patricia Hill, 118–119
Community in classroom, 36–39, 57

Community of Writers, A (Elbow and Bela-
    noff), 75
Complexities of an Urban Classroom (Smith
    and Geoffrey), 150–151
Computers, xii
Conference on Teacher Research, 106
Confidentiality, 83, 85, 139
Connor, D., 20
Consequences, of action research, 79
Consultants, dilemmas of, xii
Cook, Kathleen, 70
Copley, C., 148
Cornett, J., xv, 161
Corporal punishment, 65–67
Cowan, Gil, 89
Critical consciousness, 71
Critical subjectivity, 5
Cultural issues, 105
    cultural invisibility, 113–122
    diversity, xii
    "other people's children," xii, 114–118
    second-sight and, 118–119
    seeing own culture and, 119–122
Curriculum development, 21, 27–30, 46–47,
    52

Darrow, C. N., 95
Darwin, Charles, 94
Data collection, by university-based research-
    ers, 64–68
Davidoff, Sue, xiv, 87
Days of Courage (Kelso), 117
DeCharms, Richard, 126
Delpit, Lisa, xii, 78, 105, 114
Democratic approaches, 85
Dialogic encounters, 3–4, 71
*"Difficult to Reach, Maintain, and Help" Ur-
    ban Families in PAT* report, 92–104
DuBois, W. E. B., 118–119
DuPont, Laura, 45–54
Dwyer, D., 96

Early Theory of Conflict (Anderson), 99–
    101
Educational Action Research (journal), xiv, xx
Educational Researcher (journal), 5
Eisner, Elliott W., xvi, 83–84
Elbow, P., 75
Elliott, J., xiv
Ellison, Ralph, 114
Ely, Margot, 84
Emancipatory research, 76, 79–81
Empowerment
    action research and, 79, 97
    in group activities of researchers, 39
Erickson, Fred, 56

Esterhuyse, Jan, 87
Ethical Dilemmas in Feminist Research
    (Kirsch), xvii–xviii
Ethical guidelines for school-based researchers,
    3–12
    dialogue in classroom, 3–4
    first draft, 7–10
    input from colleagues, 4
    process for, 11–12
    quality and, 10–12
    revising, 5–7
Ethic of care, in action research, 81
Ethics
    defined, xv, 24–25
    leadership in, 20–21, 25–26
    negotiating authority and, 26–30
    in practitioner research, xi, xvi–xviii, 19–20,
        24–34
    principles behind, xvi
Ethics review committees, xi, 21
Ethnography in Education Research Forum,
    xiv
Experienced teachers, in action research,
    145–147

Factual issues, 101–102
Faden, R., xvi
Fairfax County Public Schools Teacher-
    Researcher Network (Virginia), 8
Feminist theory, 118
Fishman, S., xx
Fontaine, S., 81–82
Foster, W., 71
Freire, P., 35, 69, 71
Frenkel-Brunswick, E., 101
Fullan, M. J., 84, 86

Gannett, C., 72
Gates, Victoria Purcell, 36
Gateway Writing Project (GWP), xii, 126, 127,
    129, 131, 132–133, 155
Geertz, C., 113
Geismar-Ryan, Lori, 45–54
Gender equity, 21
Gentile, J., 66, 70
Geoffrey, William, 70, 150–151
Gerstung, M., 70
Getting Smart (Lather), 76
Gilligan, Carol, 81
Goliath, Donavon, 88–89
Greenfield, T., 68
Gregory, T. B., 156
Group activities of researchers
    collaboration among school teams, 37
    collaboration with subjects, 87–91
    empowerment in, 39

formal arrangements for, 39
impact on practice, 41–43
negotiating fellowship, 30–33
partnerships beyond school district, 53–54
resistance to, 73. *See also specific professional organizations and research groups*
Grumet, Madelaine, 74–75
Guba, E., xvi

Hajj, Linda, 35–44, 55, 56, 57, 106
Hale-Benson, Janice, 118–119
Halpin, A., 68
Hamilton, David, 97–98
Hammersley, M., 160–161
Harris, Jacquelyn C., 105, 123–135, 149, 152
Harris-Stowe State College, 124, 125, 128, 131
Harvard Family Research Project, 95
Harwayne, Shelley, 36
Hegemony in an Elementary School (Lee), 62
Henke, Linda, 45–54, 46, 47, 49, 58
Herndon, James, 124
Hill, Anita, 69
Hodgkinson, C., 68, 71
Hollingsworth, Sam, 13
Hollingsworth, Sandra, xix, 150
Holmes, Deborah, 140, 148
Holt, John, 124
House, E. R., 159
Hubbard, R. S., xiv, 157, 161–162
Huberman, A. M., 85
Human subjects
    alternative review, 155–156
    impact of research on, 159–160
    as term, xi, xxi n. 1, 108–109
Hunter, Peter, 87
Hunter, S. M., 81–82

Illuminative evaluation, 97–98
Inclusion model, 37–39
Informants, 69
Informed consent, 53, 76, 83–84, 106–107, 138–139
In Forsaken Hands (Rosow), 36
Insider research. *See* Practitioner research
Institutionalization
    defined, xviii
    and school-based researchers, 57–58
    and school-university partnerships, 152
    and university-based researchers, 107–109
Institutional review board (IRB), xvi, 21, 153, 158, 163
Integrative resolution (Anderson), 99–101
International Conference on Teacher Research, xiv, xix, 57
Interpretation/definition

defined, xvii
and school-based researchers, 56–57
and school-university partnerships, 149–152
and university-based researchers, 68–69, 106–107
Interviews
    anonymous data from, 84
    with parents, 65
    with students, 65
Invisible Man (Ellison), 114

Jeffries, Fran, 8

Keith, P., 96
Kelso, Richard, 117
Kemmis, S., 33–34
Kimmel, A. J., xv, xvi
Kirkpatrick, Suzanne, 136–148, 137, 148, 152
Kirkwood High School, 136–148, 145–147
Kirsch, Gesa, xvii–xviii, 55, 157
Klein, E. B., 95
Kohl, Herbert, 124
Kohl, Seena, 69, 70, 160
Kozol, Jonathan, 124
Krater, Joan, xii–xiii, 114, 119, 150

Lather, Patti, 76, 163
Lazarus, Sandy, 87
Leadership, by school-based researchers, 20–21, 25–26
Lee, Sharon Shockley, 61–71, 62, 63, 67, 69, 70, 105, 106–107, 160
Letts, N., 117
Levinson, D. J., 95, 101
Levinson, M. H., 95
Lewin, K., 100–101
Lincoln, Yvonna S., 5, 83, 162
Lippitt, K., 100–101
Lives on the Boundary (Rose), 77
Location
    defined, xvii
    and insider research, 157
    and school-based researchers, 55–56
    and school-university partnerships, 149
    and university-based researchers, 105–106
Lock, R. S., 21
Lowenstein, Michael, xiii, 105, 123–135, 149, 152
Lytle, Susan, ix–x, xiv, xix, xx, 36, 56

MacLean, M. S., xiv
Manchey, Theresa, 8
Mason, Jennifer, xvi, 84, 156
Mathison, S., xv, 161
McCallie, Franklin, 140
McCarthy, L., xx

McKee, D., 95
McKerrow, Kelly, 70
Meerkotter, Dirk, 87, 89
Miles, M. B., 85
Mills College, 20
Minarik, Leslie Turner, 13–23, 21, 55, 56, 57
Mirror Images (Krater et al.), xiii, 114–118, 119–122, 150
Missouri Historical Society, 70
Missouri Writing Project, 126
Mohr, Marian M., xiv, xix, xvi, 3–12, 55, 56, 57, 164
Moral role of teachers, 19–20
Morgan, T., 70
Morrow, Wally, 87
Multiage classrooms, 47–49

National Council of Teachers of English (NCTE), 124, 126, 162
National Writing Project (NWP), xiii, xx, 123, 150
Nelson, Donna, 57
Newman, D. L., xv, xvi, 79–82
Noddings, Nel, 81
Noffke, S. E., xv, 25
Nuremberg Trials, xvi

Office for Protection from Research Risks (OPRR), xvii, 158
Office of Civil Rights (OCR), 67
Office of Educational Research and Improvement (OERI), 151–152
Oliver, D., 101–102, 104
O'Malley, Rebecca K., 76–78
Oral History Association, 155
Outsider research, xii, 154. *See also* School-university partnerships; University-based researchers

Paradigm Dialog, The (Guba), xvi
Parents
    interviews with, 65
    parental consent, 53
Parents as Teachers (PAT) program, 92–104
    consequences of meeting, 94–95
    "Difficult to Reach, Maintain, and Help" Urban Families in PAT report, 92–104
    issues in, 95–98
    key meeting, 92–94
    literature-based interpretation of, 98–102
Parlett, Malcolm, 97–98
Participants, 69–71
Peshkin, A., xvi
Pfannenstiel, J., 96
Phillips, Minnie, 113–122, 114, 119–120, 122

Pierce, Kathryn Mitchell, 45–54, 47, 48, 49, 53
Pitcock, Vicki, 8
Power
    allocation of, 62, 66
    nature of, 36
    between subject and researcher, 84–85
    in "white knight" as gatekeeper project, 62–71
Power, B. M., xiv, 157, 161–162
Practice of Theory, The (Ray), 74
Practitioner research
    defined, xiv–xv
    dilemmas of, xii–xiii
    ethics in, xi, xvi–xviii, 19–20, 24–34, 45–54, 153–165
    growth in popularity, xi. *See also* School-based researchers; School-university partnerships; University-based researchers
Prince William County Institute (Virginia), 8
Principals, "white knight" as gatekeeper project, 62–71
Privacy of subjects, xx, 48, 53, 83, 85
Professional development, 47, 52, 145–147
Professional Development School Collaborative (PDSC), 145
Prophete, Myrtho, 113–122, 115–118, 121
Pseudonyms, 53, 76
Publication
    defined, xvii
    insider research and, 162–163
    school-based researchers and, 10, 48–49, 53, 57
    and school-university partnerships, 149–152
    and university-based researchers, 95, 107–109

Qualitative Inquiry in Education (Eisner and Peshkin), xvi
Qualitative research, 85–86, 161–162
Quantitative research, 153–154

Rawls, J., 62
Ray, Ruth, 74
Reed, M., 99
Reflective approach
    resistance to, 74
    school-based research and, 14–18, 27–34, 38, 41, 43, 55–58
    school-university partnerships and, 149–152
    self-reflective inquiry, 71
    shift from teaching to research and, 50–51
    university-based research and, 76–78, 81–82, 88–89, 90–91, 105–109

writing of teacher-researchers, 14–18, 27–34, 38, 41, 43
Relationships
  defined, xvii
  and school-based researchers, 56
  and school-university partnerships, 149
  and university-based researchers, 106
Reporting data, by university-based researchers, 68–69
Rief, Linda, 36
Rights, in action research, 80–81
Rose, Mike, 77, 78
Rosow, La Vergne, 36, 44
Ross, E. W., xv, 161
Routman, Regie, 36
Royce, A., 70

St. Louis Action Research Collaborative, xi, xii, xx, 76, 106, 134, 145, 155
St. Louis Gateway Writing Project (GWP), xii, 126, 127, 129, 131, 132–133, 155
St. Louis Professional Development School Collaborative (PDSC), 145
Sanford, R. N., 101
Santucci, Victoria, 8
Schlechty, Philip C., 20
School-based researchers, 1–58
  Clayton (Missouri) Research Review Team, 45–54, 55
  drafting ethical guidelines for, 3–12
  evolution of practice, 35–44
  leadership by, 20–21, 25–26
  reflections on, 14–18, 27–34, 38, 41, 43, 55–58
  vision of, 20, 46, 49–51
  voice of teacher-researcher in, 13–23, 27–34, 38, 41, 43. See also School-university partnerships
School desegregation, 70
School reform, 20
Schools for the Twenty-First Century (Schlechty), 20
School-university partnerships, 111–152
  cultural invisibility and, 113–122
  reflections on, 149–152
  Urban Sites Writing Network (USWN), xiii, 123–135, 152
  Washington University/Kirkwood High School project, 136–148
Schubert, W. H., 38–39
Scott, Rosalynde, xiii, 105, 123–135, 149, 152
Seltzer, D., 96
Shannon, Patrick, 36, 43, 44
Shaver, J., 101–102, 104
Smith, Louis M., xvi, 24–25, 62, 64, 70, 83,

92–104, 94, 96, 105, 106–107, 150–151, 161
Sockett, Hugh, 19, 79–80
Soltis, J. F., xvi–xvii
Spiegel, Dixie Lee, 36
Squires, A., 20
Steinbeck, John, 98–99, 104
Stevenson, R. B., 25
Stoecklein, Phyllis, 47
Students. See also Subjects, research
  advocacy for, 18
  interviews with, 65
  privacy of, xx, 48, 53, 83, 85
Student teachers, in action research, 143–145
Subjects, research, 69
  anonymity of, 83, 84, 85, 139, 161–162
  collaboration with, 87–91
  informed consent of, 53, 76, 83–84, 106–107, 138–139
  privacy of, xx, 48, 53, 83, 85
Systemic reform, 20

Taylor, Patricia, 8
Teacher evaluation, 52
Teacher research
  defined, xiv
  dilemmas of, xii, 33
  impact on practice, 35–44. See also Practitioner research; School-based researchers; School-university partnerships
Teacher-Researcher Network (Fairfax County, Virginia), 39
Teacher Research (journal), xiv
Teacher Research & Urban Literacy Education (Hollingsworth), 13
Teaching Public Issues in the High School (Oliver and Shaver), 101–102
Teel, K., 13
Thomas, Clarence, 69
Travels with Charley (Steinbeck), 98–99, 104
Tuskegee syphilis experiment, xvi

University-based researchers, 59–109
  accountability of, 83–91
  action research by graduate teaching assistants, 72–82
  data collection, 64–68
  initiating study, 62–64
  interpreting and reporting data, 68–69
  Parents as Teachers (PAT) program, 92–104
  personal ethical principles in, 62
  reflective approach and, 76–78, 81–82, 88–89, 90–91, 105–109
  researcher/researched contradiction, 69–71
  in schools outside university, 62–71, 92–104
  within university, 72–82

University-based researchers (*Continued*)
   "white knight" as gatekeeper project, 62–71.
      See also School-university partnerships
University of Missouri at St. Louis (UMSL),
   xiii, 107–108, 126, 131, 151
University of Western Cape (South Africa),
   xiii, 86, 87–88
Unmasking the White Knight (Lee), 62
Urban Parent Education (Smith and Wells), 95
Urban Sites Writing Network (USWN), xiii,
   123–135, 152
   impact of, 133–135
   initial responses of researchers, 127–130
   issues and problems in, 130–133
   prior experience of researchers and,
      123–127

van den Berg, Owen, xiii, xiv, 83–91, 86, 88–
   89, 105–106, 107, 108
Virginia Polytechnic University, 35
Vision, of school-based researchers, 20, 46,
   49–51
Voice
   importance of, 5
   nature of, xviii–xix
   of school-based researchers, 13–23, 27–34,
      38, 41, 43
Von Hatten, Catherine, 45–54

Wallace, R., Jr., xvi
Walters, L., xvi
Washington University, 86–90
Washington University/Kirkwood High School
   project, 136–148
   assessing action research in, 143–
      147
   authentic stories in, 141–143
   historical context and institutional demo-
      graphics, 137–138
   respect for others in, 141–143
   tensions in, 138–141
Webster Groves High School, 114, 119–122,
   150
Wells, Gordon, 108–109
Wells, Wilma, 92–93
Westervelt, B. J., 8
White, R., 100–101
Wilson, Suzanne M., 6
Wong, E. David, 6
WritingLands (Zeni), xii

XTAR (listserv), xix, 106

Zeni, Jane, xi–xxi, xii–xiii, 21–22, 46, 47, 48,
   49, 113–122, 114, 119, 120–122, 150,
   153–165
Zone of accepted practice, 158